CRUCIFIED *IN THE* MEDIA

FINDING THE
REAL JESUS
AMIDST TODAY'S
HEADLINES

C. Marvin Pate and Sheryl L. Pate

BakerBooks
Grand Rapids, Michigan

Published by Baker Books
a division of Baker Publishing Group
P.O. Box 6287, Grand Rapids, MI 49516-6287
www.bakerbooks.com

Printed in the United States of America

Library of Congress Cataloging-in-Publication Data
Pate, C. Marvin, 1952–
    Crucified in the media : finding the real Jesus amidst today's headlines / C. Marvin
Pate and Sheryl L. Pate.
       p.   cm.
    Includes bibliographical references.
    ISBN 0-8010-6548-8 (pbk.)
    1. Jesus Christ—Person and offices. 2. Jesus Christ—Historicity. I. Pate, Sheryl Lynn,
1955– II. Title.
BT203.P38 2005
232—dc22
                                                    2004023766

CRUCIFIED *IN THE*
MEDIA

We lovingly dedicate this book
to David T. McCallum (1985–2002)
who, although his stay on earth was brief,
taught us what it means to be like Jesus.

CONTENTS

ACKNOWLEDGMENTS

There are a number of individuals without whom this book never would have seen the light of day. First, we would like to thank Robert Hosack and his colleagues at Baker Books not only for giving us the opportunity to write this book but also for their excellent guidance along the way. Next, our thanks go to the faculty and students of the Pruet School of Christian Studies, Ouachita Baptist University, for their encouragement and support regarding this project. We also wish to express our appreciation to Jason Hentschel for lending us his expertise in both technology and in J. R. R. Tolkien's *The Lord of the Rings*. To our dear friends Robert and Diann McCallum, we say thank you for ministering to us and for being model Christian parents. And finally, we thank our lovely daughter, Heather, and our wonderful son-in-law, Corey, for cheering us on and providing a listening ear throughout the writing process.

INTRODUCTION

Crucified in the Media

||||||||||||||||||||||||||||||||||||||||||||||||||||||||||||||||||||

Jesus is getting top billing in the news these days, some two thousand years after he walked this earth. One might expect it on Christmas and Easter. But what's up these days with news coverage that continues to swirl around the person of Jesus seemingly all the time?

We witnessed an amazing incident in March 2004. Arriving at the cinema over one and a half hours before the next showing of Mel Gibson's *The Passion of the Christ*, we were stunned to see the enormous parking lot filled to capacity and cars parked along the street to the main highway. Soon, people began streaming from the movie theater. No chatting, smiling patrons strolled from the building like most moviegoers after viewing a film. They were subdued and appeared preoccupied with their own thoughts. Some dabbed at their eyes with Kleenex as they walked past our car; others, also sober faced, quietly proceeded to their vehicles, looking thoughtful and even in shock.

The contrast from the usual moviegoers extended to the exit from the parking lot, no small challenge since approximately three thousand people were all attempting to leave at the same time. Drivers did not rudely honk their horns; there were no obscene gestures. Rather, they routinely deferred to one another, patience and courtesy prevailing in a way we have never before witnessed. We saw one reaction to Jesus that day.

Another response was evident in the vehemently negative reviews of many movie critics. As these bastions of "objectivity" railed against the film, their emotion was just as pronounced as that of the viewers we had seen. With seething anger in their voices and pens, these critics denounced Gibson and his film, branding him everything from anti-Semitic to mercenary.

Intense emotion has surrounded the film, generating extremes that seem to defy logic. In some ways it is the very thing one would expect. Why? Because there is no neutral reaction to Jesus. There was no neutral reaction to him when he walked this earth. How can we expect something different now? Jesus's life, death, and even resurrection have sparked controversy that extends to this day. You either love him or despise him; ultimately there is no middle ground.

> *With seething anger in their voices and pens, these critics denounced Gibson and his film, branding him everything from anti-Semitic to mercenary.*

Jesus is front and center in the news. And this will not end anytime soon. As soon as one controversy regarding Jesus seems to wane, another takes its place. Was Jesus the lover of Mary Magdalene, as some claim? Have his brother James's bones been found? Did Jesus actually say and do the things recorded in the Gospels? Are there newly discovered Gospels that deserve canonical status? These and other timely questions will be addressed in this book.

In the end, every person must decide who this Jesus is. We each stake our lives and eternal future on that decision.

With all the theories and issues that keep emerging about the life and ministry of Jesus, keeping up with it all can be overwhelming. Keeping oneself informed is difficult, let alone sorting out fact from fiction. Numerous experts tell us they have made new discoveries that reveal the truth about Jesus. On the surface, they make convincing arguments to that effect. They seem to have done a lot of research and know more than the general public about their area of expertise. We may come away thinking that their view deserves our allegiance because it all seems so convincing. Knowing who and what to believe can be confusing, especially when the scholars themselves contradict one another, as later we will document.

Opinion Poll: Do you think *The Passion of Christ* is:

A. too violent?

B. more Catholic than Protestant?

C. accurate?

D. just a savvy marketing strategy?

Whom can we believe, and how do we make that decision? We need a guide through the maze of interpretations about Jesus in the media.

We believe there is a right perspective of Jesus, which is found in the Bible, especially the Gospels. We intend to show that these ancient testimonies are inspired accounts by eyewitnesses of the historical Jesus and are therefore reliable. The Old Testament says, "There is nothing new under the sun." Is this true about Jesus too? Are current attempts to redefine who Jesus is merely old approaches with a facelift? Read this book and see for yourself. To better prepare you for the adventure that follows, we offer here a survey of the topics to be covered.

Chapter 1 wrestles with the Jesus Seminar's radical approach to color coding the words and works of Jesus of Nazareth as recorded in the Gospels. What did Jesus really say and do? We begin with this topic because it is foundational to all other questions about Jesus.

Chapter 2 interacts with Elaine Pagels's best-selling book *Beyond Belief*, which argues that the *Gospel of Thomas* was originally part of the New Testament but was replaced by the Gospel of John due to the later church's subversive tactics.

Chapter 3 discusses old and more recent attempts to appeal to New Testament apocryphal gospels (e.g., the *Infancy Gospel of Thomas*) in order to reconstruct the silent years of Christ's early life.

In chapter 4 we enter the fray of debate over whether or not the recently revealed ossuary of James is that of the brother of Jesus, and what all of this means for Catholics, the Eastern Orthodox Church, and Protestants.

> *Whom can we believe, and how do we make that decision? We need a guide through the maze of interpretations about Jesus in the media.*

Chapter 5 summarizes and discusses Dan Brown's runaway best-seller and soon-to-be-released movie, *The Da Vinci Code*. Were Jesus and Mary Magdalene lovers? Does Jesus have a royal bloodline today?

Chapter 6 answers, among other quandaries, the question raised by Mel Gibson's mega-hit movie *The Passion of the Christ*: Who killed Jesus? Jews? Romans? Who?

Chapter 7 speaks to a perennial controversy regarding Christ: Is the Shroud of Turin his burial cloth? More specifically, is the moment of Jesus's resurrection indelibly burned onto the shroud?

Speaking of resurrection, chapter 8 evaluates the evidence for and the arguments against the New Testament's claim that Jesus rose from the dead.

Chapter 9 takes a break from the debates surrounding Jesus in the media by identifying themes about Christ's second coming in the movie adaptation of J. R. R. Tolkien's trilogy, *The Lord of the Rings*, an Oscar-winning cinematic wonder.

In chapter 10, we take up one of the most fascinating controversies surrounding Jesus today: Do Michael Drosnin's two internationally best-selling

Opinion Poll:

If you saw them, which movie did you like the best: *The Lord of the Rings* or *The Passion of the Christ*?

Do you plan on seeing *The Da Vinci Code* movie?

Did you know a movie called *The Gospel of John* was recently in theaters?

books on "The Bible Code" enable us to set the date of the return of Christ and the end of the world?

Chapter 11 answers the critical question facing our pluralistic society today: Is Jesus the only way to God?

At the conclusion of this work, we pose Jesus's age-old question for a new day: "Who do you say that I am?"

So keep one eye on the Bible and the other eye on CNN as we enter the storm center of Christianity today: Who is the real Jesus?

DISCUSSION QUESTIONS

1. Do you think people in Jesus's day responded to him in the contrasting ways that people today react to Jesus?
2. Why do you think there is so much interest about Jesus in the media these days?
3. Do you perceive an overarching logic to the organization of this book?

THE JESUS SEMINAR

What Did Jesus Really Say and Do?

|||||||||||||||||||||||||||||||||||||||||||||||||||||||||||||||||||||||||||||||||||||||||||||||||

Like us, you might have been presented with a Bible as a child. Within those gilded pages, many of us quickly discovered two kinds of words—red ones and black ones. While both kinds were certainly important, the red words, we soon learned, were the *especially* important ones because they were the very words of Jesus. It was a treat to turn to a particular page and find *red words*—the things Jesus actually said!

It never occurred to us growing up that there would be a Bible with pink, red, gray, and black words. After all, we grew up believing that what the Gospels reported Jesus did and said, he did and said. End of story. There is now, however, an influential scholarly movement that claims many of the red words are highly suspect.

In this chapter, we will sort out the confusion as we answer questions including: Who decided on this change? Are they right? Does it really matter whether Jesus said each word and performed each action that has been traditionally attributed to him?

If the followers of the Jesus Seminar are indeed correct, we have been deluded: The red words may have faded to pink, gray, or even black before our very eyes.

What is the Jesus Seminar anyway and who are the people involved in it? The term "Jesus Seminar" *sounds like* a nationwide conference where people from all denominations and walks of life go to learn more about Jesus—in essence, a spiritual-growth retreat for those who are spiritually hungry to increase the depth of their knowledge and experience of Jesus. Is this what the Jesus Seminar is really about?

To answer this and other questions, we will tell the story of the Jesus Seminar, discuss its biases, and offer a critique of the methods that the members use to arrive at their conclusions.

> *If the followers of the Jesus Seminar are indeed correct, we have been deluded: The red words may have faded to pink, gray, or even black before our very eyes.*

THE STORY OF THE JESUS SEMINAR

"The Fellows." That is the self-assigned name of some eighty biblical scholars who convened twice yearly from 1985 to 1996.[1] How does one get to be a Fellow? The group is not sponsored by or affiliated with any university, nor is it composed of theologians representing diverse backgrounds or beliefs. The Fellows are a group of North American theologians whose views about the Gospels are far to the left, in line with those of the founding father, Robert Funk.

What was the purpose for which these self-appointed Jesus scholars convened? It was to offer a new translation and commentary on the four New Testament Gospels, along with the *Gospel of Thomas* and the *Gospel of Peter*.

You may wonder, "Where are the *Gospel of Thomas* and the *Gospel of Peter* in my Bible? Those don't sound familiar!" If so, you are in good company. They are not in the Bible and date no earlier than the second century AD, almost a hundred years after the New Testament was completed. This fact, however, has not deterred the Jesus Seminar from according to these two supposed gospels a place with the four canonical (inspired) Gospels. We'll discuss these two extra gospels later in this chapter.

The Fellows' ten years of research have produced two controversial books: *The Five Gospels: What Did Jesus Really Say? The Search for the Authentic Words of Jesus*[2] and *The Acts of Jesus: What Did Jesus Really Do? The Search for the Authentic Deeds of Jesus*.[3]

Hearing these titles for the first time, most Christians are apt to respond, "Why search for Jesus when he was never lost?" But the Fellows of the Seminar beg to differ, for in their opinion the New Testament Gospels as we know them are not faithful, inspired accounts of the words and works of the historical Jesus but rather sayings and actions the church later invented about him.

Who are the heroes of the scholars of the Jesus Seminar, those whom the Seminar in general identifies as mentors? And why do these heroes have this status? One has to look no further than the dedication in their *Five Gospels* translation to answer these questions:

This report is dedicated to
GALILEO GALILEI
who altered our view of the heavens forever
THOMAS JEFFERSON
who took scissors and paste to the gospels
DAVID FRIEDRICH STRAUSS
who pioneered the quest of the historical Jesus

Let's take a brief look at these three individuals. Galileo, however reverent he may have been, published findings on astronomy that forever pitted the Scriptures against science. He has been the poster boy ever since for those who want to replace the Bible with science. President Jefferson cut out anything in the Gospels that smacked of supernaturalism;[4] while Strauss was a prominent eighteenth-century radical German theologian who doubted the historical reliability of the portrait of Jesus painted in the four Gospels.[5]

To read Jefferson's anti-miracle translation of the Gospels, just type "Jefferson's Bible" in any search engine on the Internet. You will see a number of websites that reproduce the first chapter of the president's translation of the life of Jesus.

It helps to know where the Fellows are coming from, doesn't it? Not surprisingly, most mainstream biblical scholars today characterize Jefferson and Strauss as radicals, and the Fellows of the Jesus Seminar as, indeed, their theological descendants.[6] If that weren't alarming enough, these Fellows of the Seminar are convinced that their research cannot be denied, as we will take up later in our discussion of the "seven pillars of scholarly wisdom" to which they adhere.

Getting a Bead on Jesus: The Jesus Seminar at Work

The Fellows arrived at their color-coded translation via the American way: they voted on whether or not the five hundred references comprising Jesus's words and works in the four canonical Gospels were authentic, meaning actually spoken and performed by Jesus. The vote on each saying and act went basically like this:

A red bead to indicate "Jesus surely said or did this";
A pink bead for "Jesus probably said or did this";
A gray bead for "he probably didn't say or do that";
A black bead for "it's very unlikely that Jesus said or did that."[7]

It does not take much to imagine the following Saturday Night Live–style spoof based on this voting system.

A group of theologians are sitting around talking about the translation of the Gospels they wish to create.

"Okay," says Fellow A. "We vote on each of the verses. Either yes, Jesus said it, or no, he didn't. Simple. Straightforward."

"No!" states Fellow B. "What if he *might* have said it? Then what?"

They argue back and forth, with others joining in: "He might *not* have said it!" counter Fellows C and D.

"That's the same thing. Might have, might not have!" replies Fellow A, exasperated.

"It's not!" respond Fellows C and D.

Finally, the peacemaker of the group chimes in: "How about *probably* said it and *probably didn't* say it?"

After much debate the group decides on four categories—Jesus either surely, probably, probably didn't, or very unlikely said and did a particular thing.

> **What were the Fellows' final results? Only 18 percent of Jesus's sayings and acts in the Gospels were deemed authentic and colored red!**

"If we're having all those categories, it's going to take us forever to vote," Fellow A grumbles.

They think about this for some time, until the bright idea of beads is brought up. "We could have different color beads, one for each category!" Fellow E volunteers.

This is a fine idea, so they debate the colors. The suggestions are numerous. White, purple, blue, orange, red, pink, gray, and black are all discussed.

"Pink!" Fellow F says with disgust. "I would feel just plain silly voting with a pink bead."

"What about me? I'm color blind!" one of the Fellows utters with exasperation.

After many hours of debate, they finally settle on red, pink, gray, and black beads.

Results of the Voting System

What were the Fellows' final results? Only 18 percent of Jesus's sayings and acts in the Gospels were deemed authentic and colored red!

While this voting technique at first glance appears to be reasonable, the reported results hide the true nature of the tally in two ways. First, the eighty or so scholars participating in the Jesus Seminar represent only a fraction of New Testament scholars in the world. The vast majority of biblical scholars have registered their own vote—against the Jesus Seminar's radical perspective.[8] Second, not even the majority of the Fellows in the Jesus Seminar are in agreement with the vote results as to choice of color in the translation.

Let's look at one example. The vote on Matthew 25:29 ("For to all those who have, more will be given, and they will have an abundance; but from those who have nothing, even what they have will be taken away" [NRSV]) was as follows: 25 percent of the Fellows thought it should be colored red because Jesus said it and another 11 percent gave it a pink rating, affirming that Jesus probably said it. Thus, 36 percent of the Fellows voted that the saying possessed some degree of authenticity.

The rest of the Fellows voted for colors gray and black. The verse was colored black in the Jesus Seminar version of the Gospels. However, as Ben Witherington III points out, when one looks at the percentage of votes for the black bead only, it represents the *minority* because the other three colors outnumbered the black. Thus, even though there could have been substantial votes for all four color beads, the gray or black category was assigned rather than red (authentic) or pink (probably authentic).[9]

What are the implications of this approach? Does it really matter whether Jesus said and did the things traditionally attributed to him?

Take the case of a young adult, a student, who is studying the translation of the Gospels according to the Fellows of the Jesus Seminar. Following the color-coded guidelines, the college student sees that very little is attributed to Jesus. Much of what the Christian tradition has taught now becomes suspect. Of the five major doctrines in the Bible regarding Jesus—his virgin birth, virtuous life, vicarious death for our sins, victorious resurrection, and visible return—*only* Jesus's virtuous life remains in red print in this translation as being really true. The rest is relegated to stories or myths that the church created. The student concludes the following: Jesus was simply a good person, deluded about his mission in life but well-intentioned. Thus the student rejects the Christian faith. After all, why commit one's life to a bunch of myths?

This example reveals the great importance of whether or not the words and actions of Jesus are deemed authentic, for why would a person make a commitment to one who was a good man but essentially not very different from any number of noble people throughout history?

Critical Criteria for Finding Jesus

What criteria did the Fellows use to determine what Jesus genuinely said and did? Two assumptions—technical sounding, but really very simple—guided them in their decision-making: the criterion of dissimilarity and the criterion of multiple attestation. Let's begin by defining them:

The *criterion of dissimilarity* states that a Jesus saying or deed which stands out both from his Jewish heritage and from his later followers (the church) truly goes back to Jesus. In other words, the saying or deed has to be unique,

Two assumptions guided them in their decision-making: the criterion of dissimilarity and the criterion of multiple attestation.

thus dissimilar, from Jesus's Jewish culture or what his followers would say or do. The saying or deed only "counts" if it is in opposition to both groups.

The *criterion of multiple attestation* assumes there are four separate sources that make up the Gospels: Mark, "Q" (sayings of Jesus not in Mark but in Matthew and Luke), "M" (material only in Matthew), and "L" (material only in Luke). (They omit John from the discussion; see below.)

If a saying or deed attributed to Jesus occurs in two or more of these sources it is thought to be authentic. If it only occurs in one source, it is not thought to be attested to, and therefore is not considered authentic.

Jesus, the Talking Head

When all is said and done, what is left of the Gospels? Michael J. Wilkins and J. P. Moreland leave us in no doubt:

> In the entire Gospel of Mark, there is only one red-letter verse: "Give to Caesar what is Caesar's and to God what is God's" (Mark 12:17). Only fifteen sayings (not counting parallels) are colored red in all of the Gospels put together, and they are all short, pithy "aphorisms" (unconventional proverb-like sayings) or parables (particularly the more "subversive" ones). Examples of the former include Jesus's commands to turn the other cheek (Matt. 5:39; Luke 6:29) and love your enemies (Matt. 5:44; Luke 6:27), and his blessing on the poor (Luke 6:20; *Thos.* 54). Examples of the latter include the parables of the good Samaritan (Luke 10:30–35), the shrewd manager (Luke 16:1–8a), and the vineyard laborers (Matt. 20:1–15). Seventy-five different sayings are colored pink, while at the other end of the color spectrum, several hundred appear in black, including virtually the entire Gospel of John and all of Jesus's claims about himself (e.g., "I am the way and the truth and the life"—John 14:6; "I and the Father are one"—10:30; and so on).[10]

So what portrait of Jesus emerges? When the preceding two criteria, especially the principle of dissimilarity, are applied to Jesus, he ends up with no connection to his Jewish heritage and no ties to the church he founded. In other words, the Jesus Seminar portrays Jesus as a "talking head" with no body.[11]

So this "talking head" Jesus appears to be nothing more than a Greek-style philosopher who utters mere moral maxims about how to treat each other, but who makes no claim to be the Messiah; announces no kingdom of God;

makes no proclamation against sin; and subverts no religious establishment. One wonders in all of this, however, why was *this* Jesus ever crucified? The Jesus of the seminar might have ruffled some feathers among his fellow Jews but he would not have undermined their core beliefs.

THE SEMINAR'S BIASES

By now you will probably be aware that the Fellows' translation of the sayings and acts of Jesus is driven by their agenda to reinvent Jesus for the modern world. Two biases are driving this agenda: historical skepticism and political correctness.

The Jesus Seminar makes no bones about being skeptical of the reliability of the Bible in general and of the Gospels in particular.

Historical Skepticism

The Jesus Seminar makes no bones about being skeptical of the reliability of the Bible in general and of the Gospels in particular. They express such suspicion in the "Seven Pillars of Scholarly Wisdom," which form the introduction to their two books.

What are these "seven pillars"?

1. The Jesus of history (the real Jesus who walked this earth) is *not* the Christ of faith (the Jesus of the four Gospels and the church).
2. The Jesus of the Synoptic Gospels (Matthew, Mark, and Luke) is not the same as the Jesus of the Gospel of John.
3. The Gospel of Mark was the first Gospel to be written (about AD 64–68) while Luke (AD 80) and Matthew (AD 90) relied on Mark in their portrait of Jesus.
4. The "Q" document (*Quelle*—German for source) refers to some 235 purported statements by Jesus; it was also used by Luke and Matthew.
5. Jesus was not a Jewish fiery preacher of the inbreaking kingdom of God (so said by Albert Schweitzer) but rather a Greek philosopher-type who went around Palestine uttering proverbial niceties about the need for people to treat each other with equality.[12]

Study the account of Jesus's baptism in Mark 1:9–11; Luke 3:21–23; Matthew 3:13–17. Underline words which are in common between two or three Gospels and use dotted lines where they are different. Who is borrowing from whom? Do we learn what distinguishes one Gospel account from another?

6. The written Gospels of the New Testament were pieced together from oral tradition that had circulated in the churches a generation earlier, which attracted legends and myths after each retelling (that is, elements of the supernatural).
7. The burden of proof that the Jesus of history is the Christ of faith now rests squarely on conservative Christians. It is they who are under the gun to demonstrate the historical reliability of the Gospels.[13]

Are the Fellows' "scientific findings" and "assured results" (as they would refer to them) indeed foolproof? The following examination will demonstrate otherwise.

First, is the Jesus of history different from the Christ of faith? The heart of this issue is the question of the reliability of the Gospels. Millions of Christians and thousands of theologians for the past two thousand years have said yes to the dependability of the Gospels. Consider these facts:

1. The New Testament Gospel authors were either eyewitnesses to the historical Jesus or close associates of those who were. Thus Mark relied upon the apostle Peter to write his Gospel; Matthew was one of the twelve disciples; John was the "beloved" disciple; and Luke wrote under the direction of Paul, who encountered the risen Jesus several times.

> Even though their remarks about Jesus and the early church are polemical in nature, non-Christian ancient writers inadvertently confirm the storyline found in the canonical Gospels.

2. The four canonical Gospels report the same basic story line: Jesus was baptized by John the Baptist; he claimed to be the Messiah; declared the kingdom of God had come in his person; began his ministry in Galilee; confronted Jewish and Roman authorities; was tried and crucified by the same, but arose on the third day after his death, after which he was seen by those very ones who would later write the four Gospels.
3. The above basic storyline is confirmed by Jewish and Roman writers outside the New Testament who lived in or shortly after the first century AD. Even though their remarks about Jesus and the early church are polemical in nature, they inadvertently confirm the storyline found in the canonical Gospels.[14]

Second, are the Jesus of the Synoptic Gospels (Matthew, Mark, and Luke) and the Jesus of the Gospel of John contradictory? No, for as the first point above noted, the four Gospels follow the same basic storyline. Furthermore, it is now recognized by many biblical scholars that the Gospel of John adds supplemental material to the Synoptics' presentation of Jesus; for example, the seven sign miracles, the seven "I am's," the upper room discourse. In addition, the passion narrative in John is close to Luke's presentation.[15]

Third and fourth, many conservative biblical scholars do accept that Mark was the first Gospel written, with Matthew and Luke using Mark and a different source for sayings of Jesus (Q) to compose their Gospels. But this need not suggest that the Gospels are unreliable, especially if Mark wrote his Gospel under the auspices of Peter, and Matthew was the author of Q. What we have in that case is one writer building on an apostle's testimony—Mark using Peter, Luke using Matthew.[16]

Fifth, if there is any assured scholarly result (what the Fellows were seeking) today in Gospel studies, it is that Jesus was indeed an apocalyptic preacher who believed that the kingdom of God was breaking into history through his Messianic ministry (see Matt. 6:9–13; Mark 1:15; 4; 9:1; Luke 11:1–4; 17:20–21). Albert Schweitzer demonstrated this in the early twentieth century; it has now become a near consensus among New Testament experts.[17] Little wonder, then, that the first instance Jesus mentions the presence of the kingdom of God, Mark 1:15—"The kingdom of God is near. Repent and believe the good news!" (NIV)—is colored in black, and thereafter, in *The Five Gospels*.[18] To admit this to be an authentic saying of Jesus would undermine the whole enterprise of the Jesus Seminar! They refuse to admit that Jesus is the heavenly Son of Man who calls for an end to this world as we know it.

Sixth, did the story of Jesus as passed on by word of mouth by the first Christians look much different by the time the second generation of Christians wrote it down? That is, were myths and legends added with each retelling of the story of Jesus? No, for a number of reasons.

1. The Jesus Seminar Fellows, like some liberal German theologians before them, assumed that the sayings and deeds of Jesus were passed along in oral form in the same way the Grimm brothers' fairy tales were handed down—over hundreds of years, with each new telling embellishing the account with more dramatic flair. They thought of it like the kids' game "Telephone," where one child whispers a secret to the next, who whispers it to the next child until the oft-told secret reaches the last person, who reveals a secret that bears little resemblance to the original. But more recent biblical scholars recognize that this approach foists a Western mindset upon the Gospels, which were, after all, ancient Jewish Christian writings. That is to say, Jewish culture was

adept at passing along accurate information in oral form, even as large blocks of African cultures do today.[19]

2. The disciples, who were eyewitnesses to the historical Jesus, lived into the second generation of Christians. They were the gatekeepers of the "Jesus tradition" to ensure it was faithfully passed on. The only way the early church could have been free to tamper with the words and deeds of Jesus was if the apostles had died and gone to heaven with Jesus, assuming the early church wanted to do so in the first place.

3. Jesus himself promised that he would send the Holy Spirit to remind the disciples of what Jesus said and did precisely to make sure they got his story right (John 14:25–26). This last point won't convince the skeptic of the reliability of the Gospels, but for the believer today, Jesus's promise that his apostles would be inspired by the Spirit as they passed along the memoirs of their Messiah is a reassuring word.

4. Thirty or so years between the time of Jesus and the writing of the Gospels is not much time for myths and legends to have been added to the Gospels. Not only that, but Paul's story of Jesus, which jibes with the story of Jesus as found in the Gospels, was written less than fifteen years after Jesus's resurrection (see 1 Cor. 15:3–11; Gal. 3:1).[20]

The **Jesus Seminar** is the product of the school of form criticism. Conservative Christians criticize this approach on five points:

(1) It imposes a Western mindset (especially German) on the Gospels, which are near Eastern in orientation.

(2) There was not sufficient time between Jesus's life and the writing of the four Gospels for the church to make up stories and sayings about Jesus.

(3) The apostles served as eyewitnesses to vouchsafe the oral account of the life, death, and resurrection of Jesus.

(4) Followers of Bultmann (the founder of New Testament form criticism) parted company with his approach due to its radical nature.

(5) The presence of the Holy Spirit ensured that the apostles accurately remembered what Jesus said and did (John 14:26).

Seventh, Christians have no problem accepting the burden of proof when it comes to substantiating the reliability of the Gospels. Bring it on! More than one skeptic who started out to disprove the Gospels has become a follower of Jesus. There's Frank Morrison, Josh McDowell, and Lee Strobel, to name a few. Ironically, even Germany, home of much biblical skepticism in the past, in part has done an about face on the subject, as the writings of Ernst Käsemann and Martin Hengel demonstrate. These scholars cannot be accused of being conservatives, yet their research again and again has confirmed the Gospels' reliability.[21]

Political Correctness

The second bias of the Jesus Seminar we wish to expose is their desire to offer us a politically correct Jesus. Not that being politically correct is wrong. But it is incorrect to read a North American mentality back into the first-century Gospels. This becomes clear when one realizes that the Jesus Seminar places the *Gospel of Thomas* alongside the canonical Gospels, even according it priority over them.[22] The *Gospel of Thomas* is a second-century AD Gnostic reinterpretation of Jesus. The Gnostics were a group of Christians who were considered heretical by the mainstream church; akin to the Greek philosopher Plato, they taught that the human body is evil and only the soul is good. According to them, in the beginning, there was one cosmic spirit-being and no matter. But an evil creator god turned from the one true God and created the world.

Gnostics believed that they were not of this world, but descendants of the one true God. They thought of themselves as sparks of divine light entrapped by the evil creator god in the material world of his creation. Their goal—their salvation—was to escape this world and re-ascend to the heavenly realm of their origin.

In Christian gnosticism, the redeemer figure was identified with Christ. He comes, as in other Gnostic systems, to remind Gnostics of their true nature, to awaken them from forgetfulness, and tell them of their heavenly home. This Christ shares with them secret knowledge—*gnosis*—which is the means by which they can escape the world of evil and return to God.

The *Gospel of Thomas* reflects the outlook of the Gnostic movement in significant aspects. Jesus, for example, speaks as the redeemer come from God. He reminds his followers of humanity's forgetfulness and tells how it is in need of enlightenment (*Thomas* 28). He deprecates the world (*Thomas* 21:6; 27:1; 56:1–2; 80:1–2; 110; 111:3). He reminds people of their origin (*Thomas* 49) and tells them of their needed return to the heavenly home (*Thomas* 50). He also speaks of his own return to the place from which he has come (*Thomas* 38).[23]

In addition, the *Gospel of Thomas* is *individualistic*—each person follows his or her own innate intuition, because that intuition is divine. That's how they follow Jesus. Thus saying 49 reads, "Blessed are the solitary and the elect, for you will find the kingdom. For you came forth from it, and you will return to it." In other words, Thomistic "Christians" individually possess the true knowledge of their origin. Related to this, saying 70 reads, "Jesus said: If you gained this [truth] within you, what you have will save you. If you do have this in you, what you do not have in you will kill you." So Thomistic "Christians" understand that the truth is within them, namely, their origin is heaven, not earth, and it is this knowledge that will save them. It is also *pantheistic*—God is in the material universe, the spark of divine in humans. Saying 77 makes this clear: "Jesus said: I am the light that is above them all. I am the all; the all came forth from me, and the all attained to me. Cleave a [piece of] wood, I am there. Raise up a stone, and you will find me there."

Furthermore, the *Gospel of Thomas* consists of 114 purported sayings of Jesus—with no passion narrative: Jesus does not die for sin and his body is not resurrected. In other words, this apocryphal work is *moralistic* in orientation. One is saved by following the light within, not by revelation from God from without.

The Jesus Seminar appeals to the *Gospel of Thomas* to prove that early Christianity was *pluralistic*. That is, they say that some Christians followed the four New Testament Gospels and others followed the Gnostic *Gospel of Thomas*. The Fellows are pleased to find that early Christianity was tolerant of alternative types of Christian faith. They see the Council of Nicea in Asia Minor (Turkey) in AD 325 as the turning point, when the orthodox view won out over the Gnostic approach, wrongly branding the latter heretical.

Individualistic—Each individual follows his or her innate intuition.

Pantheistic—Intuition is divine and therefore resides within humans, not in God's revelation to us.

Moralistic—What is important is to follow your own moral code and not to worry about a future judgment day.

Pluralistic—There is no absolute truth about Jesus, or God, for that matter.

> "Beware of finding a Jesus entirely congenial to you."

The Jesus Seminar makes quite an opening statement in its two books, "Beware of finding a Jesus entirely congenial to you."[24] The ironic thing about this comment is that the Jesus Seminar has found in the five "gospels" precisely the picture of Jesus they wanted to find—an individualistic, pantheistic, moralistic, pluralistic, North American Jesus.

CRITIQUING THE METHODS USED BY THE FELLOWS

Robert Funk is the guru of the Jesus Seminar. His forceful presence and drive formed a publishing group that in turn was responsible for producing *The Five Gospels* and the *Acts of Jesus*. Funk, like Rudolph Bultmann,[25] ardently believes that there are two criteria for determining whether or not purported words and acts of Jesus are genuine: the criteria of dissimilarity and multiple attestation, mentioned earlier in the chapter. What about these two criteria? Do they have merit?

Criterion of Dissimilarity

Remember that this guideline says that for something to be authentically attributed to Jesus, it has to be different from both ancient Judaism and the practices of the early church. But there are at least two problems with this procedure. First, it is logically absurd. Darrell L. Bock expresses this criticism well:

> If both sides of the dissimilarity are affirmed, so that Jesus differs from *both* Judaism *and* the early church, then Jesus becomes a decidedly odd figure, totally detached from his cultural heritage *and* ideologically estranged from the movement he is responsible for founding. One wonders how he ever came to be taken seriously. He becomes an eccentric if only that which makes him different is regarded as authentic. The criterion may help us understand where Jesus's teaching is exceptional, but it can never give us the essential Jesus.[26]

Second, the Jesus Seminar is inconsistent in applying the criterion. On the one hand, the Fellows use the criterion when it works to their advantage. They believe John the Baptist did indeed baptize Jesus, because (1) John the Baptist performed the baptism of Jesus himself whereas other Jewish groups, like the Dead Sea Scrolls Community, had the candidates baptize themselves, and (2) the later church was embarrassed by John's baptism of Jesus because it made the latter subservient to the former.[27]

But, other times, when the results of the application of the criterion of dissimilarity confirm evangelical convictions about Jesus, the Fellows reject the conclusions. Luke 5:33–35 says that Jesus did not fast. The Seminar argues that although Jesus's action is different from Judaism and early Christianity, both of which practiced fasting, the remark is nevertheless not genuine. Second, while most Gospel scholars accept the title "Son of Man" as coming from Jesus, many of them because (1) it was not a title for the Messiah in the Judaism of Jesus's day and (2) the early church did not use the name "Son of Man" for Jesus, nevertheless the Jesus Seminar rejects it as authentic.[28] It becomes clear in all of this that the Fellows

> *It becomes clear in all of this that the Fellows want to have their cake and eat it too. As long as the criterion of dissimilarity supports their liberal bias, it is okay. If it doesn't, they disregard the guideline's application.*

want to have their cake and eat it too. As long as the criterion of dissimilarity supports their liberal bias, it is okay. If it doesn't, they disregard the guideline's application.

Truthfully, the criterion of dissimilarity itself can strike the reader as ludicrous because we recognize in ourselves that our words and deeds reflect in some way our culture. How can one possibly arrive at true portraits of individuals by stripping them of their heritage and considering only those acts and deeds as genuine which appear to be entirely dissimilar from their culture? While Jesus certainly was not merely a collection of words and actions reflecting the ethos of his day, and he surely opposed the religious system of the time, he nevertheless lived in the midst and partook of his native Jewish environment.

Multiple Attestation

Multiple attestation occurs when a purported saying or act of Jesus occurs in multiple sources: Mark, "Q" (the 235 sayings Jesus, Luke, and Matthew share in common), "M" (Matthew's special material), "L" (Luke's special material). Here, again, the Fellows used the guideline inconsistently. On the one hand, they believe Jesus's praise of John the Baptist in Matthew 11:7–8 is probably genuine, because it is found in "Q" and in the *Gospel of Thomas*. But, on the other hand, though Mark 10:45 ("For even the Son of Man did not come to be served, but to serve, and to give his life as a ransom for many"[NIV]) is similar to Matthew 26:24, Luke 22:19–20, and 1 Corinthians 11:24–25, the Jesus Seminar declares it to be probably inauthentic.[29] This conclusion is all the more lamentable since "Son of Man," as we saw before, meets the criterion of dissimilarity.

But even if this criterion is applied perfectly, it simply fails to convince. Just because it is recorded in only one Gospel, why would that make the saying or action inauthentic? Why does it have to be corroborated in order to be authentic? Certainly the Gospels are not meant to be simply identical copies of one another.

CONCLUSION

When one learns where the Fellows of the Jesus Seminar are coming from—their heroes, "seven pillars of scholarly wisdom," and agenda—it is not difficult to see why they arrived at the color-coded translation of the Gospels that they did. This is not a group of biblical scholars who represent the gamut of theological beliefs, but rather a group of people who fit the Gospels into their own left-wing theological perspective, thus going against their own premise that one must not create a portrait of a "Jesus who is congenial to you."

Their methodology is flawed, including the two criteria they use to determine the authentic words and deeds of Jesus and the high status they give to the *Gospel of Thomas* and the *Gospel of Peter*. From their perspective, only Jesus's virtuous life remains as being historically accurate. The rest—Jesus's virgin birth, his vicarious death, victorious resurrection, and visible return—is judged to be mere stories or myths perpetuated by the church.

This matter has enormous implications. We do not commit our lives simply to a good, well-intentioned, but deluded man. Rather, as Christians, we commit our lives to the risen Christ, to one who is all he claimed to be, and one who will one day return to fully establish his kingdom.

> *Their methodology is flawed, including the two criteria they use to determine the authentic words and deeds of Jesus.*

DISCUSSION QUESTIONS

1. In the Jesus Seminar's two books, what do the following colors represent? Red? Pink? Gray? Black?
2. Was the Jesus Seminar's voting technique regarding the words and works of Jesus objective?
3. What were the two major criteria employed by the Jesus Seminar to arrive at what Jesus "really" said and did?
4. What are the two biases driving the Jesus Seminar agenda?
5. How would you counter the skeptical attitude of the Jesus Seminar to the four Gospels?

BEYOND BELIEF

Should the *Gospel of Thomas* Replace the Gospel of John?

||||||||||||||||||||||||||||||||||||||||||||||||||||||||||||||||||||||||||||||

INTRODUCTION

The gloves come off in this chapter: It's historic Christianity versus Gnosticism! Gnosticism, traditionally understood, was a second- to third-century AD interpretation of early Christianity. It taught that in the beginning there was God, the perfect one, the Spirit, who created an original primal man, who was a figure composed of light. Unfortunately, this man fell into sin, leading his body to disintegrate into myriads of particles of light, which were then seeded in the souls of humans in this dark world. The plight of humanity, therefore, is the struggle for individuals to remember the heavenly origin of their souls. God solved this problem by sending his Son, Jesus Christ the Redeemer, whose task was to bring this knowledge (*gnosis*) to people. On recollecting their true nature, those souls are led back to their heavenly home, no longer encumbered by their sinful bodies.

Thus Gnosticism refers to the *gnosis*, or knowledge, that one is ultimately spiritual, not physical, in origin. The goal, therefore, is for one to rid the soul of the prison house of the body and return to the Spirit-being. On the surface, such a belief appears to be super-spiritual and thus desirable. It conjures up images of a person being so in touch with God that the physical no longer matters; only the desire to return to be with God counts. Is Gnosticism the ultimate spirituality? Far from it.

In fact, such teaching poses dire consequences for historic Christianity, because in devaluing the body, Gnosticism ultimately denies the humanity of Jesus and thereby the reality of the incarnation (see 1 John 1:1; 2:22; 4:2–3).

Moreover, the Gnostic's dim view of the human body could wreak havoc in one's ethical life, leading to one of two contrasting reactions. It could result in ascetic treatment of the body by abusing oneself to attain supposed "spirituality" (see Col. 2:21–23). Or, just the opposite, it could produce sexual license (see 1 John 2:16; 3:4; 2 Peter 2:1–22; Jude 7), because anything done with the body doesn't matter since the "real" person is only spiritual, not physical.

It took the combined efforts of the apostles Paul, John, Peter, and the brother of Jesus, Jude, along with the church fathers Irenaeus (second century AD), Athanasius (fourth century AD), and even Emperor Constantine himself at the Council of Nicea (AD 325), to stem the tide against the pervasiveness of the Gnostic movement.

But the twentieth and twenty-first centuries have witnessed a resurgence of the Gnostic threat to historic Christianity. In 1945, numerous Gnostic texts were discovered at Nag Hammadi in upper Egypt. Fifty-two secret gospels and apocryphal works were among the cache of texts discovered there. These writings were most probably composed by fourth-century AD Gnostic monastic Christians who hid their treasure trove so it would not be destroyed by the now established church, perhaps in defiance of the Alexandrian Bishop Athanasius, who ordered the burning of all such materials.[1]

Thus Gnosticism refers to the gnosis, or knowledge, that one is ultimately spiritual, not physical, in origin.

One of the most fascinating writings that surfaced at Nag Hammadi is the *Gospel of Thomas*,[2] a gospel purported to have been written by the apostle Thomas and consisting of some 114 sayings of Jesus. We met this piece in our last chapter, but we need to focus upon it in this chapter because it has become the rallying flag for theologians who are virtually calling for the replacement of historic Christianity with Gnosticism.

One such scholar is Dr. Elaine Pagels, Harrington Spear Paine Professor of Religion at Princeton University. Professor Pagels has long championed the Gnostic cause in American religion, writing best-sellers on the subject: *The Gnostic Gospels*,[3] *The Gnostic Paul*,[4] and *Adam, Eve, and the Serpent*.[5] In her most recent best-seller, *Beyond Belief: The Secret Gospel of Thomas*,[6] she eloquently and passionately argues that the *Gospel of Thomas* has received a bad rap thanks to the canonical Gospel of John. Her title reflects the thesis of her book: the Gospel of John presents only one part of the story of early Christianity, and not a very legitimate one at that. She asserts that the Gospel of John promotes a religion in which individuals should cognitively believe a set of dogmas about Jesus (that he is the only Son of God, uniquely existing in eternity past, born of the virgin Mary, that he died for sinful humanity and arose in bodily form), and anything other than these formulations are to be categorically rejected as heresy. The *Gospel of Thomas*, on the other hand, argues Pagels, presents a more promising path, a religion in which truth is not revelation from God outside the individual, but rather truth about God is within the individual, waiting to be discovered and experienced. The content of that truth is that Christians are actually none other than Christ, newly created in the image of God! Pagels vociferously claims that the Gospel of John was written precisely to squash the growing popularity of *Thomas* in the first-century church.

There is no neutral ground in this debate: one is either for historic Christianity or for Gnosticism as portrayed in the *Gospel of Thomas*. And the stakes are high. Should we replace the Gospel of John with the *Gospel of Thomas*? To answer that question, we will uncover four assumptions driving the *Gospel of Thomas* that attract scholars like Pagels to it. These four assumptions are diametrically opposed to the Gospel of John and early Christianity; they are even at odds with the Jewish-Christian ethic that has made America great. Those four assumptions deal with issues of:

> *Pagels vociferously claims that the Gospel of John was written precisely to squash the growing popularity of Thomas in the first-century church.*

Authority—where does it come from?

Anthropology—what is the nature of humanity?

Methodology—how should we interpret the Gospel of John and, for that matter, the Bible itself?

Morality—what would happen to the church if the *Gospel of Thomas* prevails?

Before we enter the debate, let's discuss where Elaine Pagels is coming from, as well as factors that may have contributed to her arrival at the position she holds. Pagels had a life-changing experience as an adult when her first son became ill and died when he was a child. Apparently, Pagels did not receive emotional support and encouragement from the conservative Christian community at the time of this tragedy—one can surmise they were simply not there for her in her time of need. It appears that Pagels felt deeply hurt by these individuals. Understandably, this would have a significant impact, not only upon her life, but also upon her view of the religion of the people who failed her. Is it surprising that she has arrived at the polar opposite belief system theologically? One wonders—have her biases due to her personal experience contributed to her position religiously? Of course we do not want to oversimplify the situation. She is a scholar who is Ivy League–school trained, but knowing some of the background may offer insight into one of the possible contributing factors to her campaign against orthodox Christianity.

AUTHORITY: WHERE DOES IT COME FROM?

With this question Pagels goes for the jugular of historic Christianity, arguing that Gnosticism was (and is) just as legitimate an expression of Christianity as, if not more so than, orthodoxy. Her question basically is, "Who made historic Christianity the final say in matters of faith and practice?" The key issue behind this question has to do with the New Testament canon, the books that are traditionally included in the New Testament. "Canon" means rule or measuring stick. Discussions of the final formation of the Bible center on at least two important questions: When were the books of the Bible determined to be inspired? And what were the criteria for including the present books in the Bible?[7] For our purposes, we will focus only on the New Testament canon.

Pagels's thesis is two-fold: Before Irenaeus there was diversity of opinion about the nature of Christ, even in the New Testament itself. In other words, the New Testament canon was open. But from Irenaeus on, an artificial uniformity was imposed on Christianity regarding who Jesus was. Consequently, the historical winners (the four Gospels) were officially admitted into the canon, while the historical losers (the *Gospel of Thomas*, for example) were shunned. After summarizing Pagels's arguments below, we will offer a rebuttal of them, point by point.

> In reality, claims Pagels, there were at least three major competing interpretations of who Jesus was at that time, reflected in the Synoptic Gospels, the Gospel of John, and the *Gospel of Thomas.*

The Gospel(s) According to Pagels

Pagels wastes no time in her book *Beyond Belief* debunking the idea that there was a uniform witness to the nature of

Christ early on in the history of Christianity. In reality, claims Pagels, there were at least three major competing interpretations of who Jesus was at that time, reflected in the Synoptic Gospels, the Gospel of John, and the *Gospel of Thomas.*

The Synoptics

Pagels wants to pit the Gospel of John against the Synoptic Gospels (Matthew, Mark, and Luke) in order to support her theory that there were diverse, contradictory views about Christ in the New Testament. Thus she mentions the well-known differences between the Synoptics and John: the former places Jesus's cleansing of the temple in the passion week while John situates it at the beginning of Jesus's ministry (John 2); and the Synoptics equate the last supper with the Passover meal while John does not, for he wishes to equate Jesus's death on the cross with the time of the slaying of the Passover lamb.[8] Most evangelicals are not threatened by these dissimilarities, attributing them to John's poetic license. But Pagels goes on to insist that the Synoptics' view of the nature of Christ is that, though labeled the "Messiah," the "Son of Man," and "Son of God" therein, Jesus was no more than God's *human* agent! These titles were but metaphors not to be pressed literally. According to Pagels, only Luke's Gospel says that Jesus was made Lord, but only at his resurrection, not before.[9]

The Gospel of John

According to Pagels, the portrait of Jesus dramatically changes with John, for that Gospel elevates him to equal status with God. It is only in the

Two Portraits of Jesus	
The Synoptic Gospels	**The Gospel of John**
1. Begins with John the Baptist/birth and childhood of Jesus	1. Begins with creation/no birth or childhood stories
2. Jesus is baptized by John	2. Baptism of Jesus assumed but not mentioned
3. Jesus speaks in parables	3. Jesus speaks in discourses
4. Jesus preaches the kingdom of God	4. Jesus preaches eternal life
5. Jesus's public ministry lasts one year	5. Jesus's public ministry lasts three years
6. The cleansing of the temple occurs toward the end of the Gospels	6. The cleansing of the temple occurs early on
7. Jesus eats the last supper with his disciples	7. Jesus washes the disciples' feet

Gospel of John that Jesus is the unique Son of God, the light of the world, and without parallel among humans.[10] Pagels labels this "higher Christology" (Jesus is God) as opposed to the Synoptics' "lower Christology" (Jesus is mere man.)[11]

The Gospel of Thomas

The *Gospel of Thomas*, unlike the Gospel of John, teaches that God's light shines not only in Jesus but, potentially at least, in everyone. Thomas's gospel encourages the hearer not so much to believe in Jesus (as John 20:3–31 does), but rather to seek to know God through one's own divinely given capacity, since all are created in the image of God.[12]

> The Kingdom is inside you, and outside you. When you come to know yourselves, then you will be known, and you will see that it is you who are the children of the living Father. But if you will not know yourselves, you dwell in poverty, and it is you who *are* that poverty.[13]
>
> *Gospel of Thomas*, 3, our emphasis

When the would-be followers of Jesus look within themselves they discover that not only does Jesus come from the light, so do they:

> If they say to you, "Where did you come from?" say to them, "*We came from the light, the place where the light came into being by itself,* and was revealed through their image." If they say to you, "Who are you?" say, "We are its children, the chosen of the living father."
>
> *Gospel of Thomas*, 50, our emphasis

The *Gospel of Thomas* equates humans with Christ: "Whoever drinks from my mouth will become as I am, and I myself will become that person, and the mysteries shall be revealed to him" (108).

Pagels then asserts:

> This, I believe, is the symbolic meaning of attributing this gospel to Thomas, whose name means "twin." By encountering the "living Jesus," as Thomas suggests, one may come to recognize oneself and Jesus as, so to speak, identical twins.[14]

She then approvingly quotes *Thomas* in that regard:

> Since you are my twin and my true companion, examine yourself, and learn who you are . . . Since you will be called my [twin], . . . although you do not understand it yet . . . you will be called "the one who knows himself." For whoever has not known himself knows nothing, but whoever has known himself has simultaneously come to know the depth of all things.[15]

While Pagels believes that early Christianity offered various contradictory perspectives on Jesus (the Synoptics, John, and *Thomas*), she resonates only with the *Thomas* perspective.

She bemoans that the complexity and richness of early Christianity was lost with Irenaeus, second-century bishop of Lyons, France, who imposed, she believes, an artificial uniformity onto the church. Irenaeus was an ardent combatant against Gnosticism, prompting his five volume polemical work, *Refutation and Overthrow of Falsely So-Called Knowledge*, commonly referred to as *Against Heresies*. In those five volumes, the bishop affirmed the notion of "apostolic tradition," that is, the orthodox view of Jesus Christ that had been handed down by the apostles to each succeeding generation, namely, his birth from a virgin, his passion and resurrection in the flesh, and all unique revelatory events that provided atonement for sin.[16] As such, Irenaeus asserts that this apostolic tradition represents the canon of truth, the grid through which to filter out false teaching about Jesus.

According to Pagels, Irenaeus was among the first to champion the Gospel of John as the true interpretation of Jesus, linking it to the Synoptics, even interpreting the Synoptics through John's perspective.[17] Consequently, Irenaeus declared that these four Gospels exclusively conveyed the true message about Jesus—that he is the unique Son of God whose sacrificial death alone provides forgiveness of sin. Irenaeus secured such a privileged position for the four Gospels (read through John's perspective) by mounting a campaign against all apocryphal gospels, demanding they be destroyed.[18]

Irenaeus set the church on a path that led to the victory of orthodoxy over alternate expressions of Jesus, culminating in the official approval of the four Gospels and the apostolic tradition by Athanasius, fourth century champion of orthodoxy. Such a development was aided by the Roman Emperor Constantine, whose conversion to Christianity in AD 313 paved the way for the legalizing of Christianity. Using Christianity as the unifying principle for his empire, Constantine convened the bishops of the churches in Nicea, on the Turkish coast, in AD 325 for the purpose of composing a common set of beliefs among Christians—the Nicene Creed.[19]

In the spring of AD 367, Bishop Athanasius of Alexandria, Egypt, wrote his most famous letter. In his Easter letter to the churches, Athanasius clarified the picture of Christ that had been sketched out two hundred years before, starting with Irenaeus. First the bishop censured the heretics. They

> have tried to reduce into order for themselves the books termed apocryphal and to mix them up with the divinely inspired Scripture . . . which those who were eyewitnesses and helpers of the Word delivered to the fathers, it seemed good to me . . . to set forth in order the books included in the canon and handed down and accredited as divine.[20]

Pagels remarks:

After listing the twenty-two books that he says are "believed to be the Old Testament" [based on the Hebrew reckoning], Athanasius proceeds to offer the earliest known list of the twenty-seven books he called the "books of the New Testament," beginning with "the four Gospels, Matthew, Mark, Luke, and John," and proceeding to the same list of writings attributed to apostles that constitute the New Testament today. Praising these as the "springs of salvation," he calls upon Christians during this Lenten season to "cleanse the church from every defilement" and to reject "the apocryphal books," which are "filled with myths, empty, and polluted"—books that, he warns, "incite conflict and lead people astray."[21]

> Pagels makes essentially two arguments. First, she maintains that before Irenaeus, diversity characterized not only early Christianity, but even the New Testament. Second, she argues that a forced uniformity became the mark of the church's teaching from Irenaeus on.

The Argument against Pagels

Pagels makes essentially two arguments. First, she maintains that before Irenaeus, diversity characterized not only early Christianity, but even the New Testament. Second, she argues that a forced uniformity became the mark of the church's teaching from Irenaeus on.

We now take issue with those two claims:

First, it simply is not true that diversity to the point of contradiction characterizes the Synoptics' relationship to John. Not only does the Gospel of John teach that Jesus is God, but so do the Synoptics. This is clear from the Synoptics' titles for Jesus, *contra* Pagels: Messiah, Son of Man, and Son of God. "Messiah" is the Hebrew term for "anointed one" ("Christ" is the Greek term for the same). It is clear from Psalm 2:2, 7 that the term does not refer to a mere man, for there the Lord's anointed one (Messiah–v. 2) is proclaimed the Son of God (v. 7). Even in a Jewish work written close in time to the New Testament, *4 Ezra*, we see God call the Messiah "my son."[22]

A similar dynamic exists for the title "Son of Man," Jesus's favorite self-reference. This title originated in Daniel 7, where it is the *heavenly* Son of Man who receives the kingdom of God (Dan. 7:13).[23] "Son of God," as we saw in Psalm 2, elevates the Messiah far above humans. Furthermore, in ancient Egyptian and Mesopotamian thought as well as in the Roman Empire, the pharaoh or king was declared to be the Son of God—one divinely begotten of God. The use of these three titles for Jesus in the Synoptics, then—Messiah, Son of Man, and Son of God—surely demonstrates that they view Jesus as more than a mere man.

Moreover, Pagels asserts that the Gospel of John consciously opposed the *Gospel of Thomas*. She says this, although most scholars date *Thomas* in the second century AD, because she believes that *Thomas* dates back to around AD 50. The proof of this, according to Pagels, is that the *Gospel of Thomas* must have been extant in the first century because John criticizes it and paints such a negative picture of the apostle Thomas. Thus Thomas does not understand that Lazarus will rise from the dead (John 11:16); he does not comprehend that Jesus is the way to heaven (John 14:5–6); and most importantly, he has to see the risen Jesus before he will believe Jesus is no longer dead (John 20:24–28).[24] But there is no need to draw the conclusion from these failings of Thomas that John was criticizing a *written* document about Thomas; after all, the first two responses were typical of the misunderstandings of the disciples toward Jesus in general during the life of Christ.

Furthermore, John 20:24–28 serves the purpose of confirming that Jesus arose bodily from the dead, so Thomas was able to see and touch Christ. But the "target" for this passage need not have been the *Gospel of Thomas*, for the beginning forms of Gnosticism in the first century AD denied the bodily resurrection of Jesus, and John 20:24–28 is better suited as a barb against it. Scholars date the beginnings of Gnosticism—but not the full blown system presumed in *Thomas*—to the late first century AD, with *Gospel of Thomas* following decades later. If this is so, then Pagels's entire thesis collapses to the ground; for it

> **Athanasius's List of the Twenty-seven Books of the New Testament**
>
> "There must be no hesitation to state again the [books] of the New Testament; for they are these: Four Gospels: According to Matthew, according to Mark, according to Luke, according to John. Further, after these, also [The] Acts of [the] Apostles, and the seven so-called Catholic Epistles of the Apostles, as follows: One of James, but two of Peter, then, three of John, and after these, one of Jude. In addition to these there are fourteen Epistles of the Apostle Paul put down in the following order: The first to the Romans, then two to the Corinthians, and after these, [the Epistles] to the Galatians, and then to the Ephesians; further, [the Epistles] to the Philippians and to the Colossians and two to the Thessalonians, and the [Epistle] to the Hebrews. And next two [letters] to Timothy, but one to Titus, and the last [being] the one to Philemon. Moreover, also the Apocalypse of John."[25]

cannot uphold a first century dating of the *Gospel of Thomas*.[26] All of this to say, the four canonical Gospels espouse a consistent message about Jesus Christ—though he was fully human, he was fully God.

To summarize, Pagels states that the Synoptics do not agree with John, nor do they agree with the *Gospel of Thomas*. However, the real picture that emerges is that the Synoptics are very similar to John in their portraits of Jesus and together they disagree with the non-canonical *Thomas*'s presentation of Jesus as Gnostic.

The bottom line is that it's the non-canonical *Thomas* versus the Synoptics and John.

Neither will Pagels's second thesis do—that only from Irenaeus on was there a forced uniformity on the church's teaching about Jesus. In other words, she believes Gnostic writings like *Thomas* were held in high regard among Christians, along with the Synoptics and John, until Irenaeus messed things up. But this assumption overlooks a crucial fact: orthodoxy runs throughout the New Testament and is witnessed to consistently up to Irenaeus and far beyond. In the Pastoral Epistles—1 and 2 Timothy, Titus, written circa AD 64—the author admonishes pastors Timothy and Titus to preserve and protect the "sound doctrine" (1 Tim. 1:10; 6:3; 2 Tim. 1:13; 4:3; Titus 1:9). This sound teaching is no doubt the teaching of the apostles (Acts 2:42) concerning Jesus's birth, death, and resurrection. Second Peter (ca. AD 64) vows to protect that same truth (1:1; 2) as does Jude (ca. AD 80) urge the believers to defend "the faith which was once for all delivered to the saints" (v. 3 RSV). Most likely, these biblical authors were combating the beginning expressions of Gnosticism. First John (ca. AD 95) rounds out the discussion by providing a more sustained criticism of Gnostic teaching (1:1; 2:22; 3:4; 8–10, 4:2–3).

> However, the real picture that emerges is that the Synoptics are very similar to John in their portraits of Jesus and the four together disagree with the non-canonical Thomas's presentation of Jesus as Gnostic.

This is all in keeping with the message of the Gospel of John that Jesus is the God-man (see especially the opening statement 1:1–14). Irenaeus and Athanasius were not the first to "impose" the canonical rule of faith. In reality, the church fathers all the way from Justin Martyr (early second century AD) to Augustine (early fifth century AD) attest to the orthodox belief in Jesus. We see this from the fact that, while the fathers quote the twenty-seven New Testament books some 36,000 times (!) their treatment of the New Testament Apocrypha is negligible by way of comparison. They also chose to read and preach on the twenty-seven New Testament books in their worship services.

The necessary conclusion to be drawn from all of this is that it looks very much like orthodox Christianity was far and away the dominant view of early Christianity, beginning from New Testament times and continuing with the church fathers all the way to the Council of Nicea in AD 325 and beyond. By way of contrast, Gnosticism and the writings it spawned (the *Gospel of Thomas* and the other fifty apocryphal documents discovered at Nag Hammadi in 1945) were the view of a few extremists whose message the collective church rejected—and rightly so.

It would be fitting for us to conclude this discussion of authority by briefly stating what most biblical scholars—minus Pagels and her colleagues[27]—say about the New Testament canon. The answers to the two questions that began this section are as follows.

First, when were the twenty-seven books of the New Testament recognized to be inspired (in other words, from God)? Answer: AD 200. By then the churches were reading and the church fathers were preaching from all twenty-seven books that now comprise the New Testament. This prior practice was later confirmed at the Council of Carthage (AD 397). That assembly of church leaders, held in Carthage, North Africa, determined that only canonical works should be read in the churches. It then listed the twenty-seven books now comprising the New Testament as inspired writings.

Second, what were the criteria for including the present books in the New Testament and no more? Five criteria were applied by the church fathers:

> **When it comes to the proper view of Jesus, the New Testament is our sole authority—not Gnostic books like the *Gospel of Thomas* that tried unsuccessfully to force themselves upon the people of God.**

1. Does it have apostolic authority?
2. Does the writing in question go back to the first century?
3. Does the writing subscribe to orthodoxy?
4. Was the book read in the churches?
5. Did the people of God sense the book was inspired?[28]

The simple result of the application of these tests in the second to the fourth centuries AD was that the books of the New Testament were admitted into the canon while writings by the Gnostics and others (the *Gospel of Thomas* included) were not. And there is no reason for the modern church to do anything different now. When it comes to the proper view of Jesus, the New Testament is our sole authority—not Gnostic books like the *Gospel of Thomas* that tried unsuccessfully to force themselves upon the people of God.

ANTHROPOLOGY: WHAT IS THE NATURE OF HUMANITY?

Knowledge versus sin: That's the key issue when deciding between the *Gospel of Thomas* and the Gospel of John. In a lengthy statement, Pagels notes the contrasts between the two:

> Now we can see how John's message contrasts with that of Thomas. Thomas's Jesus directs each disciple to discover the light within ("within a person of light there is light"); but John's Jesus declares instead that "I am the light of the world" and that "whoever does not come to me walks in darkness" [John 8:12]. In Thomas, Jesus reveals to the disciples that "you are from the kingdom, and to it you shall return" and teaches them to say for themselves that "we come from the light"; but John's Jesus speaks as the only one who comes "from above" and so has rightful priority over everyone else: "*You are from below; I am from above. . . . The one who comes from above is above all*" [John 8:23]. Only Jesus is from God, and he alone offers access to God. John never tires of repeating that one must believe in Jesus, follow Jesus, obey Jesus, and confess him alone as God's *only* son. We are not his "twin," much less (even potentially) his equal; we must follow him, believe in him, and revere him as God in person: thus John's Jesus declares *"you will die in your sins, unless you believe that I am he"* [John 8:24].
>
> We are so different from Jesus, John says, that he is our only hope of salvation. Were Jesus like ourselves, he could not save and deliver a human race that is "dying in sin." What gives John hope is his conviction that Jesus descended into the world as an atonement sacrifice to save us from sin and from eternal damnation, and then rose—bodily—from the dead. As John tells it, the story of Jesus' baptism reaches its climax not, as in Mark, when Jesus announces the coming of God's kingdom, but when John the Baptist announces that Jesus has come: "Behold—the lamb of God, who takes away the sin of the world" [John 1:29].[29]

One gets the distinct impression from this that Pagels thinks the *Gospel of Thomas* got it right. The author of that writing has Jesus say, "If you bring forth what is within you, what you bring forth will save you. If you do not bring forth what is within you, what you do not bring forth will destroy you" (*Thomas*, 70).[30] This is perhaps the key statement in the *Gospel of Thomas* for it expresses the essence of human nature—humans are divine, though they need to become aware of this *gnosis* (knowledge). When that happens they are reborn; they recognize that their true destiny is the Spirit-being, not the material world. From this it follows that the *Gospel of Thomas*, like the Gnostic leaders Valentinus and Ptolemy, pinpoints the problem with humanity: not sin but lack of knowledge.[31]

This, then, is the basis of *Thomas*'s rejection of revelation as the source of truth and authority: one has those things within. Such confidence proceeds from the Gnostic assumption that there is no original sin passed along since Adam. Rather, what is passed down from generation to generation is ignorance of one's true innate goodness. If this sounds suspiciously like modern secular humanism's attempt to overthrow the concept of original sin, we should not be surprised.

But the leaders of historic Christianity were not so confident in the goodness of human nature. Though Pagels disagrees with Irenaeus's rejection of the Gnostics' exaltation of human nature, she accurately says of him:

> Nevertheless Irenaeus had to respond to a question that many people—Jews as well as "heretics"—apparently asked him: What is *wrong* with seeing Jesus as if he were simply "one of us"? Haven't we all—ourselves as well as he—been created in the image of God? Irenaeus agrees but adds that the original affinity between God and ourselves was obliterated when the human race surrendered to the power of evil. "Although by nature we belonged to the all-powerful God," he explains, the devil, whom he calls "the apostasy," captured and came to dominate the human race and "alienated us [from God], contrary to nature, and made us his own." Thus we were all in a desperate situation and would have been utterly destroyed had not the divine *word* descended from heaven to save us; for "there is no other way we could have learned about God unless our Master, existing as the word, had become man" and shed his blood to redeem us from the evil one.[32]

But, ironically, while the *Gospel of Thomas* appears to champion the image of God, it actually is an affront to humankind because it sees genderlessness as the ultimate experience. According to *Thomas*, male and female distinctions are not divine in origin. The first human being was androgynous, that is without sexual distinction. It is the goal of humanity to return to this state, which is true spirituality:

> But, ironically, while the *Gospel of Thomas* appears to champion the image of God, it actually is an affront to humankind because it sees genderlessness as the ultimate experience.

Jesus saw some babies nursing. He said to his disciples, "These nursing babies are like those who enter the Kingdom."

They said to him, "Then shall we enter the Kingdom as babies?"

Jesus said to them, "When you make the two into one, and when you make the inner like the outer and the outer like the inner, and the upper like the lower, and when you make male and female into a single one, so that the male will not be male nor the female be female, when you make eyes in place of an eye, a hand in place of a hand, a foot in place of a foot, an image in place of an image, then you will enter [the Kingdom]."[33]

Unfortunately, the concept of the image of God renewed through Christ in the *Gospel of Thomas* is further degraded when the author equates it with pantheism, the teaching that God is not separate from his creation but in it. Saying 77 puts it this way:

Jesus said, "I am the light that is over all things. I am all. From me all came forth, and to me all extends. Split a piece of wood, and I am there. Lift up the stone, and you will find me there."

All of this is far removed from the biblical concept of the image of God.

METHODOLOGY: HOW SHOULD WE INTERPRET THE GOSPEL OF JOHN AND, FOR THAT MATTER, THE BIBLE ITSELF?

How could the *Gospel of Thomas*, and Gnosticism in general, come up with such bizarre interpretations of early Christianity? Why is it that they distort the intended message of the Gospel of John? Simply put, the answer is hermeneutics. Hermeneutics has to do with the interpretation of literature in general and, for our purposes, the Bible in particular. Throughout the history of the church, a battle has raged as to how one should read sacred Scripture: literally or allegorically.

From the beginning, Jewish exegesis, or interpretation, was based on the literal (*peshat*) approach to reading the Bible. The goal of this method was to grasp what the original authors meant in their writings. The process for discovering the authorial intent of the biblical text involved locating the passage in its historical setting, identifying the cultural background of the text, and analyzing its grammar.[34] The New Testament authors continued that approach to the Old Testament, starting with Jesus himself.[35] And that stream of traditional interpretation continued on with the church fathers who lived in Antioch, Syria (for example, Theodore of Mopsuestia, ca. 350–428), and, especially through the greatest of the church fathers, Augustine of Hippo (ca. 354–430). It was sustained by the Victorines in Paris, France, and blossomed in Reformation exegesis, particularly in the works of Martin Luther and John Calvin. The literal reading of the Bible (now defined as the historical-grammatical-cultural principle) has proceeded up to this very day, notably through the Protestant heritage, but also in the modern period through Roman Catholicism.[36] In other words, the literal interpretation of the Bible has been the preferred approach of historic Christianity.

Pitted against the literal regard for the Bible is the allegorical method, which argues that the historical, cultural, and grammatical details of the text lead only to the surface meaning. Rather, what is most important is the underlying, symbolic meaning of the passage. This perspective was championed early on by the Jewish philosopher, Philo of Alexandria, Egypt (ca. 20 BC–AD 50). For example, Genesis 12 and following records Abraham and Sarah's obedience to God in departing from Mesopotamia, their temporary residence in Haran, and their permanent dwelling in Palestine. Bernard Ramm cites how Philo allegorizes this account, making it say things never intended by the writer of Genesis:

> Abraham's trek to Palestine is *really* the story of a Stoic philosopher who leaves Chaldea (sensual understanding) and stops at Haran, which means "holes," and signifies the emptiness of knowing things by the holes, that is the senses. When he becomes Abraham he becomes a truly enlightened philosopher. To marry Sarah is to marry abstract wisdom.[37]

Thereafter, because of Philo's influence, Alexandria, Egypt, became the home of the allegorical interpretation of the Bible, including famous Christian theologians such as Clement of Alexandria (ca. 150–215) and Origen (ca. 185–254). This interpretation gained a foothold in the medieval church (600–1500). It was rightly defeated by the Reformers.[38] But

Augustine's Principles for Interpreting the Bible

1. The interpreter must possess a genuine Christian faith.

2. The literal and historical meaning of Scripture should be held in high regard.

3. The task of the expositor is to understand the meaning of the author, not to bring his own meaning to the text.

4. The interpreter must consult the orthodox creed (the rule of faith).

5. A verse should be studied in its context, not in isolation from the verses around it.

6. If the meaning of a text is unclear, nothing in the passage can be made a matter of orthodox faith.

7. The Holy Spirit is not a substitute for the necessary learning to understand Scripture. The interpreter should know Hebrew, Greek, geography, and other subjects.

8. The obscure passage must yield to the clear passage.

9. The expositor should take into account that revelation is progressive.

the allegorical approach is rearing its ugly head again due to the rediscovery of Gnostic writings like the *Gospel of Thomas.*

Let's examine a couple of examples of Gnostic writings, especially their allegorical misinterpretations of the Gospel of John.[39] Valentinus, the leading Gnostic theologian in the second century AD, seems to have written the *Gospel of Truth.*[40]

> But the allegorical approach is rearing its ugly head again due to the rediscovery of Gnostic writings like the *Gospel of Thomas.*

This writing's first line is, "The gospel of truth is joy to those who receive from the Father the grace of knowing him."[41] So, "the grace of knowing him" is the Gnostic way. We can see how the *Gospel of Truth* draws on the prologue of John (1:1–18), with its emphasis on the Word: "the word of the Father . . . Jesus of the infinite sweetness . . . goes forth into all things, supporting all things," and finally "restoring all things to God . . ."[42] Similar to what we observed regarding the *Gospel of Thomas,* the *Gospel of Truth* seems to say that Jesus proceeded from God and inhabited all things, including rocks, trees, etc. Obviously this interpretation is far removed from John 1:1–18, especially verses 1–5.

> Allegorization— reading something into the text not originally intended by the sacred author. And it is in that world that the *Gospel of Thomas* fits.

The *Apocryphon of John*, another second-century Gnostic work, does something similar to John 1:5–17. In that allegorization of John's prologue, it has Jesus the light appealing to John the apostle saying, "John, John, why are you astonished and why are you afraid? . . . I am the one who is with you always. I am the Father; I am the Mother; and I am the Son."[43] After a moment of shock, John recognizes Jesus as the one who radiates the light of God and appears in various forms.[44] This is a far cry from the portrayal of Jesus in John 1:11–18—Jesus is certainly not portrayed as a mother-figure version of the Holy Spirit.

This clearly is allegorization, reading something into the text not originally intended by the sacred author. And it is in that world that the *Gospel of Thomas* fits.[45]

MORALITY: WHAT WILL HAPPEN TO THE ETHICS OF THE CHURCH IF THE GOSPEL OF THOMAS PREVAILS?

At this point, perhaps the reader is tempted to ask, "What's the big deal anyway? Isn't this another one of those picky debates that is relevant only to ivory tower theologians?" Not at all, because belief dictates behavior and behavior determines destiny. When it comes to ancient Gnosticism, biblical scholars have long noted that the Gnostics' dim view of the body resulted in two contrasting ethics: asceticism (self-denial or mistreatment of the body) and libertinism (doing whatever you want because the body doesn't matter anyway). The former is present in the *Gospel of Thomas*. Saying 27 says, "If you do not fast from the world, you will not find the Kingdom. If you do not observe the Sabbath day as a Sabbath day, you will not see the Father." Saying 49 pronounces, "Blessed are those who are solitary and chosen, for you will find the Kingdom. For you have come from it, and you will return there again." These remarks conjure up images of ascetic Christianity that later dominated the medieval monasteries. Such asceticism is sustained in the Gnostic writings.[46]

The other ethic, or lack thereof, espoused in ancient Gnostic works is libertinism, immorality in particular. The historian E. M. Yamauchi writes of this:

> Since salvation was not dependent upon faith or works but upon the knowledge of one's nature, some Gnostics indulged deliberately in licentious behavior. Carpocrates, for example, urged his followers to participate in all sins; his son Epiphanes taught that promiscuity was God's law.[47]

In this regard, one fears that the statements in the *Gospel of Thomas* and other Gnostic books about the need for humanity to return to a primeval, androgynous state puts one on the slippery slope to devaluing the genders to the point of obliterating sexual distinctions altogether.

Asceticism (and libertinism), then, inform the ethical perspectives of Gnosticism in general, and the *Gospel of Thomas* in particular. That is what potentially awaits the modern church if historic Christianity loses the day in its most recent battle with Gnosticism.

CONCLUSION

The casual observer browsing in the bookstore may pick up a copy of *Beyond Belief* by Elaine Pagels, surmising this is a book about how to move beyond one's current belief system into higher spirituality. Or he or she might assume this is a brand new take on spirituality unique to Pagels. Neither assumption would be accurate. The spirituality Pagels advocates is neither higher nor new: it is a recycled Gnosticism, whose beginnings were present in the late first century AD and fully developed in the second to third centuries.

Her advocacy of placing the *Gospel of Thomas* on par with the four traditional Gospels may also appear new, exciting, and tolerant in a day when "flexibility" in spiritual matters is attractive. Pagels, although she does not acknowledge it, is in the minority of scholars who date the *Gospel of Thomas* to the first century. She does not reveal this, although this fact is pivotal to her argument.

> **The Gnostic belief system that Pagels advocates is nothing short of life-threatening to historic Christianity today.**

She also does not disclose the lifestyle of the Gnostics, the behavioral outcome of the belief system she advocates, which is characterized by self-harm to the body in asceticism or by immorality resulting from libertinism. The Gnostic belief system that Pagels advocates is nothing short of life-threatening to historic Christianity today.

Regarding the *authority* of the Scriptures, the *Gospel of Thomas* does not meet the five criteria determined by historic Christianity for it to be included in the canon. Futhermore, the *Gospel of Thomas* was not a document contemporary with the four Gospels, for it was written in the mid- to late second century AD. In terms of *anthropology*, we, as humans, are simply not divine. Although we are created in the image of God, we are not duplicates of Jesus. And we do not arrive at the truth apart from Jesus. Examining the *methodology* for interpreting the Bible, the literal interpretation that is representative of orthodox Christianity is in direct opposition to the allegorical interpretation which Pagels advocates. Finally, and perhaps most importantly, the *morality* which is reflective of the Gnostic tradition and is the behavioral result of the position which Pagels holds has the potential of leading to two outcomes: asceticism or libertinism.

Pagels is on a mission to replace traditional Christianity with Gnosticism. If historic Christianity loses this battle, Christian faith and practice as we know it will be obliterated and the damage to individuals and society as a whole will indeed be "beyond belief."

DISCUSSION QUESTIONS

1. Please summarize the teachings of Gnosticism.
2. What are Pagels's two main claims about early Christianity?

3. How do the authors counter those two assertions?
4. What were the criteria for admitting a book into the New Testament canon?
5. What is the essential difference between reading the Scripture literally and allegorically?
6. Would the effect of the *Gospel of Thomas* upon the church today be benign if it were recognized as canonical?

3

THE NEW TESTAMENT
APOCRYPHAL GOSPELS

Are They the Missing Pieces
of Jesus's Silent Years?

||||||||||||||||||||||||||||||||||||||||||||||||||||||||||||||||||

INTRODUCTION

Have you ever wondered what Jesus was like growing up? The New Testament tells us comparatively little about his life from infancy through his late twenties. It would be fascinating to know, for example, was he kind? Was he mischievous? Did he play with other children? What was he like around his family? You may be surprised to learn there are sources outside the Bible that do claim to tell us about the boyhood of Jesus—the New Testament apocryphal books. In this chapter, we will discuss these writings and their reliability in teaching us about the "silent years" of Jesus.

Let's begin with a little true or false quiz to test your knowledge about Jesus. Some of the following come from Scripture, while others are from New Testament apocryphal books. Can you tell them apart?

1. Jesus was born in a cave.
2. Mary placed the baby Jesus in a manger.
3. Animals such as an ox, donkey, and other beasts worshipped the infant Jesus.
4. A small child played a musical instrument for the infant Jesus and was rewarded with a smile.
5. A bright light surrounded both the face of the infant Jesus and his mother Mary.

51

6. Jesus was virgin born.
7. Mary was also virgin born and remained a perpetual virgin.
8. Jesus astounded the religious authorities in his visit to the temple at age twelve.
9. Jesus's bath water as a child cleansed a girl of leprosy.
10. A child fell off a roof and died. The boy Jesus raised the child from the dead.
11. Jesus, as a child, tamed lions and leopards.
12. As Jesus, Mary, and Joseph traveled together during his childhood, they were attacked by two robbers. Jesus told Mary that one day he would be crucified between those very two men.
13. Jesus raised his friend Lazarus from the dead.
14. Jesus walked on water to the amazement of his disciples.
15. A woman who touched the hem of Jesus's garment was instantly healed.

If you aren't already secure in your answers, you will be by the end of this chapter. What is the New Testament Apocrypha anyway? Does it differ from the four Gospels (Matthew, Mark, Luke, and John)? How reliable are these documents?

Origen, a third-century church father, expressed the majority opinion of Christianity in his day about what came to be called the New Testament Apocrypha contrasted to the four Gospels:

> I know a certain gospel which is called "The Gospel according to Thomas" and a "Gospel according to Matthias," and many others have we read—lest we should in any way be considered ignorant because of those who imagine that they possess some knowledge if they are acquainted with these. Nevertheless, among all these we have approved solely what the Church has recognized, which is that only the four Gospels should be accepted.[1]

Origen was speaking of the New Testament Apocrypha. "Apocryphal" means "hidden" or "mysterious" and was first applied to some fifteen extra books the Roman Catholic Church adds to the Old Testament, including *1 and 2 Maccabees, Wisdom of Solomon,* and *Bel and the Dragon.* Although there is a debate between Protestants and Catholics over whether those books are canonical, until recently all major expressions of Christianity rejected the New Testament Apocrypha. Philip Jenkins, in an exhaustive study of these works, concludes, much like Origen, "Far from being the alternative voices of Jesus's first followers, most of the lost gospels should rather be seen as the writings of much later dissidents who broke away from an already established orthodox church."[2]

So what are the New Testament apocryphal books and why were they written? Furthermore, are they of any value to the church? First, the New Testament Apocrypha are various writings imitating the New Testament, produced from the second century up to the middle ages. These works are often written under the assumed names of the twelve apostles and the associates of Christ. Thus some are Gospels, recounting events from the life of Christ before he began his public ministry. Others are similar to Acts, claiming to record episodes from the lives of the apostles after Jesus's ministry. Still others are apocalypses, modeling the format of Revelation, while a few are letters patterned after the New Testament epistles.[3]

> *Until recently all major expressions of Christianity rejected the New Testament Apocrypha.*

The table below classifies the majority of the New Testament Apocrypha, including the Nag Hammadi documents:

I. Gospels and Related Forms

A. Narrative Gospels
1. *Gospel of the Ebionites*
2. *Gospel of the Hebrews*
3. *Gospel of the Nazoreans*
4. *Gospel of Nicodemus (Acts of Pilate)*
5. *Gospel of Peter*
6. *Infancy Gospel of Thomas*
7. Papyrus Egerton 2 (a fragment of an unknown narrative Gospel)
8. Papyrus Oxyrhyncus 840 (a fragment of an unknown narrative Gospel)
9. *Proto-Evangelium of James*
10. *Arabic Infancy Gospel*
11. *Gospel of Pseudo-Matthew*

B. Revelation Dialogues and Discourses
1. *(First) Apocalypse of James* (NHC V)
2. *(Second) Apocalypse of James* (NHC V)
3. *Apocryphon of James* (NHC 1)
4. *Apocryphon of John* (NHC II, III, IV, and BG 8502)
5. *Book of Thomas the Contender* (NHC II)
6. *Dialogue of the Savior* (NHC III)
7. *Epistula Apostolorum*

Nag Hammadi Manuscripts

A group of twelve papyrus codices plus eight leaves written in Coptic (a language of the Egyptian Christians) were found at Nag Hammadi, located in Upper Egypt, in December 1945. They came from an ancient monastery at Chenoboskion; the vast majority contain Gnostic ideas.

8. *Gospel of the Egyptians*
9. *Gospel of Mary* (BG 8502)
10. *Gospel of Philip* (NHC II)
11. *Letter of Peter to Philip* (NHC VIII)
12. *Pistis Sophia*
13. *Questions of Mary*
14. *Questions of Bartholomew*
15. *Second Treatise of the Great Seth* (NHC VII)
16. *Sophia of Jesus Christ* (NHC III and BG 8502)
17. *Two Books of Jeu*
18. Bodlian Coptic MS d54 (a fragmentary dialogue between Jesus and John)
C. Sayings, Gospels, and Collections
    1. *Gospel of Thomas* (NHC II)
    2. *Teachings of Silvanus* (NHC VII)

II. Treatises

1. *On the Origin of the World* (NHC II)
2. *(Coptic) Gospel of the Egyptians* (NHC III and IV)
3. *Gospel of Truth* (NHC I and XII)
4. *Hypostasis of the Archons* (NHC II)
5. *Treatise on Resurrection* (NHC I)
6. *Tripartite Tractate* (NCH I)

III. Apocalypses

1. *(Coptic) Apocalypse of Elijah*
2. *(Arabic) Apocalypse of Peter*
3. *(Coptic) Apocalypse of Peter* (NHC VII)
4. *(Greek/Ethiopic) Apocalypse of Peter*
5. *(Coptic) Apocalypse of Paul* (NHC V)
6. *(Latin) Apocalypse of Paul*
7. *Apocalypse of Sophonias*
8. *Apocalypse of Thomas*
9. *Ascension of Isaiah* (chaps. 6–11)
10. *Christian Sibyllines*

Apocryphon of James

"Do not let the kingdom of heaven wither away. For it is like a date-palm shoot whose fruit fell down around it. It put forth buds, and when they blossomed its productivity was caused to dry up. So it also is with the fruit that came from this singular root; when it was picked, fruit was gathered by many. Truly, this was good. Is it not possible to produce such new growth now? Cannot you discover how?"[4]

Dialogue of the Savior

"[Judas] responded, saying, 'Tell me, Lord, [how it is that . . .] . . . which shakes earth moves.' The Lord picked up a [stone and] held it in his hand, [saying, 'What] am I holding [in] my [hand]?' He said, '[It is] a stone.' He [said] to them, 'That which supports [the earth] is that which supports the heaven. When a Word comes forth from the Greatness, it will come on what supports the heaven and the earth. For the earth does not move. Were it to move, it would fall. But it neither moves nor falls, in order that the First Word might not fail. For it was that which established the cosmos and inhabited it and inhaled fragrance from it.'"[5]

    11. *Concept of Our Great Power* (NHC VI)
    12. *Book of Elchasai*
    13. *V and VI Ezra*
    14. *Melchizedek*
    15. *Mysteries of Saint John the Apostle and the Holy Virgin*

IV. Acts
    1. *Acts of Andrew*
    2. *Acts of Andrew and Matthias*
    3. *Acts of John*
    4. *Acts of Paul (and Thecla)*
    5. *(Coptic) Acts of Peter* (BG8502)
    6. *(Greek) Acts of Peter*
    7. *Acts of Peter and the Twelve* (NHC VI)
    8. *Acts of Philip*
    9. *Acts of Thomas*
    10. *Kerygmata Petrou*

V. Letters
    1. *Abgar Legend*
    2. *Correspondence between Paul and Seneca*
    3. *Epistle of Pseudo-Titus*
    4. *Paul's Letter to the Laodiceans*

VI. Liturgical Materials
  A. Homilies
    1. *Interpretation of Knowledge* (NHC XI)
    2. *Kerygma of Peter*
    3. *Testimony of Truth* (NHC IX)
    4. *A Valentian Exposition* (NHC XI)
  B. Psalms
    1. *Odes of Solomon*
  C. Prayers
    1. *On the Anointing* (NHC XI)
    2. *On Baptism A* (NHC XI)
    3. *On Baptism B* (NHC XI)
    4. *On the Eucharist A* (NHC XI)
    5. *On the Eucharist B* (NHC XI)
    6. *A Prayer of the Apostle Paul* (NHC I)

Key to abbreviations:
NHC = Nag Hammadi Codex
BG = Berlin Gnostic Papyrus[6]

Why were the New Testament Apocrypha written? Everett Harrison points out the twofold motivation behind the writing of these works:

Two factors are largely responsible for the creation of these writings. One was the desire for further information about the life of Jesus and the careers of the apostles. Scripture has little to say about our Lord prior to the opening of his ministry. This gap was an invitation and even a challenge to supply the deficiency by calling upon the resources of the imagination. . . .

A second factor was the desire of those with heretical tendencies to foist their ideas on the church with the alleged endorsement of Christ or the apostles. By far the most common of these tendencies was the Gnostic. . . . It was rather easy to claim the authority of Jesus for teaching that went beyond that of the New Testament, since he himself had hinted that he had much to say that he was unable to impart to his disciples at the time (John 16:12). This was an open door for Gnostic propaganda, especially as it was put in the lips of the resurrected Saviour.[7]

But if the New Testament apocryphal books are not canonical, then what value are they to the church? Actually, there are several reasons Christians can benefit from studying these "hidden" writings.

First, they bear witness to customs, ideas, and philosophies prevalent during early Christianity. For example, we learn much about Greek philosophy, especially Plato, from these works. And also about how Jesus was presented as the Word of God. This background enabled the orthodox church to formulate its creeds and beliefs about the Trinity.

Second, the New Testament Apocrypha remind us that early Christendom was diverse and complex, which might better inform Christians today how to live in a pluralistic society. Third, some of the early New Testament apocryphal books just might contain an authentic word from Jesus here and there that did not get recorded in the four Gospels. These *agrapha*, nonwritings, occur in the New Testament, but not in the Gospels. Thus Acts 20:35 states "remembering the words the Lord Jesus himself said: 'It is more blessed to give than to receive'" (NIV). In 1 Corinthians 7:10, 9:14, and 11:24–25, Paul

> *"Two factors are largely responsible for the creation of these [apocryphal] writings. One was the desire for further information about the life of Jesus and the careers of the apostles. . . . A second factor was the desire of those with heretical tendencies to foist their ideas on the church with the alleged endorsement of Christ or the apostles."*

records words of Jesus given to him not mentioned in the four Gospels. So one should not be surprised to find *agrapha* in the New Testament Apocrypha. Otfried Hofius, a leading expert on the subject, has convinced many that there are perhaps three of these authentic utterances to be found in the New Testament Apocrypha:

1. The *Gospel of Thomas* 82, which says: "Whoever is near me is near the fire; whoever is far from me is far from the kingdom."
2. A phrase from the *Gospel of the Hebrews* quoted in Jerome, which says, "And never be joyful, save when you look upon your brother in love."[8]
3. The fragment in the Oxyrhynchus Papyrus 1224, which states, "And pray for your [ene]mies, For he who is not [against yo]u is for you. [He that] stands far off [today] will tomorrow be [near you]."[9]

We should hasten to add, however, that recognizing these three utterances as authentic statements by Jesus is a far cry from placing the New Testament Apocrypha en mass on par with the New Testament.

This leads us to a fourth "contribution" made by these hidden writings. By way of contrast, they underscore the distinctiveness of the New Testament canon. Harrison rightly notes that

> the student is able to compare this literature with the acknowledged books of the New Testament. If he has misgivings about the formation of the canon, feeling that perhaps the endorsement of the books was somewhat arbitrary, it is morally certain that he will be won to a position of complete confidence in the superiority of the New Testament books on the basis of comparison.[10]

THE NEW TESTAMENT APOCRYPHA AND JESUS'S SILENT YEARS

We now focus on those New Testament apocryphal gospels and related literature that purport to supply events from Jesus's silent years. Four stages of Jesus's life before his public ministry will be highlighted from those fascinating works: infancy—the *Proto-Evangelium of James*; two-year stay in Egypt after his birth—the *Arabic Infancy Gospel* and the *Gospel of Pseudo-Matthew*; childhood from ages five to twelve—the *Infancy Gospel of Thomas*; and teenage years and early adulthood—*The Unknown Life of Jesus Christ: From Buddhistic Records*. We will discover that these materials reveal their respective motives for their stories about Jesus. After summarizing the contents of these works, we will critique them in the next section.

Jesus's Infancy: The Proto-Evangelium of James

"Proto-Evangelium" means proto or first gospel, as related by James, most likely the brother of Jesus. The author of this Greek manuscript tells his readers that he wrote an early history of Jesus's infancy and especially regarding his mother Mary (25.1).[11] James would know because he was the son of Joseph by a former marriage (9.2). The author asserts that he wrote his book right after the death of Herod Antipas (Herod the Great's son), which occurred in AD 44. In fact, *Proto-Evangelium of James* dates no earlier than AD 150, for it clearly draws on Jesus's infancy accounts in Luke (ca. AD 70–80) and Matthew (ca. AD 80–90). We know it was written by mid- to late second century AD, though, because there are indications that Clement of Alexandria (second century) and Origen (second/third century) probably knew of *Proto-Evangelium*.[12]

The story begins by telling of the sadness of Joachim and his wife, Anna, because they could not have children (1.1–3.2). But, reminiscent of God's answer to Hannah's cry for a child (1 Samuel 1), the angel of the Lord told Anna that she would give birth to a baby girl (4.1–4). Shortly after that, Anna miraculously conceived (nothing is said of Joachim's part in the conception) and nine months later delivered Mary. In grateful response Anna promised she would take her baby girl to the Jerusalem temple to be raised unto God (5.1–6.1). Then, at the age of two, Anna and Joachim took little Mary to the temple where she was raised by the priests as a virgin, separated unto the Lord (6.2–8.2). When Mary reached the age of twelve, God told the priests that she should be married to Joseph, a widower with children (9.1–10.2). "And the priest said to Joseph: 'Joseph, to you has fallen the good fortune to receive the virgin of the Lord; take her under your care'" (9.1). But some time later, Joseph discovered with horror that his wife Mary was pregnant. Like the account of Matthew, Joseph struggled to know what to do with Mary, but an angel of the Lord assuaged his fears by telling him Mary's conception was by the Holy Spirit of God (9.2–16.2).

Following the account in Luke, *Proto-Evangelium of James* then relates Augustus's census and

Four stages of Jesus's life before his public ministry will be highlighted from those fascinating works: infancy, two-year stay in Egypt after his birth, childhood from ages five to twelve, and teenage years and early adulthood.

"Christ traveled through many countries teaching and performing all kinds of miracles before arriving to Judea to teach the doctrine formulated in Japan. This provoked the Romans who sentenced Jesus to death by crucifixion, but Jesus's brother, Isukiri, voluntarily sacrificed himself on the cross. At the age of 36, Christ went on a four-year journey to northern Europe, Africa, Central Asia, China, Siberia, Alaska, down through both Americas and back to Alaska. He then arrived at Matsugasaki Port in Japan . . . on 26 February in the 33rd year of Suinin, together with many followers from all the countries he had visited on the way. Christ's final years were spent in Herai, where he died at the age of 118."[13] Is this true?

the holy couple's journey to Bethlehem (17.1–19.1). Unique to *Proto-Evangelium*, however, Mary rested in a cave, where the glory of the Lord appeared and then a brilliant light, which prevented the onlookers from seeing the actual birth of Jesus. The light left the cave after Jesus was born (19.2–3). Then there follows the story about the midwife who was with Mary, who convincingly testifies to others that Jesus was virgin born (19.3–20.3). At that point, the story pretty much resumes Matthew's infancy account, relating the incidents of the Magi's visit to Jesus and Herod the Great's failed attempt to kill Jesus (21.1–4). In retaliation Herod had Jewish males under two years old killed, as well as Zecharias, father of John the Baptist (22.1–24.4).

There are two motives for the writing of *Proto-Evangelium of James*: First, it is a defense of the virgin birth of Jesus, perhaps in contrast to Jewish accusations that Jesus was the illegitimate child born out of Mary's sexual relations with a Roman soldier by the name of Panthera.[14] Second, it purports that Mary was also virgin born and she remained a perpetual virgin. Oscar Cullmann writes of this work:

> All the future themes of Mariology are already propounded: the "immaculate conception" of the mother of Jesus is not indeed yet taught, but her birth, in itself miraculous, is recorded. The virgin birth of Jesus, in contrast to the more unbiased views of Tertullian and Origen, is already understood as implying Mary's perpetual virginity. This is harmonized with the existence of brothers of Jesus

> There are two motives for the writing of *Proto-Evangelium of James*: (1) It is a defense of the virgin birth of Jesus, and (2) it purports that Mary was also virgin born and she remained a perpetual virgin.

in the primitive tradition by postulating an earlier marriage of Joseph, an explanation which was accepted as plausible down to the time of Jerome. Yet this very assumption provoked Jerome, who wished to have the brothers of Jesus regarded as his cousins, into a sharp polemic against the *Protev. of James*, which was then taken up by the popes.[15]

The belief in Mary's perpetual virginity continues to be a cherished doctrine in Roman Catholicism.

Jesus's Stay in Egypt: The Arabic Infancy Gospel and Pseudo-Matthew

If *Proto-Evangelium of James* is a defense of one aspect of Jesus's infancy, the next two works are born out of concerns to present Jesus as solely God. The *Arabic Infancy Gospel* and *Pseudo-Matthew* claim that Jesus as a young child during his sojourn in Egypt was every bit the supernatural Son of God that he was in adulthood, performing miracles that were sometimes bizarre in nature.

The first of these, the *Arabic Infancy Gospel*, is an Arabic work probably based on a Syriac text, which does not date any earlier than the fifth century AD. The first edition of the Arabic translation appeared in 1697, and became familiar to Muslims.[16] We will only comment on the part of the text that speaks of Jesus's stay in Egypt. (The other part of the work deals with the miracles of Jesus as a boy in Israel, but because these are also recorded in the *Infancy Gospel of Thomas*, which we will soon discuss, we will not treat that section here.)

The *Arabic Infancy Gospel* relates several legends associated with Jesus's childhood in Egypt.[17] Jesus's bath water cleansed a girl of leprosy (17–22). In an Egyptian desert, Joseph, Mary, and Jesus came upon a band of robbers, led by two thieves, Titus and Dumachus. Titus took compassion on the holy family and granted them safe passageway. When Dumachus objected, Titus paid him forty drachmae to let them go, which he did. After the family safely left, the young Jesus prophesied to his mother that in thirty years he would be crucified between those very two men. And Titus would be taken to paradise because of his kindness to Jesus and his parents (23). After that incident, the holy family stopped under a sycamore tree and Jesus caused a spring to gush forth from it. Mary then washed his shirt in the water, and the sweat wrung out from the shirt caused balsam to appear in that place (24).[18] The last miracle recorded in this document has Jesus change children into three-year-old goats because they hid from him. But Jesus showed mercy on the children by changing the goats back into children, after which they played with Jesus. The onlookers thereby proclaimed Jesus to be the good shepherd and the Lord (40).

The second work which highlights Jesus's childhood in Egypt is *Pseudo-Matthew*. This work was probably written in the eighth or ninth century, but rumor had it that the great Latin translator, Jerome, identified it as being written by Matthew. But no scholar today believes that to be true; hence the name *Pseudo* (false) *Matthew*.[19] This writing, too, ascribes supernatural miracles to the young Jesus, moving from one legend to the next.

After his birth in the cave at Bethlehem, Mary moved Jesus to a manger in a stable, where an ox, donkey, and other beasts worshipped him (14.1–2).[20] In Egypt, Jesus cast out dragons from a cave so Mary and Joseph could rest in it (18.1). Lions and leopards were tamed by Jesus. In his presence, wild beasts walked peacefully with domesticated animals (18.2–19.2). In the hot Egyptian desert, little Jesus commanded high palm tree branches to bend down and give its fruit to Mary to nourish her, which they did, only resuming their upright posture at Jesus's command. Next, Jesus commanded the roots of the tree to spring forth water to drink (20.1–2). The next day, Jesus commanded that an angel take one of the palm branches to be in heaven's paradise (21). Because the desert was so hot and Mary and Joseph were dehydrated, Jesus miraculously fast-forwarded their journey to the city of Hermopolis, compressing a thirty-day trip into one day (22.1). When the holy family reached that pagan Egyptian city, the 365 idols in its temple fell and shattered on the ground as Jesus passed by. This prompted the governor, the priests, and all of the people of Hermopolis to worship Christ (22.2–24). After these things, an angel told Joseph to go back to Judea because Herod was dead (25).

> *Pseudo-Matthew ascribes supernatural miracles to the young Jesus, moving from one legend to the next.*

Jesus from Age Five to Twelve: The Infancy Gospel of Thomas

Second in popularity only to *Proto-Evangelium of James,* the *Infancy Gospel of Thomas* (not to be confused with the *Gospel of Thomas*) has attracted much attention throughout the centuries. Knowledge of this work goes as far back as Irenaeus (*Against Heresies* 1:13, second century), who criticizes it. It has come to us in various languages, including Greek (probably the original language of the text), Syriac, and Latin.[21] The *Infancy Gospel of Thomas* has a distinct purpose—to prove that Jesus was a child prodigy. Oscar Cullmann notes of this:

> All the miracles he was later to perform are here anticipated in a particularly blatant fashion. There is, however, a great difference between those miracles

and those reported in the canonical Gospels. Here the extraneous material is simply imported into the story of Jesus, without the slightest attempt to make it fit, even remotely, the portrait of Christ. If the name of Jesus did not stand alongside the description "child" or "boy," one could not possibly hit upon the idea that these stories of the capricious divine boy were intended to supplement the tradition about him. Parallels from the legends of Krishna and Buddha, as well as all kinds of fables, can here be adduced in particular quantity. The cruder and more startling the miracle, the greater the pleasure the compiler finds in it, without the slightest scruple about the questionable nature of the material. In this respect there is a vast difference also between the [infancy] *Gospel of Thomas* and the *Protoevangelium of James.*[22]

Not only Christ the miracle-worker but also Christ the teacher is fore-shadowed in the boy Jesus. He possessed all the wisdom of this age and was highly esteemed as a Gnostic teacher.[23] This is why he could confound the Jewish sages in his temple visit at age twelve (19.1–5). This is the ultimate motive behind the "account of Thomas the Israelite philosopher concerning the childhood of the Lord," the opening title of the work.

Here is a list of the miracles and teachings of Jesus from ages five to twelve, as portrayed in the *Infancy Gospel of Thomas*:

Age 5

2.1: Jesus miraculously gathered the water of a ford into pools, and purified them by his word.

2.2–5: Jesus made twelve live sparrows from soft clay on the Sabbath. Jesus clapped his hands and the sparrows flew away.

3.1–3: The son of Annas the Scribe was disturbed with this happening on the Sabbath, so he stirred up the pools of water. Jesus cursed the lad and he withered up like a tree.

4.1–5.2: Jesus pronounced a death curse on a boy who inadvertently ran into Jesus. The boy died. When the parents of the deceased boy rebuked Jesus, he struck them blind.

6.1–8.2: The teacher Zacchaeus saw in Jesus great promise, so he tried to teach him the Greek and Hebrew alphabet. But Jesus confounded the teacher by providing an allegorical interpretation of the alphabet.

9.1–3: Jesus raised to life a child who fell off a roof and died.

10.1–2: Jesus healed the foot of a young man who split it with an axe.

Age 6

11.1–2: Jesus fell and broke a pitcher of water, but he supernaturally gathered the water in his cloak and brought it to his mother.

12.1–2: Jesus miraculously multiplied one kernel of wheat into a hundred-fold.

13.1–2: The six-year-old carpenter miraculously caused a leg of a table to grow.

14.1–3: Another teacher attempted to teach Jesus Hebrew and Greek, but Jesus again told mysteries about the languages, angering the instructor. The teacher rebuked Jesus, only to have Jesus curse the teacher, who then died.

15.1–4: A third teacher attempted to teach Jesus. But this instructor marveled at Jesus's wisdom. Jesus rewarded that man by bringing to life the second teacher cursed by Jesus.

16.1–2: A poisonous snake bit Jesus's brother, James, but Jesus breathed on the bite and his brother was healed.

17.1–2: Jesus raised a child from the dead who had been sick.

18.1–2: Jesus raised a construction worker from the dead who had met with an on-site accident.

Age 12

19.1–5: Jesus appeared in the temple and amazed the teachers with his knowledge of the law and the prophets.

So what we find in the *Infancy Gospel of Thomas* is a rather misbehaved miracle-working boy, who possessed knowledge that confounded the teachers of Israel. Two Gnostic themes inform this portrait. First, Jesus did not (like Luke 2:52 says) grow in wisdom; he had it instantly. The Docetics held that Jesus only appeared to be human, that he was really only God from the start. One will recognize in this description the aversion that Gnostics had for human flesh. Second, Jesus possessed special knowledge (*gnosis*) that set him apart from even the brightest in ancient Israel. Later forms of Gnosticism would connect these two ideas: thus Gnostics believed true knowledge recognized that spirituality resides in the soul not the body. Thus, the *Infancy Gospel of Thomas* was propaganda for Gnosticism.

Two Gnostic themes inform this portrait. First, Jesus did not (like Luke 2:52 says) grow in wisdom; he had it instantly. Second, Jesus possessed special knowledge (gnosis) that set him apart from even the brightest in ancient Israel.

From Jesus as a Teenager until His Public Ministry (Age 30)—The Unknown Life of Jesus Christ, from Buddhistic Records

In the early twentieth century, Nicholas Notovich published his work *The Unknown Life of Jesus Christ: From Buddhistic Records*. In that book, the author claims that on his trip to Tibet he found numerous sermons by Jesus. Supposedly, Jesus had delivered these sermons in India while a teenager. News of Notovich's claim attracted much attention in the 1920s.[24]

Notovich's work is but one of a number of twentieth-century books that want to demonstrate that Jesus's teaching ultimately is not Judeo-Christian in orientation but rather is permeated by Asian thinking, even New Age–like teaching.[25] As such, the movement's motive is polemical in nature: that the orthodox, established church has until recently managed to suppress the "authentic" sources of the life and work of Jesus. For Notovich, the authentic source is clear: Jesus was Buddhist.

Pagels herself, in *The Gnostic Gospels*, accepts the supposed connection between Jesus and Buddha, basing it in the *Gospel of Thomas*, which we examined in chapter 2. Pagels writes, "One need only listen to the words of the *Gospel of Thomas* to hear how it resonates with the Buddhist tradition . . . these ancient gospels tend to point beyond faith toward a path of solitary searching to find understanding, or *gnosis*." She asks, "Does not such teaching—the identity of the divine and human, the concern with illusion and enlightenment, the founder who is presented not as Lord but as spiritual guide—sound more Eastern than Western?" She suggests that we might see an explicitly Indian influence in *Thomas*, perhaps via the Christian communities in southern India, the so-called Thomas Christians.[26]

"When we were in Srinigar, we were told of a book written by a European [Notovich] who advanced a strange theory. The author claimed to have found documentary evidence in Himis that Jesus Christ had been to Ladakh in his lifetime. After the crucifixion, so the tale goes, Christ was not buried in the Holy Land, but was brought secretly to Little Tibet, brought to life by Himalayan herbs and later ascended to heaven from the Himalayas. We were also told that this author mentioned going to Himis and seeing the document with Father Gergen. But the venerable old gentleman [Father Gergen] assured us he knew of no such evidence. Though he remembered the author, he had never been to Himis with him. After reading the book, several European church dignitaries wrote to Father Gergen asking for corroboration and details of this matter. When we visited Himis, we asked about the document [Notovich's sermon scrolls], but the lamas didn't know what we were talking about. It was Greek to them."[27]

Never mind that Notovich's work was exposed as a forgery; the seed had been planted and the twenty-first century is experiencing its harvest of ideas.[28]

A RESPONSE TO NEW TESTAMENT APOCRYPHAL GOSPELS

> *Never mind that Notovich's work was exposed as a forgery; the seed had been planted and the twenty-first century is experiencing its harvest of ideas.*

Two damaging pieces of evidence have emerged in our discussion of New Testament apocryphal gospels that claim to fill in the missing pieces of Jesus's silent years. First, the late dating of these works prohibits their inclusion in the New Testament canon, the latter of which was completed by AD 100. The *Arabic Infancy Gospel* dates no earlier than the fifth century AD. *Pseudo-Matthew* only goes back to the eighth or ninth century AD. Assertions in *The Unknown Life of Christ* that sermons Jesus preached in India have been found are recognized by all biblical scholars to be forgeries dating to the early twentieth century. That leaves us with the *Infancy Gospel of Thomas* and *Proto-Evangelium of James*. They date to the mid-second century AD, but even these were written fifty years after Revelation, the last book of the Bible. Furthermore, the church fathers from the second century up to the fifth century AD have left us their sermons and quotations of the books considered by the early church to be inspired, and they are our current twenty-seven books of the New Testament. These they draw on over 36,000 times! The only times they mention the New Testament Apocrypha, such as we discussed in this chapter, is for the purpose of criticizing them. In other words, it is clear that books like those we have analyzed in this chapter were never highly regarded in early Christianity.

Second, it has also become clear that the writings evaluated in this chapter are driven by agendas other than historical fact. Thus *Proto-Evangelium of James* obviously plays loose with the truth when it attempts to defend the perpetual virginity of Mary, the mother of Jesus. The author's claim that Joseph was a widower who had children from a first marriage fares no better to convince the reader than those who say the brothers and sisters of Jesus were only his cousins, not his natural siblings. The Gospels (see Mark 3:31–33 and its parallel passages) and Paul (1 Cor. 15:7) are quite clear on the matter: Mary and Joseph had children after the virginal conception and birth of Jesus. Mary was a human being who later gave birth to other children. More on this in our next chapter when we discuss the ossuary box of James, the brother of Jesus.

The repeated, and sometimes bizarre, miracle stories in the *Arabic Infancy Gospel* and *Pseudo-Matthew* are obviously born of motives to portray Jesus as solely God, not at all human. While we certainly agree that Jesus was God in all phases of his life, one is left with the distinct impression that these two writings are docetic in perspective; that is, they will not let Jesus be human as well. This is in contrast to Luke 2:52, which tells us that Jesus grew in wisdom and knowledge and in favor with God and humans. He was divine as a child but undeveloped; he had to grow and mature like all other humans. Likewise, the propaganda conveyed in the *Infancy Gospel of Thomas* plays down the human nature of young Jesus in typical docetic fashion, while its portrayal of Jesus as an ethereal, mystic teacher combines to portray him as the first Gnostic. Such a picture demeans the Gospels' message that Jesus was fully God and fully human.

And the agenda behind *The Unknown Life of Christ*—that orthodox Christianity has not been able to suppress the true message that Jesus was a Buddha—has no place in serious biblical study.

> *The New Testament apocryphal gospels are an off-shoot of orthodox Christianity, not merely a collection of supplementary and complementary materials to the canonical Gospels.*

CONCLUSION

The New Testament apocryphal gospels are an off-shoot of orthodox Christianity, not merely a collection of supplementary and complementary materials to the canonical Gospels. Do you recall our quiz at the beginning of this chapter? You may have already found some of the answers contained in the chapter. The following are from the four canonical Gospels (Matthew, Mark, Luke, and John):

Mary placed Jesus in a manger.

Jesus was virgin born.

Jesus astounded the religious authorities in his visit to the temple at age twelve.

Jesus raised his friend Lazarus from the dead.

Jesus walked on water to the amazement of his disciples.

A woman who touched the hem of Jesus's garment was instantly healed.

The remainder are from the New Testament apocryphal gospels:

Jesus was born in a cave.

Animals such as an ox, donkey, and other beasts worshipped the infant Jesus.

A small child played a musical instrument for the infant Jesus and was rewarded with a smile.

A bright light surrounded both the face of the infant Jesus and his mother Mary.

Mary was also virgin born and remained a perpetual virgin.

Jesus's bath water as a child cleansed a girl of leprosy.

A child fell off a roof and died. Jesus, as a boy, raised the child from the dead.

As Jesus, Mary, and Joseph traveled together during his childhood, they were attacked by two robbers. Jesus told Mary that one day he would be crucified between those very two men.

Jesus, as a child, tamed lions and leopards.

A reading of the apocryphal gospels is fascinating and is beneficial from the standpoint of understanding the culture, customs, and complexity of the early days of Christianity, and because there are therein perhaps several authentic utterances of Jesus not recorded in the four canonical Gospels. In addition, and more importantly, they serve as a contrast to the canonical Gospels, for the stories contained within are clearly legends, not based in fact. They are interesting documents, but they exist to paint a very different portrait of Jesus than that of historic Christianity. We see that although they claim to have been written as contemporaries of the canonical Gospels, they were actually written much later, which negates their reliability.

> *We see that although they claim to have been written as contemporaries of the canonical Gospels, they [the New Testament Apocrypha] were actually written much later, which negates their reliability.*

DISCUSSION QUESTIONS

1. What are the New Testament Apocrypha?
2. For what two reasons were they written?

3. What does *Proto-Evangelium of James* say about Mary the mother of Jesus?
4. Can you name two purported miracles by Jesus recorded in the *Arabic Infancy Gospel*?
5. Can you do the same for *Pseudo-Matthew*?
6. How is the *Infancy Gospel of Thomas* Gnostic in orientation?
7. Is there any value in studying the New Testament Apocrypha?

THE BONES OF JAMES, BROTHER OF JESUS

Are They Bona Fide?

||||||||||||||||||||||||||||||||||||||||||||||||||||||||||||||

In the fall of 2002, an ossuary (bone box used for burial) bearing the inscription, "James, son of Joseph, brother of Jesus" created an uproar among academics and popular audiences alike. For scholars, the controversy centered on the fact that the ossuary had not been excavated by qualified archaeologists. Apparently, it had come to its dealer via the antiquities (underground) market. For the general public, the debate focused on the relationship between James, the leader of the Jerusalem church from AD 40s to 62, and Jesus.

Hershel Shanks, the editor of *Biblical Archaeology Review*, first broke the story on October 21, 2002, at a press conference held in conjunction with the Discovery Channel. The next morning, a color picture of the ossuary appeared on the front pages of the *New York Times*, *Washington Post*, and numerous other major newspapers around the world. Shanks appeared on the evening news with Peter Jennings, Tom Brokaw, and Jim Lehrer. Voice of America and CNN broadcast the story around the globe.[1]

Shanks registered a number of questions that accompanied the discovery:

> But the initial excitement has been followed by a barrage of questions. Where did it come from? How did the collector get it? Is it a fake? How do we know that it refers to Jesus of Nazareth? Did Jesus have a brother? Who, really, was James, and why is he so significant in understanding the earliest forms of Christianity?
>
> And what are the theological implications of this extraordinary find? Does it cast doubt on the doctrine that Mary was a perpetual virgin? Does it challenge the Roman Catholic identification of James as only a cousin of Jesus?[2]

> "The simplest explanation is the likeliest... the James ossuary is what it seems, the earliest recorded reference to Jesus of Nazareth."

These questions reveal how significant the ossuary of James is. Thus on the book cover of Shanks and Ben Witherington's book, *The Brother of Jesus*, the *New York Times* said of this discovery, "This could well be the earliest artifact ever found relating to the existence of Jesus." *Newsweek* chimes in on the back cover:

Although Jesus of Nazareth is a universally recognized figure, no one has ever found any evidence for his existence apart from texts. Now, in the form of a twenty-inch-long limestone ossuary, a box used by first-century Jews to hold the bones of the dead, biblical archaeologists may have found their holy grail.

To those who doubt the authenticity of the ossuary, the *Wall Street Journal* asserts this on the back cover: "The simplest explanation is the likeliest . . . the James ossuary is what it seems, the earliest recorded reference to Jesus of Nazareth."

The purpose of this chapter is to enter into the fray of debate over this ossuary by covering three points: the discovery of the bone box, the controversy surrounding it, and the significance of it. Regarding the last point, what would it mean if the bone box is bona fide? (Pardon the pun.) And what facts remain if it is not?

THE DISCOVERY OF THE JAMES OSSUARY

It appears that there were three steps in the process whereby the James ossuary was brought to the notice of the public, a fascinating story with unexpected twists and turns.

Oded Golan, a successful Israeli engineer and entrepreneur, has collected thousands of ancient artifacts since he was eight years old. In recent years he has stored them in his Tel Aviv apartment. Golan bought the ossuary in question when he was twenty-three from an Arab antiquities dealer in Jerusalem's Old City. When it was purchased is significant here because if he acquired the box before 1978, as he claims, his findings would legally belong to him. But after a law passed in 1978, Israel by right is the owner of archeological findings made in that country.[3]

Back to the story. The dealer told him that the box had been found in Silwan, an Arab village south of the Mount of Olives and in plain view of the Temple

Mount. Interestingly enough, the limestone ossuary matched the limestone bedrock flanking the Kidron Valley, the valley separating the Temple Mount from the Mount of Olives.[4]

In the late spring of 2002, Golan invited André Lemaire, one of the world's leading experts on ancient Semitic scripts, to visit his apartment to peruse some of Golan's artifacts. Lemaire did so; while examining the items, Golan showed him a photograph of an inscription on an ossuary. Ossuaries are relics of Jewish burial practices from 20 BC to AD 70 in Jerusalem. Corpses were placed in family tombs and, after the body decayed in about a year, the bones of the relative were gathered together in a bone box and left in the tomb. Some 900 ossuaries have been catalogued from this period of time, with about 250 of them bearing inscriptions that identify the deceased.[5]

On this particular ossuary the letters were carefully engraved, the significance of which had not yet impressed its owner. But when Golan showed the photograph to Lemaire, the latter was awestruck. If the find was authentic, the words "James, son of Joseph, brother of Jesus" would possess astounding importance. Here was the first archaeological confirmation that James and Jesus lived and were brothers![6] Later, when Golan was asked why he failed to recognize the significance of the inscription, he responded with a now famous quip: "I didn't know the Son of God could have a brother!"[7]

Although there were no indications that the ossuary still contained bones, the James ossuary would be an incredible find. Clearly, Lemaire recognized this.

After studying the photograph, Lemaire, a leading epigrapher (one who studies ancient letters), became convinced the bone box was authentic. Some time after his meeting with Golan on May 22, 2002, Lemaire had lunch with Hershel Shanks, editor of *Biblical Archaeology Review*, in Jerusalem and mentioned that he would like to publish an article on the ossuary of James.[8] With Golan's permission, and with two excellent photographs he supplied, Lemaire wrote the article and sent it to Shanks. So now collector/owner Golan and discoverer Lemaire had set in motion the unveiling of the ossuary.

Shanks represented the third stage of the making known of the James ossuary when he published Lemaire's article in *Biblical Archaeology Review* in November. Before publishing the article, however, Shanks solicited the input of experts on Aramaic, the language of the inscription. Aramaic is a sister language to Hebrew and was spoken by Jesus and most Jews in the first century AD in Palestine. Thus Kyle McCarter, Professor of Bible and Ancient Eastern Studies at

> **Here was the first archaeological confirmation that James and Jesus lived and were brothers!**

> **All three of these scholars concluded that the Aramaic inscription dates to the first century AD, the time of Jesus and James, and that it was not a forgery.**

Johns Hopkins University in Baltimore, Ada Yardeni, Israel's leading expert on Semitic scripts, Father Joseph A. Fitzmyer, another leading Aramaic expert and professor emeritus at Catholic University of America in Washington, D.C., were asked to register their expert opinions about the box. All three of these scholars concluded that the Aramaic inscription dates to the first century AD, the time of Jesus and James,[9] and that it was not a forgery.

Next, Shanks, with the permission of Golan, had the ossuary sent to the Geological Survey of Israel in Jerusalem to test the composition of the ossuary. Shanks writes:

The tests were performed by Amnon Rosenfeld and Shimon Ilani of the Geological Survey of the State of Israel. They examined the stone, the dirt that still clings to the sides of the ossuary, and, most important, the patina, a film formed from chemicals that seep out of or drip onto the stone over hundreds of years as it lies in a damp cave. The chemical makeup of the patina is thus dependent on the nature of the stone. . . .

They found the ossuary to be made of chalk limestone of the Menuha Formation of the Mount Scopus Group and noted that the lower part of this formation "was exploited around Jerusalem during the 1st and 2nd centuries CE [AD]." Indeed, several quarries of this particular limestone and from this period have been found in the Jerusalem area. . . .

Most tellingly, the patina found inside the incised letters of the inscription was the same as the patina on the side of the ossuary. This eliminated the possibility that the inscription was a modern forgery on a genuine ancient ossuary.

Could patina have been taken from another ossuary and applied to this one, both on the side and within the carved letters? The geologists considered this possibility. But they found that the patina "adheres strongly to the stone," and they found no trace of a modern adhesive. . . .

The ossuary inscription, they concluded, was ancient and authentic. I now felt confident in publishing Lemaire's article in BAR. The inscription had passed every test we could devise.[10]

THE CONTROVERSY OVER THE JAMES OSSUARY

Even before the unveiling of the James ossuary, at least one of the experts who later approved of the artifact expressed some concerns about the inscription in particular. Paleography (the study of shapes and forms of ancient letters in order to determine their date) is a specific branch of epigraphy. McCarter, the paleographer referred to earlier, judged the inscription to be ancient, though he thought it possible that two hands were involved. One person may have carved the first half ("James, son of Joseph") and a century later a second hand might have carved the second half ("brother of Jesus").[11] But this fear was allayed by the later inspection conducted by officials at the Royal Ontario Museum in Toronto, Canada, and confirmed by the Geological Survey of Israel. They determined that the same patina occurs inside the letters of both halves of the inscription, which matched the patina on the side of the ossuary.[12]

McCarter was also concerned that three of the twenty letters in the inscription were cursive—yod, dalet, aleph—while the others were not. This might suggest those three letters originated at a later date. But Lemaire seemingly answered that doubt by noting that it is rather common in ossuary inscriptions to see a mixture of cursive and formal letters.[13]

In summary of its authenticity, Shanks appealed to five major arguments which combine to indicate the ossuary contained the remains of James, son of Joseph and brother of Jesus. First, the shape and form of the letters (paleography) point to a first century AD date. Actually, according to Lemaire, the three cursive letters (yod, dalet, aleph) matched the shape of those letters precisely in the decades before the fall of Jerusalem in AD 70. And James the brother of Jesus died in AD 62.[14] Second, the inscription is in Aramaic, the spoken language of Jews in first-century Palestine. Third, geological analysis showed that the patina is consistent on the side of the box and in both halves of the inscription. Fourth, statistically, Lemaire estimates that only twenty men lived in Palestine in the first century who were named James and connected with a Joseph and Jesus. But Camil Fuchs, a professor of statistics at Tel Aviv University in Israel, estimated that there were only between two and four men who fit the description of the inscription. Fifth, from a psychological point of view, neither buyer (Golan) nor seller (unknown to the public) knew the worth of the ossuary; it was only revealed to Golan by Lemaire.[15]

And so it was that on Sunday evening, November 24, 2002, Shanks, Lemaire, McCarter, Fitzmyer, Harvard University emeritus professor Frank Cross (the unofficial dean of paleographers), and other scholarly notables enjoyed a private showing of the James ossuary while it was on display at the Royal Ontario Museum. They all agreed that nothing about the inscription suggested it was a modern forgery.[16]

Yet from the beginning of its unveiling to the public, the James ossuary had its detractors. Eric Meyers, professor of archaeology at Duke University, spoke for many when he criticized the find because it was "unprovenanced."[17] In the world of scholarship, artifacts obtained through the antiquities (underground) market rather than by professional archaeologists have no context. The location of the find, the method of excavating it, and the identity of the

> Yet from the beginning of its unveiling to the public, the James ossuary had its detractors.

discoverer are unknown. These omissions predispose scientists to reject any such artifact as fake. Thus the two leading scholarly archaeological journals, the *American Journal of Archaeology* and the *Bulletin of the American Schools of Oriental Research*, will not even comment on unprovenanced finds much less promote them.[18] But the flip side of this argument is that where would scholarship be without the unprovenanced materials like the Dead Sea Scrolls[19] or the Rosetta Stone?[20]

So controversy mounted regarding the bone box, reaching a fever pitch on June 18, 2003, when the Israel Antiquities Authority, after three months of investigating the evidence, held a news conference to announce that the James ossuary and another artifact in Golan's possession (the Jehoash inscription)[21] were forgeries. The report rejected both the patina on the inscription as well as the inscription itself, stating that they were not authentic, but later additions. The committee, however, seemed to indicate the ossuary itself dates to the first century AD.[22]

As if to put an exclamation point on the report, not long thereafter Israeli police took Golan into custody, strongly suspecting him of forgery of both the James ossuary and the Jehoash inscription, though he was not formally charged. He was then released.

But the debate did not end there. Lemaire responded in *Biblical Archaeology Review* that the Israel Antiquities Authority's (IAA) report was seriously flawed. He detailed what he believed are erroneously drawn conclusions from the data regarding the inscription and the patina chemical deposit. Moreover, he pointed out that the committee contradicted itself, some arguing that the first half of the inscription was authentic but not the second half, while others argued precisely the opposite.[23] Shanks went so far as to assert that the committee had prejudged the ossuary before objectively analyzing the evidence.[24] By April 2004, there was a growing sense that the IAA might have rushed to judgment. Four Israeli scholars have called for another, more careful investigation, without prejudice. David Merling, professor of archaeology at Andrews University and president of the Near East

> As if to put an exclamation point on the report, not long thereafter Israeli police took Golan into custody.

Archaeological Society, said archaeology must be done without an agenda: "We need to make sure that we draw the theories from the data and not evaluate the data based on theories."[25]

> By April 2004, there was a growing sense that the IAA might have rushed to judgment.

SIGNIFICANCE OF THE JAMES OSSUARY

Why all the fuss about an ancient burial box? After all, do we really need archaeology to prove the Bible? Do we not walk by faith and not by sight? These are good questions, and the answers to them are no and yes. No, we don't absolutely need archaeology to prove the Bible and yes, we do walk by faith, not by sight. But it is always helpful to have corroborating evidence for the Bible. The Judeo-Christian tradition is a reasonable faith. We base our convictions on historical fact not fiction. The discipline of apologetics has for centuries provided a very useful service to the people of God by helping to present the evidence for our biblical beliefs.

And archaeology does the same. A number of spectacular digs quickly come to mind in this regard: the discoveries of the Hittite kingdom in modern-day Turkey, the Philistine civilization in what is today the Gaza Strip in Israel, and the Dead Sea Scrolls. These findings confirm the reliability of the Old Testament. To these could be added New Testament–related finds, such as Pilate's inscription at Caesarea by the Sea, the warning inscriptions forbidding Gentiles to enter the Jerusalem temple, and Gallio's inscription in Corinth, which is the foundation for dating the apostle Paul's letters and journeys. These discoveries help to confirm the reliability of the New Testament. So, if the James ossuary turns out to be authentic, it, too, could be very helpful in this regard.

But how so? What is its significance? Well, if genuine, the James bone box would be highly important in at least two major ways. First, it would be the first archaeological proof of Jesus's existence. There are extra-

Archaeology

Like the information about Jesus, the Gospels, and early Christianity that comes from literary sources, archaeology assists us in better understanding the Scriptural text. The material remains of a culture—its public buildings, private houses, furniture, dishes and containers, utensils, tools, toys, coins, religious symbols, and funeral practices—help moderns to identify the beliefs and behavior of the ancients. While Christians need not depend on archaeology to "prove" their faith in the Bible, discoveries from the world of antiquity often help confirm the trustworthiness of Scripture.

canonical references to Jesus attesting to his historicity in the writings of Josephus, Suetonius, Tacitus, and the Talmud. But even though these literary testimonies confirm the general facts about Jesus's life and death (even if by way of criticism), they are not archaeological in nature. In the 1960s, the bones of a first-century AD crucified man excavated in Israel bore testimony to the hideous nature of that form of execution by the Romans at that time—just as the Gospels depicted Jesus's death. It would be nice to have in our hands another archaeological artifact confirming Jesus's life.

Second, there are a number of aspects about James that the disputed os-suary would confirm should it prove to be bona fide.[26]

It would confirm that James and family probably spoke Aramaic, which scholars have recognized as Jesus's first language.[27] The James ossuary lends credence to this claim, for it is likely that the language spoken by the family is the language of the inscription.

It would also confirm that James, originally of Galilee, continued to live in or near Jerusalem, where the ossuary was discovered. This coincides with the data on James found in Acts 15:13–21, Galatians 2:9–13, and 1 Corinthians 15:7. Those New Testament writings provide a composite picture of James's role in the Jerusalem church. It seems that, after Jesus's post-resurrection appearance to his younger brother, James in AD 30 became the leader of the church in Jeru-salem. James's leadership skills were showcased when, along with the guidance of the Holy Spirit, he helped the early church to recognize at the Jerusalem Council in AD 49 that both Jew and Gentile were justified before God through faith in Christ alone, apart from the works of the Old Testament law. This was a historic decision for early Christianity, for had Gentiles been expected to obey the Torah, the gospel may never have reached non-Jews en mass.

Tradition has it that James was known for his holiness, hence his nick-name, "James the Just." As such, he led the Jerusalem church to be faithful to Christ. This stance on James's part brought him into disfavor with the religious leaders in Jerusalem, especially the Sadducees. In AD 62, after the death of the Roman procurator of Palestine, Festus (see Acts 25), and just before the arrival of Albinus, the new Roman procurator, to Caesarea by the Sea, Ananus, the Jewish high priest, plotted to kill James. Josephus, the Jew-ish historian, reports the incident:

> The younger Ananus, who as we have said, had been appointed to the high priesthood, was rash in his temper and usually daring. He followed the school of the Sadducees, who are indeed more savage than any of the other Jews, as I have already explained, when they sit in judgment. Possessed of such a character, Ananus thought that he had a favorable opportunity because Festus was dead and Albinus was still on the way. And so he convened the judges of the Sanhedrin and brought before them a man named James, the brother of Jesus, who was called the Christ, and certain others. He accused them of having

transgressed the Law and delivered them up to be stoned. Those of the inhabitants of the city who were considered to be the most fair-minded and who were strict in observance of the Law were offended at this. They therefore secretly sent to King Agrippa urging him, for Ananus had not even been correct in his first step [of convening the Sanhedrin without Albinus' permission], to order him to desist from any further such actions. Certain of them even went to meet Albinus who was on his way from Alexandria, and informed him that Ananus had no authority to convene the Sanhedrin without his consent. Convinced by these words, Albinus angrily wrote to Ananus threatening to take vengeance upon him. King Agrippa, because of Ananus' action, deposed him from the high priesthood which he held for three months.[28]

It is clear from Josephus's account that James was the spokesperson of the Jerusalem church, hence the high priest wanted to do away with him in particular. It is also remarkable that strict law-abiding, non-Christian Jews protested Ananus's action against James. Elsewhere, we learn from Hegesippus, a second-century Christian leader, more details about James's life and death. Of his holy reputation, Hegesippus writes:

> **James was the spokesperson of the Jerusalem church, hence the high priest wanted to do away with him.**

Control of the church passed together with the apostles, to the brother of the Lord, James, whom everyone from the Lord's time till our own has named the Just, for there were many Jameses, but this one was holy from his birth; he drank no wine or intoxicating liquor and ate no animal food; no razor came near his head; he did not smear himself with oil, and he took no baths. He alone was permitted to enter the Holy Place, for his garments were not of wool, but of linen. He used to enter the Sanctuary alone, and was often found on his knees beseeching forgiveness for the people, so that his knees grew hard like a camel's from his continually bending them in worship of God and beseeching forgiveness for the people. Because of his unsurpassable righteousness he was called the Just and Oblias [in Greek, "Bulwark of the people and Righteousness"] fulfilling the declarations of the prophets regarding him.[29]

All of this to say that the ossuary of James, discovered as it seems to have been in Jerusalem, reaffirms the impression conveyed by certain New Testament books that James did not return to his home in Galilee, but remained in Jerusalem after Jesus's post-resurrection appearance to him.

Related to the last consideration, the James ossuary may confirm that James died in Jerusalem, as early church tradition maintains. If the ossuary was indeed discovered in Silwan, near the Temple Mount, then Hegesippus's

> **The James ossuary may confirm that James died in Jerusalem, as early church tradition maintains.**

account (similar to Josephus) would be strengthened. In a famous passage detailing the motive for, and the means of, James's death, he writes:

Representatives of the seven sects already described by me asked him what was meant by "the door of Jesus" and he replied that Jesus was the Savior. Some of them came to believe that Jesus was the Christ: the sects mentioned above did not believe either in a resurrection or in one who is coming to give every man what his deeds deserve, but those who did come to believe did so because of James. Since therefore many even of the ruling class believed, there was an uproar among the Jews and scribes and Pharisees, who said there was danger that the entire people would accept Jesus as the Christ. So they collected and said to James: "Be good enough to restrain the people, for they have gone astray after Jesus in the belief that he is the Christ. Be good enough to make the facts about Jesus clear to all who come for the Passover Day. We all accept what you say: we can vouch for it, and so can all the people, that you are a righteous man and take no one at his face value. So make it clear to the crowd that they must not go astray as regards Jesus: the whole people and all of us accept what you say. So take your stand on the Temple parapet, so that from that height you may be easily seen, and your words audible to the whole people. For because of the Passover all the tribes have come together, and the Gentiles too."

So the scribes and Pharisees made James stand on the Sanctuary parapet and shouted to him: "Just one, whose word we are all obliged to accept, the people are going astray after Jesus who was crucified; so tell us what is meant by 'the door of Jesus.'" He replied as loudly as he could: "Why do you question me about the Son of Man? I tell you, he is sitting in heaven at the right hand of the great power, and he will come on the clouds of heaven." Many were convinced, and gloried in James's testimony, crying: "Hosanna to the Son of David!" Then again the scribes and Pharisees said to each other: "We made a bad mistake in affording such testimony to Jesus. We had better go up and throw him down, so that they will be frightened and not believe him." "Ho, Ho!" they called out, "even the Just one has gone astray!"—fulfilling the prophecy of Isaiah: "Let us remove the Just one, for he is unprofitable to us." Therefore they shall eat the fruit of their works.

So they went up and threw down the Just one. Then they said to each other, "Let us stone James the Just," and began to stone him, as in spite of his fall he was still alive. But he turned and knelt, uttering the words: "I beseech Thee, Lord God and Father, forgive them; they do not know what they are doing." While they pelted him with stones, one of the descendants of Rechab the son of Rechabim—the priestly family to which Jeremiah the Prophet bore witness—called out: "Stop! What are you doing? The Just One is praying for you." Then one of them, a fuller, took the club which he used to beat the clothes, and brought it down on the head of the Just one. Such was his martyrdom. He was buried on the spot, by the Sanctuary, and his inscribed stone is still there by the Sanctuary. He had proved a true witness to Jews and Gentiles alike that Jesus is the Christ.[30]

If bones had been found in the ossuary, it would have been fascinating to see if the condition of the bones (most specifically if there was a skull fracture) corroborated this account of his death.

As Craig A. Evans observes, ossilegium burial was a Jewish custom. If the bone box is authentic, it would imply that James, though a follower of Jesus and part of a movement that became more and more oriented toward Gentiles, continued to live as a Jew, and so was buried as a Jew. Thus James's Christianity was not something separate or opposed to Jewish faith because he strictly obeyed the law of Moses.[31]

Finally, if the inscription on the ossuary is authentic—"James, son of Joseph, brother of Jesus"—then the Protestant case that Jesus had natural brothers and sisters would be clinched. The earliest reference to Jesus's brothers is found in Mark 6:3 and Matthew 13:55. Four brothers are named, and the sisters are referred to as a group. James heads the list, suggesting that he was the next eldest to Jesus. But the question of the relationship between Jesus and his siblings arises from those verses. In the history of the church, three views compete for the interpretation of these Gospel verses. Ben Witherington III outlines those three views:

> All three ancient views of this matter are still alive today in the three main components of Christianity worldwide.
>
> 1) Jerome, the fourth-century church father, taught that James and the other brothers were actually cousins of Jesus, sons of some woman and man other than the biblical Mary and Joseph. This is the most frequently enunciated position of the Roman Catholic Church proceeding from the belief that Mary was a perpetual virgin.
>
> 2) Helvidius, a contemporary of Jerome, maintained that James and the other brothers were in fact the children of Mary and Joseph, and so he denied the idea of the perpetual virginity of Mary. This is the usual Protestant view today.
>
> 3) Epiphanius held that the brothers were sons of Joseph by a previous marriage. This is the Orthodox position today.[32]

Jerome (the great translator of the Latin Bible beginning in AD 385) argued for the cousin view because the Greek word "*adelphos*" could connote the sense of spiritual brother rather than only physical brother. But, as Witherington observes, there is a Greek word for cousin (*anepsios*) and that term is not used of Jesus's family. Also, it is rather clear that Jerome was an ascetic and therefore viewed sexual relations with contempt. This might explain why Jerome advocated the perpetual virginity of Mary.[33]

One of Jerome's critics was Helvidius, who argued against the cousin theory in favor of the siblings theory. We learn of his critique of the cousin theory from Jerome's quotations:

> (1) Matthew 1.18, 25 implies that Joseph did "know" Mary (that is, have sexual relations with her) after the birth of Jesus because it says he did not know her until then. The reference to Mary being found with child "prior to when they came together" refers to prior to when they had a sexual relationship, not merely prior to when they lived in the same house. (2) The reference to Jesus as Mary's firstborn son (Luke 2.7) implies she had others later. (3) Various passages mention Jesus's brothers and sisters. (4) Tertullian agreed with his view, as did Victorinus of Pettau. (5) It was no dishonor that Mary was a real wife to Joseph, as the patriarchs all had wives.[34]

Epiphanius (AD 366) popularized the view that Jesus's brothers originated from Joseph's prior marriage, and therefore were stepbrothers. It is anticipated in *Proto-Evangelium of James,*[35] an apocryphal work we analyzed in our previous chapter. But there are problems with the view of Epiphanius, as Witherington points out:

> (1) There is no mention of the brothers of Jesus in the infancy narratives or in Luke 2:41–52. (2) Matthew 1.25 does not prohibit Mary and Joseph having a sexual relationship after the birth of Jesus. (3) The absence of Joseph from accounts of Jesus's ministry does not mean he had to be older or that he was previously married. (4) The fact that the brothers of Jesus are often associated with Mary in all four Gospels suggests she is their mother. (5) Most important, there is nothing arising in the Gospel texts to push us in this interpretive direction. This scenario has to be brought from outside and imposed on the biblical texts.[36]

On balance, the position of Helvidius, that the Gospels intend to tell us that Jesus had younger siblings born of Joseph and Mary, seems to be accurate. And, if genuine, the James ossuary would clinch the Protestant case.

In a telling remark, Father John P. Meier, a leading Catholic scholar on the Gospels, responded to the news about the bone box of James by saying that, if it is genuine, it is probably the last nail in the coffin of Jerome's view.[37]

CONCLUSION

This twenty-inch bone box is commanding extraordinary attention. Is the James ossuary genuine or is it a fake? That probably will not be determined for quite some time. Clearly, there are those who staunchly maintain that it is authentic, while others are just as convinced it is a forgery. Only time will tell whether the James ossuary is indeed the bone box of James, the brother of Jesus.

If the ossuary is indeed genuine, the implications are enormous, none the least of which is that it could be the earliest artifact with reference to James *and indeed Jesus* found to date. It would also serve to confirm aspects about James's life—the language he spoke (Aramaic), where he lived (although from Galilee, he lived in or near Jerusalem), and most importantly, that James really was the brother of Jesus.

What would it have been like to have been the brother of Jesus? It is fascinating to contemplate. The controversy surrounding the James ossuary has brought to the forefront a man who has previously been in the shadows for a number of us—James the Just. It gives us a glimpse into the life and death of this man of faith, the spiritual leader of the Jerusalem church from AD 40s–62.

DISCUSSION QUESTIONS

1. What is an ossuary?
2. Who do you think owns the James ossuary—Golan or the Israeli government?
3. What are the five major arguments Shanks appeals to in his article on the James ossuary that seem to prove its authenticity?
4. What does it mean that the James ossuary was "unprovenanced"?
5. What did the Israel Antiquity Authority's report say about the ossuary?
6. What are the two major reasons why, if genuine, the James ossuary is significant?
7. How did James receive his nickname, "James the Just"?
8. Do you think the James ossuary is genuine?

THE DA VINCI CODE

Were Jesus and
Mary Magdalene Lovers?

||||||||||||||||||||||||||||||||||||||||||||||||||||||||||||||||||||||||||||||

INTRODUCTION

Dan Brown's *The Da Vinci Code* is a runaway best-seller. It has sold millions of books, sat atop the *New York Times* best-seller list for over a year, and generated a movie directed by Ron Howard, thus creating no small stir within and outside the church. Its formula for success is the mixture of a conspiracy theory, a potent long-held secret, and a good dose of vilifying historic Christianity, especially the Catholic Church.

The basic plot of *The Da Vinci Code* is as follows: Robert Langdon, the hero of the book, is a professor of religious symbology at Harvard whose skill at cracking codes puts him on the trail of a long-held secret by the Priory of Sion. The latter supposedly is a guild with origins back to the Crusades whose task it is to protect the Holy Grail, the chalice from which Jesus drank at the Last Supper. That, however, is but a diversion from the real truth which is that Jesus of Nazareth and Mary Magdalene were lovers who married and bore children. Thus the real Holy Grail was Mary Magdalene.

The Priory of Sion included the great Sir Isaac Newton, the painter Botticelli, Victor Hugo, and none other than the master artist himself, Leonardo da Vinci; hence the book's title. These and other grandmasters of the guild preserved the secret. Supposedly, Jesus's bloodline persists even today in the person of the heroine of our story, Sophie Neveu ("New Wisdom"), though it took Langdon's expertise for her to figure that out. The Catholic Church is the foil in the plot, whose secret organization, Opus Dei ("work of God") relentlessly

> **Supposedly, Jesus's bloodline persists even today in the person of the heroine of our story, Sophie Neveu.**

and ruthlessly seeks to suppress the truth about the royal bloodline of Jesus and Mary, no matter whom it has to kill. Added to the story is the scholarly protagonist Leigh Teabing, a former British Royal Historian who moved to France, who has the disguised intent to expose historic Christianity for what it is—an institutionalized fabrication making Jesus into divinity when he is not. The revelation that Jesus was a mere human who, with Mary Magdalene, begat other humans would clearly undermine the Christian message. And with hard-hitting, fast action the book concludes in breathtaking fashion by bringing all the above themes together. There is no doubt about it; *The Da Vinci Code* is a brilliant, thrilling page turner.

However, the ire of the church need not have been raised over this book but for the way Brown presents his fictitious story; namely, he begins his work with a page labeled "FACT," which claims that "all descriptions of . . . documents . . . in this novel are accurate."[1] This gives the distinct impression that the novel is based on sound historical research. On the ABC News special *Jesus, Mary, and Da Vinci*, which aired on November 3, 2003, Dan Brown proclaimed himself a believer in these things. In an interview on *Good Morning America* the day of the special, he declared that if he had been asked to write

> **Brown begins his work with a page labeled "FACT," which claims that "all descriptions of . . . documents . . . in this novel are accurate."**

a piece of nonfiction on these things, he would change nothing about what he claimed in the novel. In his book, key characters state that Jesus was married and had children. Moreover, they say the Catholic Church lied about this and suppressed the fact that his wife and children fled to France. In that interview, Brown affirmed the views of some of his novel's characters. He told the prime-time audience of around fifteen million viewers that, "I began as a skeptic. As I started researching *The Da Vinci Code*, I really thought I would disprove a lot of this theory about Mary Magdalene and Holy Blood and all of that. I became a believer."

This chapter begs to differ with Brown's claim that his novel is rooted in fact. Accordingly, we will expose four key errors upon which the novel is based.[2]

Error 1: The true gospels are the *Gospel of Mary* (Magdalene) and the *Gospel of Philip,* not the canonical Gospels.

Dan Brown's theological perspective is expressed through the British scholar Teabing. Teabing accuses early Christianity of waging a conspiracy against the truth. He declares that "more than *eighty* gospels" were considered for the New Testament, but only four were chosen.[3] The former were the historical losers while the latter were the historical winners. The intent of this assertion is obviously to discredit historical Christianity and replace it with the New Testament Apocrypha. In reality, however, there are only about fifty non-canonical gospels.[4]

Here we discuss two more New Testament Apocrypha—the *Gospel of Philip* and the *Gospel of Mary* (Mary Magdalene). They are the foundation of Dan Brown's thesis that Jesus and Mary Magdalene were lovers who got married. The *Gospel of Philip* surfaced in the Coptic (Egyptian plus Greek) texts at Nag Hammadi. It is thoroughly Gnostic in orientation. Thus: the body is evil and only the soul is good (sayings 21–23); the first man, Adam, was androgynous, and sin came into being when Eve was separated from Adam (sayings 70–79); and the *pleroma*, or fullness, stretches from heaven to earth (saying 205) and the *archons*, or mediating angelic powers, that inhabit the fullness brought the world into being, not God (saying 166).[5]

But it is the emphasis that the *Gospel of Philip* places on Mary Magdalene that is of immediate interest to us. Two passages are critical to our discussion. The first is saying 32, where Mary Magdalene is called Jesus's "companion," a possible reference to Mary as the wife of Jesus. Ben Witherington, however, does not believe this to be the case, because it is far more likely that the word "companion" used here is not a synonym for a spouse, but rather refers to a spiritual "sister."[6]

But opponents believe "companion" does mean wife. Saying 55b in the *Gospel of Philip* is thought to confirm this interpretation:

> The S[aviour lov]ed [Ma]ry Mag[da]lene more than [all] the disciples, and kissed on her [mouth] often. The other [disciples] [. . .]. They said to him: "Why do you love her more than all of us?" The Saviour answered and said to them [. . .]: "Why do I not love you like her?"

Bear in mind that the bracketed portions represent words or portions of words not in the text, but which have been filled in due to context, etc., not necessarily the original words intended by the author. While the kiss referred to here

> The *Gospel of Mary*, like the *Gospel of Philip*, places Mary Magdalene on a pedestal above the disciples.

could be a kiss on Mary's cheek or forehead, in light of saying 32 it could also refer to a kiss on the mouth:

The perfect conceive through a kiss and give birth. Because of this we also kiss one another. We receive conception from the grace which we have among us.

What is clear from these texts is that Mary is favored by Jesus above the twelve disciples, because she shares with him the knowledge (*gnosis*) of the true nature of reality. Nevertheless, even though these nonbiblical passages seem to indicate that Jesus and Mary were married, in typical Gnostic fashion, physical marriage is made secondary in importance to the spiritual intimacy between the two of them—that is, their shared *gnosis*.

The *Gospel of Mary* (implied Magdalene) is a second-century fragment written in Greek. Like the *Gospel of Philip*, it also places Mary Magdalene on a pedestal above the disciples. The passage we are about to quote indicates that Jesus entrusted Mary with secret knowledge because he recognized her superior worth. This aroused jealousy in Andrew and Peter. Hence the ensuing tense conversation:

When Mary had said this, she was silent, so that the Saviour had spoken with her up to this point. But Andrew answered and said to the brethren: "Tell me, what think ye with regard to what she says? I at least do not believe that the Saviour said this. For certainly these doctrines have other meanings." Peter in answer spoke with reference to things of this kind, and asked them [*the disciples*] about the Saviour: "Did he then speak privily with a woman rather than with us, and not openly? Shall we turn about and all hearken unto her? Has he preferred her over against us?"

Papyrus Berolinensis 8502, p. 17.7–22

Then Mary wept and said to Peter: "My brother Peter, what dost thou then believe? Dost thou believe that I imagined this myself in my heart, or that I would lie about the Saviour?" Levi answered (and) said to Peter: "Peter, thou hast ever been of a hasty temper. Now I see how thou dost exercise thyself against the woman like the adversaries. But if the Saviour hath made her worthy, who then are thou, that thou reject her? Certainly the Saviour knows her surely enough. Therefore did he love her more than us. Let us rather be ashamed, put on the perfect Man, [form ourselves (?)] as he charged us, and proclaim the Gospel, without requiring any further command and any further law beyond that which the Saviour said."

Papyrus Berolinensis 8502, p.18.1–21

The Gnostic character of this work is evident. Right before the preceding dialogue, Jesus says, "The Son of Man is within you, follow him" (Papyrus Berolinensis 8502, pp. 8.12–9.5). This alludes to the Gnostic idea that humans are divine and need to become aware of such. Another Gnostic thought occurs in the same context, where Mary says she becomes a man, thereby affirming the androgynous nature of humanity.

This last comment needs development. Darrell L. Bock summarizes the Gnostic view that behind the unisex perspective of humanity is God. He writes:

> Many of these texts portrayed God as a dyad, with the divine mother as part of the original couple. Irenaeus, writing in *Against Heresies* 1.11.1, complained about the view of a major teacher, Valentinus, who spoke of God as a dyad. Valentinus believed that God consisted in two parts. In one part, God was the ineffable, the Depth, the Primal Father; and in the other, Grace, Silence, the womb, and "Mother of the All." This Grace and Silence was the feminine complement of God, and her womb received the seed of the Ineffable Source to bring forth the emanations of divine being.
>
> The recognition of the divine feminine distinguishes Gnosticism from the Jewish and Christian presentations of God. The Judeo-Christian tradition argued that God lacks gender. . . . The closest that these other Jewish and Christian views of God came to such feminine understandings appears in the metaphorical portrayal of Wisdom as a female (Prov. 8).[7]

> *The Gnostic thought undergirding the Gospel of Philip and the Gospel of Mary dates no earlier than the second to third centuries AD, precisely the false teaching opposed by the church fathers.*

Although the Gnostic view that God and humans are androgynous seems to argue for equality between the genders, the *Gospel of Thomas* dispels such an idea:

> Simon Peter said to them [the disciples], "Let Mary leave us, for women are not worthy of life." Jesus said, "I myself shall lead her, in order to make her male, so that she too may become a

living spirit, resembling you males. For every woman who will make herself male will enter the Kingdom of Heaven" (114).

Thus, in the Gnostic approach, women are subservient to men.

The point to be made from all of this is that the Gnostic thought undergirding the *Gospel of Philip* and the *Gospel of Mary* dates no earlier than the second to third centuries AD, precisely the false teaching opposed by the church fathers Irenaeus (ca. 130–200), Hippolytus (ca. 170–236), and Tertullian (ca. 160–220), as we saw earlier. This is in utter contrast to the message of orthodox Christianity evident in the first century AD in the four Gospels.[8]

Error 2: Jesus is a mere human in the earliest historical sources who was only later divinized at the Council of Nicea in AD 325. This was due to the oppressive tactics of Emperor Constantine, who suppressed the earlier (Gnostic) Gospels and replaced them with the four canonical Gospels.

Teabing makes the claim that Constantine "commissioned and financed a new Bible, which omitted these gospels that spoke of Christ's human traits and embellished those gospels that made Him godlike. The earlier gospels were outlawed, gathered up, and burned."[9] The earlier gospels Teabing has in mind here are the Nag Hammadi Gnostic documents. These oppressive actions were supposedly continued throughout history by the Vatican, whose agenda was "to promote the divinity of the man Jesus Christ and use His influence to solidify their own power base."[10] The story goes that, for the first four centuries after Jesus's death, numerous documents existed chronicling Jesus's life as a mere mortal, but Constantine rewrote history by replacing these with the four canonical Gospels.[11]

It might be helpful at this point to cite the Nicene Creed of AD 325, which for Teabing (and Brown) hijacked the human Jesus, offering in its place the divine Jesus:

> *Teabing makes the claim that Constantine "commissioned and financed a new Bible, which omitted these gospels that spoke of Christ's human traits and embellished those gospels that made Him godlike."*

We believe in one God, the Father All-sovereign, maker of heaven and earth, and of all things visible and invisible;

And in one Lord Jesus Christ, and the only-begotten Son of God, Begotten of the Father before all the ages, Light of Light, true God of true God, begotten not made, of one substance with the Father, through whom all things were made; who for us men and for our salvation came down from the heavens, and was made flesh of the Holy Spirit and the Virgin Mary, and became man, and was crucified for us under Pontius Pilate, and suffered and was buried, and rose again on the third day according to the Scriptures, and ascended into the heavens, and sits on the right hand of the Father, and comes again with glory to judge living and dead, of whose kingdom there shall be no end;

And in the Holy Spirit, the Lord and the Life-giver, that proceeds from the Father, who with the Father and Son is worshipped together and glorified together, who spoke through the prophets;

In one holy catholic and apostolic church;

We acknowledge one baptism unto remission of sins. We look for a resurrection of the dead, and the life of the age to come.[12]

Nothing could be further from the truth than Brown's theory. As we saw in chapter 2, the four Gospels, which undeniably date to the first century AD, equate Jesus with God. And so did the apostle Paul (see Phil. 2:9–11 where he calls Jesus "Lord," the Greek equivalent of the Hebrew *Yahweh*). Ben Witherington well summarizes the evidence for this claim:

Jesus is called *theos* (God) some seven times in the New Testament, including in the Gospel of John, and he is called "Lord" in the divine sense numerous times. No historian I know of argues that these texts postdate the Nicean council. The Council of Nicea in the fourth century and the Council of Chalcedon in the fifth century merely formalized and clarified these first-century beliefs by making them part of the creeds.[13]

Neither is it true that Constantine imposed the canonical four Gospels onto the church in AD 325. To the contrary, long before Constantine and even before the Gnostic gospels existed, the four Gospels of the New Testament were considered authoritative by the churches. Thus Irenaeus in AD 125 recognizes the "four-fold Gospels."[14] Tatian, a student of the church father Justin Martyr, combined the four Gospels into one harmony at around AD 175 (called the *Diatessaron*—Greek for "through the

> *Long before Constantine and even before the Gnostic gospels existed, the Gospels of the New Testament were considered authoritative by the churches.*

four") because they were so well received in the churches. Earlier, Justin himself attested to the canonicity of the four Gospels, calling them the memoirs of the apostles.[15] Coming from the late second century AD, the Muratorian canon (a list of the canon named after the man who discovered it) lists the four Gospels as authoritative for the church. Origen (ca. 185–254) concurs in his *Homily on Luke 1:1* that only the four Gospels should be accepted by the churches. By AD 325, Bishop Athanasius in the Eastern church and the papal see in the West recognized only four Gospels (recall Athanasius's Easter letter in our chapter 2). Eusebius, the fourth-century AD church historian who wrote *Ecclesiastical History*, quotes with approval Origen's restriction of inspired Gospels to Matthew, Mark, Luke, and John.[16]

It is, therefore, preposterous of Brown to assert through Teabing that Constantine imposed the four Gospels onto the church. The fact is, early on, the Eastern and Western churches rejected the Gnostic gospels in favor of the "four-fold Gospel." A widely recognized Roman Catholic New Testament scholar, Raymond Brown, commented that what these second- to third-century Christians did in moving to recognize these books and in rejecting others was to reject "only the rubbish of the second century," and he added, "It is still rubbish."[17] Dan Brown could learn a thing or two from Raymond Brown.

Error 3: Jesus was married to Mary Magdalene.

The most provocative claims in *The Da Vinci Code* are that Mary Magdalene (Mary from Magdala, a town on the Sea of Galilee; Luke 8:2) was the wife of Jesus and the mother of his children, and that this was a secret the church wanted to cover up to protect the divinity of Jesus. In the novel, she also is directly associated with the Holy Grail. The association with the Grail comes through the idea of Holy Blood and its bloodline,[18] the *Sangreal*. A word play on the term *Sangreal* gets us to a connection to the Holy Grail. The hypothesis is that the story of the Holy Grail really points to the holy bloodline of Jesus and Mary Magdalene coming into France. This idea was expressed earlier in the book *Holy Blood, Holy Grail*, which introduces the idea that the Holy Grail is the womb of Mary Magdalene.[19]

In *The Da Vinci Code*, Mary is said to be in Leonardo da Vinci's painting *The Last Supper*. The evidence is the V-shape to the left side of Jesus as one looks at the painting.[20] It is the symbol of the feminine, and a feminine-looking figure on the left side of the V is Mary of Magdala.[21] Leonardo knew of the genealogical secret and put a clue of it in this painting. It is from this detail that the novel gets its title, *The Da Vinci Code*. All of these ideas surface in the middle portion of the book.[22]

But even if the *Gospel of Philip* and the *Gospel of Mary* (Magdalene) wish to say that Jesus and Mary were married, there is no New Testament evidence for such a notion. We offer here two rebuttals to the preceding hypothesis: first, Jesus was not married to Mary; second, Jesus was never married.

First, the Gospels' references to Mary Magdalene show no indication whatsoever that she and Jesus were married. Here are the references:

- Jesus cast seven demons out of Mary (Luke 8:2).
- Mary witnessed Jesus's crucifixion (Mark 15:40–41; Matt. 27:55–56; John 19:25).
- She was present at the burial of Jesus (Mark 15:47; Matt. 27:57–61; cf. Mark 16:1).[24]
- She was the first to see Jesus in his resurrection body (John 20:10–17).
- She along with other women announced Jesus's resurrection to the apostles (Luke 24:10; John 20:18).

What If Jesus Were Married? Is That a Problem?

"Jesus did many things that underscored His genuine humanity. He ate, thirsted, slept, tired, lived, and died. His everyday life was that of a normal human existence. His life was exceptional because of His relationship with God, His access to divine power, and His resurrection. One of the basic beliefs of Christian faith is that Jesus was 100 percent human. So if He had been married and fathered children, His marital relationship and His parenthood would not theoretically undercut His divinity but would have been reflections of His complete humanity. Had Jesus been married, there was no need to cover it up. The whole rationale for covering up any supposed relationship has no basis in theology. Had Jesus been married, theoretically He still could have been and done all He did."[23]

The fact that emerges from these references is that, except in John 20:10–18, Mary and Jesus were consistently in the presence of other people when together. In John's account, Mary touched Jesus out of surprise and joy on the first Easter morning. There are no sexual innuendoes in the narrative at all. Mary's embrace of Jesus is born out of spontaneity and reverence. Furthermore, while Mary supported Jesus's ministry, there is not so much as a hint in the Gospels that Mary was an apostle, or enjoyed a privileged place among followers of the historical Jesus; nor was she placed on a pedestal by Jesus, contra the *Gospel of Philip* and the *Gospel of Mary*.[25] Moreover, as Darrell Bock points out, in the Gospel references to Mary and other women followers of Jesus, all the other ladies are connected to males as relatives except Mary, strongly suggesting she had no man in her life, and certainly not Jesus.[26]

So, on the one hand the Gospels do not accord to Mary Magdalene a place of superiority, but neither do they cast her in a bad light. How did the common misconception about her, that she was a prostitute, get started? This identification comes from confusing the account of the unnamed sinful woman (presumably a prostitute) anointing Jesus's feet with oil (Luke 7:37–38) with Jesus exorcising Mary (Luke 8:2). Historians seem to agree that the branding of Mary Magdalene as a prostitute was not started until the sixth century, by Pope Gregory I. But scholars today do not believe Luke 8:2 should be connected with Luke 7:37–38. Thus Luke 8:2 introduces Mary Magdalene for the first time, therefore eliminating any questionable background for her. Nor should we equate Mary with the adulterous woman in John 7. Neither should we conjecture that, because the town of Magdala was supposedly associated with prostitution, that Mary was involved in the same "livelihood." Such theories are speculation and have no basis in fact.[27]

Second, there is no good indication that Jesus was ever married. Bock nicely summarizes the evidence that Jesus was single:

> It has long been believed by Christians and scholars that Jesus was single, and there are good reasons for this belief. When He was in ministry, there was no mention of a wife. When He was tried and crucified there was no mention

It is true that the normal expectation was that Jewish males in Bible times were supposed to be married and have children, but there were notable exceptions to that norm.

of a wife. After His death and resurrection, there was no mention of a wife. Jesus's family members—His mother, brothers, and sisters—were mentioned more than once, but never a wife. Nor was there any indication that He was widowed.[28]

In *The Da Vinci Code*, the Opus Dei attempts to cover up the "fact" that Jesus had a family and children in order to protect his claim to deity. In the novel, the Opus Dei is a secret religious society whose goal is to protect the Roman Catholic Church by any means. The novel argues the case for Jesus's marriage on two primary bases: first, that it was un-Jewish to be unmarried;[29] and second, that according to Gnostic texts, Jesus kissed Mary on the mouth, and the apostles were jealous of his special relationship with her.[30]

The Celibate Essenes according to Josephus

"These Essenes reject pleasures as an evil, but esteem continence, and the conquest over our passions. They neglect wedlock, but choose out other persons' children, while they are pliable, and fit for learning; and esteem them to be their kindred, and form them according to their own manners. They do not absolutely deny the fitness of marriage, and the succession of mankind thereby continues.[31]

> *His thesis is as clear as it is provocative when he has Langdon say that the sexual union between man and woman is the only way to "achieve gnosis—the knowledge of the divine."*

We have already dispelled the myth that the *Gospel of Philip* and the *Gospel of Mary* are on a par with the four canonical Gospels. So we need not be swayed by their suggestion that Jesus and Mary had a romantic relationship or that they were married. But what about the first assertion—that Jesus was a Jew and therefore was married? It is true that the normal expectation was that Jewish males in Bible times were supposed to be married and have children (Gen. 1:26–28), but there were notable exceptions to that norm. It may well be that the Old Testament prophet Samuel was single, as well as Hosea (until God commanded him to marry Gomer). Certainly the Essenes (the probable authors of the Dead Sea Scrolls) were celibate.[32] And, no doubt, John the Baptist (who might have been raised by the Essenes)[33] was also single. These individuals apparently felt a calling to forego marriage in order to be able to devote themselves fully to the kingdom of God, as did the apostle Paul himself (1 Corinthians 7). This seems to be what Matthew 19:10–12 is saying in describing certain disciples who have chosen to be celibate for the sake of the kingdom (see v. 12). Most scholars believe this reference alludes to Jesus's own justification for remaining single.[34]

If we have indeed refuted the claim of *The Da Vinci Co*de that Jesus was married to Mary Magdalene or, even short of that, that they were lovers, then the main thesis and sub-theses of Dan Brown's book fall like a house of cards.

Error 4: The truest form of Christianity is sexual in nature, beginning with Jesus and continuing with the Gnostic gospels, but Constantine's church and beyond suppressed this truth.

Sex sells, and that undoubtedly is one of the reasons *The Da Vinci Code* has sold so well. Add religion to sex and the appeal is almost irresistible. Dan Brown's thesis is as clear as it is provocative when he has Langdon say that the sexual union between man and woman is the only way to "achieve *gnosis*—the knowledge of the divine."[35] This is what Langdon calls *Hieros Gamos* (sacred marriage).

One of the most powerful scenes in the novel takes place in early spring in windswept Normandy. Sophie Neveu discovers her grandfather, Jacques Saunière, engaging in a secret sex ritual in the basement of his old country house as masked worshipers look on, rocking back and forth and chanting. The men are dressed in black, the women in white. Later, Robert Langdon explains to a distraught Sophie that the ritual she saw was *Hieros Gamos*, "sacred marriage," and that it was "not about sex, it was about spirituality . . . not a perversion . . . [but] a deeply sacrosanct ceremony."[36]

> *Langdon himself, in The Da Vinci Code, subscribed to the notion of finding divinity during times of sex. Sex supposedly not only brings knowledge of God, it also makes the participants realize that they are androgynous—they are both male and female.*

This scene contains the only extended description of a religious experience in the entire novel. The goal of the ritual is for the man to gain, at the moment of orgasm in a sexual union with a woman, spiritual completeness and *gnosis*, or secret knowledge.[37] *The Da Vinci Code* does not say how the woman gains knowledge, since she is only a "chalice" in the rite, but the male, with the help of the chanting crowd, "could achieve a climactic instant when his mind went totally blank and he could see God."[38]

Langdon himself, in *The Da Vinci Code*, subscribed to the notion of finding divinity during times of sex, a concept he taught at Harvard University.[39] Sex supposedly not only brings knowledge of God, it also makes the participants realize that they are androgynous—they are both male and female. James L. Garlow and Peter Jones write of this, referring back to the sexual ritual that Sophia witnessed:

> The cult members are wearing "androgynous masks" (308); Jahweh is presented as an ancient name containing the idea of an "androgynous physical union"; Leonardo da Vinci's Mona Lisa is "smiling" (101). Why? Because Mona Lisa really stands for Amon and L'Isa (Isis), the androgynous pair, so that the painting presents an image that is "neither male nor female . . . [but] carries a subtle message of androgyny . . . a fusing of both" (121). The *Mona Lisa* smiles because she has *gnosis*. . . .
>
> Knowing oneself to be both male and female changes everything, according to this esoteric tradition. Reconstructing God-given sexuality appears in this spirituality to be at the top of the agenda. In undergoing this transformation, one "joins the opposites," the classic phrase for *gnosis*. This means that in the irrational state of altered consciousness, all the normal distinctions of everyday life—not merely the sexual distinctions—fall away: "*The blade and chalice. Fused as one*" (446). This concept is further expressed in Jacques Sauniére's "passion for dualism. . . . Everything in pairs . . . *Male female. Black nested within white*" (323).[40]

The driving force behind the celebration of the sacred marriage is the conviction that the sexual union between male and female joins them to the Feminine Goddess.[41] This is the mission of the Priory of Sion, the guild charged with protecting the secret of Jesus and Mary's royal bloodline; it is "the pagan goddess worship cult."[42] But Garlow and Jones well note that such a concept is thoroughly pagan, going back thousands of years before Christ:

> The Goddess certainly is pre-Christian. She emerges from the mists of time, out of the East, as the saviour from death. The Egyptian Isis, the goddess of witchcraft and magic, goes back to around 3000 BC. The pagan religion of ancient Ugarit (around 2500 BC) worshiped the goddess Anat, who restored Baal to life. The Goddess Istar, a spiritual force around 1800 BC in ancient Babylon, sup-

When Teabing says, "Jesus was the original feminist," he means that Jesus approved of sexual union as the means to getting in touch with the sacred feminine.

posedly bridged the gap between the living and the dead with her secret power. In ancient Canaan, the goddess Asherah, resembling Istar and Anat, was the consort of Baal. The Syrian goddess Cybele or Atargatis had all the qualities of Anat. Often known as the Great Mother, the Goddess under many names communicated the powers of death in the unseen spirit world.[43]

It is this background that informs Teabing's statement, "Jesus was the original feminist."[44] Rather than meaning that Jesus believed in the equality of males and females, Teabing means that Jesus approved of sexual union as the means to get in touch with the sacred feminine. This belief was contained in Gnostic writings like the *Gospel of Philip* and *Thunder, Perfect Mind*, both Nag Hammadi texts. The former speaks of "the bridal chamber" reserved for secret and private initiations of "free men and virgins," who wore clothes of "perfect light," probably an allusion to physical and spiritual nakedness; here the couple symbolized their androgyny through sexual union with the Goddess.[45] According to Irenaeus, mantras also accompanied the ceremony of the bridal chamber.[46] Early Christian teachers who witnessed this activity firsthand called it "promiscuous intercourse."[47] *Thunder, Perfect Mind*, another Gnostic work discovered at Nag Hammadi, shares a similar perspective toward sexual union and the Goddess: "I am the prostitute and the holy one, . . . the wife and the virgin . . . knowledge and ignorance, . . . bride and bridegroom . . . shame and shamelessness."[48] In this work, the feminine Goddess is cast as the Egyptian Goddess Isis who joins opposites in union with her in sex. In doing so, supposedly, humans transcend all distinctions.

But, according to *The Da Vinci Code*, this all changed with Constantine's Catholic Church and beyond. Thus,

> "For the early church," Langdon explained in a soft voice, "mankind's use of sex to commune directly with God posed a serious threat to the Catholic power base. It left the Church out of the loop, undermining their self-proclaimed status as the *sole* conduit to God. For obvious reasons, they worked hard to demonize sex

Jesus's Call Back to the Original Relationship at Creation

It is clear that Jesus affirmed the divinely ordained distinction between male and female. His Jewish heritage would not allow him to say otherwise. We see this in Matthew 19:4–6, which records Jesus's comments on the subject of divorce:

> "Haven't you read," he replied, "that at the beginning the Creator 'made them male and female,' and said, 'For this reason a man will leave his father and mother and be united to his wife, and the two will become one flesh'? So they are no longer two, but one. Therefore what God has joined together, let man not separate" (NIV).

Here we see Jesus agreeing that man and woman are rightly different in gender and yet fully equal. This is the message he called his audience to embrace. The fact that Jesus was single does not speak against this, because in such a capacity he did not see himself as the norm; his special mission set him on a different path than most. It is illuminating to scan the references to women that one finds in the four Gospels for, in doing so, one discovers that Jesus consistently treated women as equal to men. Three categories emerge: Jesus's restoration of the dignity and worth of women from sickness and sin (Matt. 8:14–15 and parallel passages; Matt. 9:18-26 and parallel passages; Luke 7:36–50; 13:11–17); his encouragement to women to be his disciples (Matt. 27:55–56; 27:61–28:1; Mark 15:40–41; 15:47–16:1; Luke 8:1–3; 23:49; 23:55–24:1; John 19:25–27; 20:1); the inclusion of women as preachers of the Gospel (Luke 1:41–45; 1:46–55; Luke 2:36–38; John 4:7–26; Matt. 28:1–8 and parallel passages; John 20:14–18).

and recast it as a disgusting and sinful act. Other major religions did the same."[49]

Consequently the church brought about a change of perspective toward sex:

> Holy men who had once required sexual union with their female counterparts to commune with God now feared their natural sexual urges as the work of the devil.[50]

The net result was that the church maintained power over the masses

> **This is not really, therefore, a work of *fiction*, but a work of *conviction* by Dan Brown.**

because it replaced communion with God through sex with communion with God through the church.

The preceding model of spirituality is not new to the Bible, for already in the Old Testament the prophets thunder forth against the pagan, especially Canaanite, fertility rites (Judges 2:11–23, 1 Sam. 7:3–4, 1 Kings 11:4–8). We gain from the Ras Shamra tablets discovered in Syria in the 1920s a firsthand look at Canaanite religion at the time of Israel's occupation of Palestine, from 1200 BC on. It was as the Old Testament said it was: The Canaanite men were expected to cohabitate with the prostitute priestesses; this act symbolized sex among the male and female deities, which ensured a bountiful harvest for their crops.

Moreover, it is also clear that the Bible affirms both the equality and the distinctions between male and female (Gen. 1:26–28). And Jesus, contrary to *The Da Vinci Code* and the bad track record that some sectors of the church have sustained over the years, confirmed the same (Matt. 19:4–6; Mark 10:6–9).

CONCLUSION

Certainly *The Da Vinci Code* has taken the world by storm and heated debate continues to swirl around it. Not only did *The Da Vinci Code* quickly climb the best-seller lists, it also generated many books written in opposition to its claims.

It would be easy to write off *The Da Vinci Code* as simply a brilliant novel had it not been for Dan Brown's assertions on more than one occasion that he believes the book to be based in fact. This is not really, therefore, a work of *fiction*, but a work of *conviction* by Dan Brown. As such, it not only vilifies the Catholic Church, but challenges the belief system of Protestants as well by painting a very different picture of Jesus, Mary, and spirituality than that of historic Christianity.

Were Jesus and Mary Magdalene lovers? Were they married with children? There is no indication that this is the case. And although it makes for fascinating reading and generates much discussion, the belief that Jesus and Mary Magdalene had a sexual relationship is not based on sound, historical evidence.

DISCUSSION QUESTIONS

1. How did *The Da Vinci Code* get its name?
2. According to *The Da Vinci Code*, does Jesus's "bloodline" persist today?

3. Does Dan Brown believe *The Da Vinci Code* is based on fact?
4. According to Dan Brown in *The Da Vinci Code*, why are the *Gospel of Mary* and the *Gospel of Philip* the true gospels?
5. Did Emperor Constantine suppress the Gnostic gospels, as Dan Brown indicates, and replace them with the four canonical gospels?
6. According to Dan Brown in *The Da Vinci Code*, Jesus was married to Mary Magdalene. Was Jesus in fact married?
7. Dan Brown indicates in *The Da Vinci Code* that the truest form of Christianity is sexual in nature, advocating androgyny. Did Jesus agree?

THE PASSION OF THE CHRIST

Who Killed Jesus?

||||||||||||||||||||||||||||||||||||||||||||||||||||||||||||

INTRODUCTION

What an irony—the number one R-rated film of all time is a religious movie! We're talking, of course, about Mel Gibson's 2004 film, *The Passion of the Christ*, whose showings turned theaters across America into worship services as millions of Christians voted with their feet for a cause they especially hold dear—getting the gospel to the world. As one of our colleagues quipped, "I have always assumed that God would use a Southern Baptist preacher to evangelize the world but instead he used a pre–Vatican II Catholic layman!" The intense media criticism of the film also became a part of the story, as both Jews and Christians (Catholic and Protestant alike) expressed their own reactions to the film: "mercenary," "anti-Semitic," "truncated version of the Gospels devoid of Jesus's life and teachings,"

> *As one of our colleagues quipped, "I have always assumed that God would use a Southern Baptist preacher to evangelize the world but instead he used a pre-Vatican II layman!"*

and "too icon-graphic" were but some of the complaints leveled at the movie and even at Gibson himself.

There is no neutral ground in opinions about this film: like the message of the cross itself, you either love *The Passion of the Christ* or you hate it. This chapter will attempt to answer three crucial questions generated by Gibson's film: Is it really too violent? Who actually killed Jesus? Why did Jesus die?

WAS MEL GIBSON'S FILM TOO VIOLENT?

Those who criticize Gibson's film, "The Goriest Story Ever Told" as one film critic labeled it,[1] for its violence often do so because they perceive it to be cast in the style of the medieval passion plays. The backdrop for these plays was the Black Death Plague in Europe during the 1300s that claimed the lives of almost twenty million people. This was followed by the Hundred Years' War; the aftermath of these two catastrophes left much of Europe in poverty and suffering. Many of the victims coped by explaining their afflictions as the consequence of being mystically united with Christ's suffering on the cross, making observances like the Fourteen Stations of the Cross and the Sorrowful Mysteries of the Rosary popular. These factors, along with Renaissance iconography, inspired *The Passion of the Christ*, so it is claimed.[2]

The question remains: is Gibson's film too violent? No, it is not. In fact, the film is not violent enough because it is simulated, not real, agony. We say this because crucifixion at the hands of the ancient Romans was unparalleled in its cruelty. So hideous was this form of execution that Roman citizens were spared from it; it was reserved for dangerous criminals, slaves, and the populace of foreign provinces. The Roman orator Cicero (ca. 40 BC) described crucifixion as the most cruel and frightful sentence. Three types of brutality related to crucifixion were inflicted on Jesus: physical, emotional, and spiritual.

Crucifixion was designed by the Romans to either deter rebellions against the empire or punish insurrectionists. The Jewish historian Josephus provides an eyewitness account of the Roman army's

> *The question remains: is Gibson's film too violent? No, it is not. We say this because crucifixion at the hands of the ancient Romans was unparalleled in its cruelty.*

siege of Jerusalem in AD 70. He observes how hundreds of Jewish prisoners were "scourged and subjected to torture of every description . . . and thence crucified opposite the city walls." Hoping that the gruesome sight might induce the Jews to surrender the city, Titus, the Roman commander, gave his soldiers freedom to continue the crucifixions as they pleased. "The soldiers out of rage and hatred amused themselves by nailing their prisoners in different positions."[3]

Preceding the crucifixion, soldiers flogged the criminal with a Roman scourge (*flagellum*)[4] that consisted of two or three thongs with pieces of bone or metal attached which were designed to rip the skin. The prisoner was stripped of his clothing, and his hands were tied to an upright post; his back, buttocks, and legs were flogged, either by two soldiers (*lictors*) or by one who alternated positions. The severity of the scourging depended on the disposition of the *lictors* and was intended to weaken the victim to a state just short of collapse or death. After the scourging, the soldiers often taunted their victim.

> **Preceding the crucifixion, soldiers flogged the criminal with a Roman scourge (flagellum) that consisted of two or three thongs with pieces of bone or metal attached which were designed to rip the skin.**

As the Roman soldiers repeatedly struck the victim's back with full force, the iron balls would cause deep contusions, and the leather thongs and sheep bones would cut into the skin and tissues. Then, as the flogging continued, the lacerations would tear into the underlying skeletal muscles and produce quivering ribbons of bleeding flesh. Pain and blood loss generally set the stage for circulatory shock. The extent of blood loss may well have determined how long the victim would survive on the cross. It was customary for the condemned man to carry his own cross from the flogging post to the site of crucifixion outside the city walls. He was usually naked. Since the weight of the entire cross was probably well over 300 pounds, only the crossbar (*patibulum*) was carried. The *patibulum*, weighing 75 to 125 pounds, was placed across the nape of the victim's neck and balanced along both shoulders. Usually, the prisoner's outstretched arms were tied to the crossbar. The procession to the site of crucifixion was led by a complete Roman military guard, headed by a centurion. One of the soldiers carried a sign (*titulus*) on which the condemned man's

> **The bones of a crucified body found in an ossuary near Jerusalem, and dating from the time of Christ, indicate that the nails were tapered iron spikes approximately thirteen to eighteen centimeters long with a square shaft one centimeter across.**

name and crime were displayed. Later, the *titulus* would be attached to the top of the cross. The Roman guards would not leave the victim until they were sure of his death.

At the site of execution, by law, the victim was given a bitter drink of wine mixed with myrrh (gall) as a mild analgesic. The criminal was then thrown to the ground on his back, with his arms outstretched along the *patibulum*. His hands could be nailed or tied to the crossbar, but nailing was apparently preferred by the Romans. The bones of a crucified body found in an ossuary near Jerusalem, and dating from the time of Christ, indicate that the nails were tapered iron spikes approximately thirteen to eighteen centimeters long with a square shaft one centimeter across.

After both arms were fixed to the crossbar, it and the victim, together, were lifted on to the stipes. On the low cross, four soldiers could accomplish this relatively easily. However, on the tall cross, the soldiers used either wooden forks or ladders.

When the nailing was completed, the *titulus* was attached to the cross, by nails or cords, just above the victim's head. The soldiers and the civilian crowd often taunted and jeered the condemned man, and the soldiers customarily divided up his clothes among themselves. The length of survival generally ranged from three or four hours to three or four days and appears to have been related to the severity of the scourging. However, even if the scourging had been relatively mild, the Roman soldiers could hasten death by breaking the legs below the knees. No longer able to lift their chests to breathe, the victims suffocated to death. Not uncommonly, insects would light upon or burrow into the open wounds or the eyes, ears, and nose of the dying and helpless victim, and birds of prey would tear at these sites. Moreover, it was customary to leave the corpse on the cross to be devoured by predatory animals.[5]

The emotional aspect of the torture of crucifixion was that of humiliation. Nakedness, scorn,
and unbearable pain combined to reduce the
strongest of men (women were not subjected
to crucifixion) to a state of helplessness. And
the more humiliated they were, the more for-
midable Rome appeared.

In addition to the physical agony and emotional shame that accompanied crucifixion,
Jesus of Nazareth suffered spiritually. He
was abandoned by God because the sin of
the world rested on him. Deuteronomy
21:23 says "anyone hung on a tree is under
God's curse," a statement that in Jesus's
day was applied to crucifixion (NRSV; see
Gal. 3:13).[6]

> *Deuteronomy 21:23 says, "Cursed is everyone who hangs on a tree," a statement that in Jesus's day was applied to crucifixion.*

WHO KILLED JESUS?

Another key criticism raised against Gibson's film is that it is potentially
anti-Semitic. More than one rabbi appeared on TV after the debut of *The*

Nonbiblical Aspects of Gibson's *The Passion of the Christ*

Although we applaud Gibson's *The Passion of the Christ* there are, however, scenes in it not found in the canonical Gospels, including the following key episodes:

1. Jesus crushed a serpent in the Garden of Gethsemane. Yet Genesis 3:15 does predict that God's anointed one will one day crush the head of the serpent after first striking at the Messiah's heel (at the cross?).

2. Demonically inspired children taunted Judas Iscariot after his betrayal of Jesus.

3. Satan held a baby with an ugly adult's head. This seems to suggest that evil has the capacity to pervert that which is precious.

4. Veronica aided Jesus on his way to the cross.

5. Pilate's wife, who related her dream to her husband warning him not to harm Jesus because he was righteous (a scene that is found in Matthew), comforted Jesus's mother during his crucifixion (which is not in the Gospels).

Except for number 1, the rest of the above episodes are a part of Roman Catholic tradition.

Passion of the Christ to decry its effects on Jewish/Gentile relations because of its similarities to medieval passion plays. These plays are well known for contributing to the climate in Europe that culminated in the Holocaust. "Christ killers" became the motto of some of those who watched such plays, which stirred up their hatred toward the Jewish race.

It is crucial at this point that we maintain an awareness of history, and work to interpret the events surrounding Jesus's passion as objectively as possible. There is no need to revise history in order to deny the role of some ancient Jews in their gross mistreatment of one of their own—Jesus of Nazareth. Surely modern Jews would categorically reject any attempt to revise recent history by denying the horrors of the Holocaust, and rightly so. But neither is it intellectually and morally permissible to explain away the culpability of those few Jews in the past who killed an innocent man. But after we arrive at the truth about the passion—that some Jewish leaders in AD 30 stirred up a crowd against one of their own—we will also see that such action should in no way justify anti-Semitism in any form.

What, then, is the historical evidence concerning the question, who killed Jesus? We begin to answer this question by observing that the source of some modern Jews' consternation about the portrayal of the death of Jesus ultimately is *not* Gibson, but the *Gospels*—for it is they that lay the blame for Jesus's death at the feet of some ancient Jews, as well as on the shoulders of the Roman governor Pilate.

> *All the Gospels indicate that the Jewish leaders initiated the plot to kill Jesus and that Pilate's attempt to release Jesus was met with the Jewish crowd's demand for Jesus's death.*

The Jews and Jesus's Death

All the Gospels indicate that the Jewish leaders initiated the plot to kill Jesus (Matt. 21:46; 26:3–4; 14–16, 47, 57–67; Mark 14:1, 43, 53–65; Luke 19:47; 20:19; 22:3–6, 47, 54, 63–65; 23:1–12; John 11:45-57; 18:2–3, 12–14). All the Gospels also indicate that Pilate's attempt to release Jesus was met with the Jewish crowd's demand for Jesus's death (Matt. 27:20-26; Mark 15:9–14; Luke 23:13–25; John 18:39–40; 19:1–7, 15–16).

The culpability of the Sanhedrin, the seventy-one Jewish leaders who governed ancient Israel, is all the more notable when one realizes how illegal the trial of Jesus was. Compared to its own laws regulating trials as recorded in the Mishnah, the ancient Jewish law code, the Sanhedrin acted improperly at Jesus's trial in at least five ways, as Bruce Corley observes:

> (1) it was improperly convened in the high priest's house (*m. Sanh.* 11:2); (2) met during the night (*m. Sanh.* 4:1); (3) on a Sabbath eve or Feast Day (*m. Sanh.* 4:1); and (4) reached a guilty verdict on the same day (*m. Sanh.* 4:1; 5:5) (5) based on inadequate grounds for blasphemy (*m. Sanh.* 7:5).[7]

The Sanhedrin broke their own laws and convicted Jesus of blaspheming for identifying himself as the Son of God (see Mark 14:61–64 and parallel passages)—a crime punishable by death. At the time, both the Jewish leaders and the Jewish people readily accepted responsibility for their part in the death of Jesus. Matthew 27:25 is particularly powerful on this point: After demanding that Jesus be crucified, the Jewish crowd cried out to Pilate, "Let his blood be on us and our children" (NIV).

Josephus on Jesus's Death

"About this time there lived Jesus, a wise man, if indeed one ought to call him a man. For he was one who wrought surprising feats and was a teacher of such people as accept the truth gladly. He won over many Jews and many of the Greeks. He was the Christ. When Pilate, upon hearing him accused by men of the highest standing amongst us, had condemned him to be crucified, those who had in the first place come to love him did not give up their affection for him. On the third day he appeared to them restored to life, for the prophets of God had prophesied these and countless other marvelous things about him. And the tribe of the Christians, so called after him, has still to this day not disappeared."[8]

But these indictments against those Jews who rejected Jesus are not to be equated with anti-Semitism for two reasons. First, the Gospels are simply condemning Jesus's disobedient generation, just like the Old Testament prophets condemned their generation of unbelievers. Second, many Jews accepted Jesus in his day and the next generation and experienced God's grace and blessing.

In a *Time* magazine article, Richard Corliss catches this distinction in both Gibson's film and in the Gospels:

> Is the film anti-Jewish? Well, which Jews? Start with the Sanhedrin, the Rabbinical senate that found Jesus guilty of violating temple law and handed him to the Roman authority for summary punishment. The rabbis had their reasons; they saw the upstart as dangerous, blasphemous, possibly insane for proclaiming

> But the Jews could not have pulled off the trial and execution of Jesus without the Romans' help, particularly Pilate's.

himself the Messiah and telling his followers they would live forever if they ate his flesh and drank his blood. The film sees the rabbis as doctrinally pure but politically corrupt. Indeed, it suggests they are a rogue cell calling a midnight caucus for a frame-up. But Gibson also shows many Jews (and no Romans) treating Jesus with a kindness and charity one might call Christian. We acknowledge, then, that *The Passion* is rabidly anti-Sanhedrin—opposed, as Jesus and other Jews were, to the Establishment of the time. But to charge the film with being anti-Semitic is like saying those who oppose the Bush Administration's Iraq policy are anti-American.[9]

The point is well taken. We should not confuse the Gospel's condemnation of some ancient Jews' mistreatment of Jesus with anti-Semitism. Bruce Corley expresses the matter more strongly:

> A lamentable feature of Christian reaction to the trial of Jesus across the centuries has been an odious persecution of the Jews for putting Jesus to death. It has been maintained above that the Evangelists did not invent the fact of Jewish involvement, but the NT never says that the Jews alone, least of all every succeeding generation, were responsible for the cross. The perennial instinct to kindle anti-Semitism by the findings of historical scholarship is deplorable in all its forms. The theological stance of the Gospels indicts us all, Jew and Gentile alike: "He was numbered with the transgressors" (Luke 22:37), yet "this man has done nothing wrong" (Luke 23:41).[10]

The Romans and Jesus's Death

But the Jews could not have pulled off the trial and execution of Jesus without the Romans' help, particularly Pilate's. John 18:31 relates how the Jewish Sanhedrin did not have the right to execute criminals, only the Roman governor did. It is interesting that at that point the Jews mixed the nature of their accusations against Jesus—he was a blasphemer (John 19:7) *and* an insurrectionist (John 19:12). Introducing the latter charge necessarily involved Pilate—for now Jesus was accused of being a revolutionary. Though they could pass a death sentence, the Sanhedrin needed Pilate's approval to carry it out because the power to execute lay only in his hands as the Roman procurator (governor). This fact is corroborated by extra-canonical Jewish testimony. Corley lists the evidence from Josephus (late first century AD) and the Talmud (ancient Israel's legal writings [second to fifth centuries AD]):

> While still competent to try religious cases, the prerogatives of the Sanhedrin changed with the beginning of direct Roman rule in Judea: (1) Coponius, the first governor (AD 6), was sent out by Augustus with full powers "extending to capital punishment" (Josephus, *J.W.* 2.8.1/117; cf. *Ant.* 18.1.1/2). (2) Tannaitic tradition confirms that "the right to try capital cases was taken from Israel forty years before the destruction of the Temple" (*y. Sanh.* 1.1; 7.2; cf. b. *Sanh.* 41a; b. *Abod. Zar.* 8b); (3) the Jewish death penalty was reinstated a week after the Romans lifted the siege of Jerusalem in September AD 66; "On the twenty-second of the month [Elul] the execution of malefactors began again" (*Meg. Ta'an.* 6).[11]

But there are scholars who disagree with the traditional view that only the Roman governor, not the Sanhedrin, had the power to execute criminals.[12] Those scholars typically appeal to the following cases: First, archaeologists have discovered two of the warning inscriptions dating to the first century AD that surrounded the Jerusalem temple, forbidding Gentiles to proceed no further on pain of death at the hands of the Jewish authorities.[13] Second, Stephen was executed by the Sanhedrin (Acts 6:8–7:60). And third, like Stephen, James, the brother of Jesus, was stoned to death at the orders of the high priest Ananus and the Sanhedrin.

But the preceding episodes are easily explained according to the traditional view. Regarding the warning inscriptions, Josephus tells his readers that Rome first gave the Sanhedrin permission to erect the barriers containing the inscriptions, and to execute trespassers.[14] In Stephen's case, while a trial procedure was initially followed by the Sanhedrin (Acts 6:11–14; 7:57–58), the proceedings were interrupted without proper sentencing. In other words, Stephen's death occurred as an act of lynch law at the hands of a mob, a violation of Jewish law.[15] And in James's case, the brother of the Lord was killed in the interval between the rules of the Roman governors Festus and Albinus (AD 62); that is, without the approval of Rome.

> *Critics of The Passion of the Christ accused the film of going easy on Pilate. But neither Gibson's film nor the Gospels let Pilate off the hook.*

Consequently, the Jewish high priest, Ananus, was deposed from office by Rome. Therefore, John 18:31 stands: the Sanhedrin had to get permission from Rome to have a criminal executed. And such was the case for Jesus. Only Pilate could make it happen.

Critics of *The Passion of the Christ* accused the film of going easy on Pilate. But neither Gibson's film nor the Gospels let Pilate off the hook. All the Synoptics include Jesus's prediction that he will be handed over to the Gentiles (Matt. 20:19; Mark 10:33; Luke 18:32); and Pilate is presumably to be numbered among them. In Matthew, Pilate yields to the crowd despite the warning of his wife's dream (27:19). His washing of his hands is an empty gesture (27:24); he can no more evade his responsibility than could Judas or the high priests (27:3–7). In Luke, Pilate pronounces Jesus's innocence three times (23:4, 15, 22). However, this serves to emphasize Jesus's innocence (23:41, 47; Acts 13:28), not to exonerate Pilate, who in Acts is numbered among those who gather against the Anointed One (4:25–28). In Mark, Pilate's resistance to the crowd's demand is minimal. In John, he is cynical and self-serving (18:35, 38; 19:8–9). Thus, no consistent exoneration of Pilate can be traced in any of the Gospels.[16]

So even though Pilate considered Jesus innocent, why did he give in to the Jewish demand to crucify Jesus? History reveals the answer. Pilate capitulated to the crowd's request to crucify Jesus because of his previous failed relationships with the Jews. Pilate, the Roman prefect of Judea from AD 26 to 36, was not well thought of by the Jews, to say the least. Josephus writes of his blundering dealings with the nation of Israel.[17] Three in particular call for comment.

First, when he became governor of Judea, Pilate sent his troops into Jerusalem with the ensigns on their standards. For the Jews, the image to Caesar was tantamount to idolatry. When the people protested Pilate's actions, he threatened them with death, but they were not intimidated. Pilate backed off from his threat.

Second, Pilate confiscated money out of the temple treasury to fund an aqueduct to bring water to Jerusalem. The Jews of Jerusalem were furious, but this time the governor carried through with his threat to kill those who opposed him. He did so by having his soldiers dress as civilians and then, at Pilate's signal, attack the protesters.

Third, as Marvin has written elsewhere,

Pilate hung votive shields engraved with emperor Tiberius's name in the palace of Herod in Jerusalem. Before Pilate the Romans had tried to respect the Jew's abhorrence of anything that remotely resembled a graven image erected in Jerusalem. Pilate's actions crossed the line, so a Jewish delegation responded by appealing directly to the emperor, who rebuked Pilate and ordered the removal of the shields. The final straw had now come with the Jews' demand for Jesus's crucifixion. Were Pilate to refuse their request, Caesar Tiberius would surely depose the governor, especially if he tolerated a rival king (see John 19:12–15).[18]

So the Gospels are clear that both some ancient Jews and Romans killed Jesus of Nazareth, innocent though he was. But are they alone responsible for Jesus's death? No, for while the Gospels provide the historical reason for Jesus's death, the apostle Paul provides the *theological* reason for Jesus's death—Jesus died because of the whole world. The sins of humanity crucified Jesus. The key word here is "delivered up" (one word in the Greek—*paradidomi*). This word is used in the Gospels to refer to the Jews and Romans "delivering up" Jesus to death (Matt. 17:22; 20:18–19; Mark 9:31; 10:33; Luke 9:44; 18:32; 20:20; 1 John 18:35; 19:16). But Paul uses the word to refer to all of humanity as being responsible for Jesus's death. Note the following references: "He [Jesus] was delivered over to death for our sins" (Rom. 4:25); "He [God] who did not spare his own Son, but delivered him up for us all" (Rom. 8:32); "by faith in the Son of God, who loved me and delivered himself up for me" (Gal. 2:20); "And [God] delivered him [Jesus] up for us as a fragrant offering and sacrifice" (Eph. 5:2); "Just as Christ loved the church and delivered himself up for her" (Eph. 5:25). All the preceding verses in this paragraph are the authors' translation based on the Greek text (*Nestle-Aland Greek-English New Testament* [Stuttgart, Germany: Deutsche Bibelgesellschaft, 1998]).

So to return to our question: Who killed Jesus? We all did, not just some ancient Jews and Romans. But the good news of the Gospel is that we can all be saved from our sins precisely because of Jesus's death and resurrection for us.

> *Christ the Victor was a theme championed by some church fathers, which held sway until about AD 1000. This viewpoint appeals to passages like Colossians 2:15, which refers to Christ's triumph over Satan and the fallen angels at his resurrection. The whole book of Revelation is a dramatization of this theme of Christ the Victor defeating Satan and the enemies of God.*

WHY DID JESUS DIE?

> According to Anselm of Canterbury, Christ's death did constitute a ransom, but not to Satan. Rather it was a ransom paid to God himself, to satisfy his holiness that had been offended by humanity's sin.

The April 12, 2004, cover of *Time* magazine featured the following: "Why Did Jesus Have to Die? As Easter arrives and millions still flock to see *The Passion*, the reasons behind his sacrifice are debated anew."[19] The article goes on to say that the answer to that question might be seen to be as simple as "Jesus loves me, but in fact has divided theologians and clergy for centuries with no end in sight; why did Christ die?"[20] The question takes us into the meaning of the atonement, the centerpiece of Christianity. Although there are a number of theories as to why Jesus died, three have been especially influential: Christ the Victor, Jesus's substitutionary sacrifice, and the imitation of Christ. Christ the Victor was a theme championed by some church fathers, which held sway until about AD 1000. This viewpoint appeals to passages like Colossians 2:15, which refers to Christ's triumph over Satan and the fallen angels at his resurrection. The whole book of Revelation is a dramatization of this theme of Christ the Victor defeating Satan and the enemies of God. Origen (AD 184–254) seems to have been one of the first to push this perspective. According to him, Christ's death was the ransom God paid to Satan. When Adam and Eve fell in the Garden of Eden, all of humanity became the possession of the devil. But Christ's death "bought" humanity out of the clutches of Satan. The church father Gregory of Nyssa (AD 335–395) further developed Origen's concept by using the metaphor of divine bait and switch: Jesus's death was the bait that the devil gobbled up, which became a hook—Satan was vanquished when Christ was revealed to be God. Saint Augustine (AD 354–430) agreed, likening the devil to a mouse, the cross to a mousetrap, and Christ to the bait. Colorful an image as this is, no theologian today really views Jesus's death in that light, because if God had to appease the devil by sending his Son to die, Origen's theory makes Satan equal to God. Though it must be said that a vestige of the theory is convincing—that Christ's cross defeated Satan—but without the ransom nuance.

A second dominant view of the death of Jesus was that of Anselm of Canterbury (eleventh century AD). According to him, Christ's death did constitute a ransom, but not to Satan. Rather it was a ransom paid to God himself, to satisfy his holiness that had been offended by humanity's sin. Jeff Chu writes of this:

> Anselm too read the New Testament lines calling Christ's death a ransom, but he could not believe that the devil was owed anything. So he restructured the cosmic debt. It was, he posed, humanity that owed God the Father a ransom of "satisfaction" (to use Anselm's feudal terminology) for the insult of sin. The problem was that the debt was unpayable: not only did we lack the means, since everything we had of value was God's to begin with, but also we lacked the standing, like a lowly serf helpless to erase an injury to a great lord. Eternal damnation seemed unavoidable, except for a miracle of grace. God "recast" himself into human form so that Christ, who was both innocent of sin and also God's social equal, could suffer the Crucifixion's undeserved agony, dedicating it to the Father on humanity's behalf. Christ "paid for sinners what he owed not for himself," wrote Anselm reverently. "Could the Father justly refuse to man what the Son willed to give him?"[21]

> *Together these two traditions form the "imitation of Christ" theme: Christ died for our sins and we must show our love for God and others by emulating his suffering in our lives.*

In the hands of the sixteenth-century Protestant Reformers Martin Luther and John Calvin, Anselm's substitutionary theory of atonement caught on and even was adopted by the Catholic Church. In the New Testament, Paul's letter to the church in Corinth (ca AD 57) thoroughly presents such a perspective toward Christ's death on the cross (cf. 2 Cor. 5:21). The Gospel of John also equates Jesus with the sacrificial lamb of the Old Testament (John 1:29; 19:14, 29, 36), as does the book of Hebrews (see chapters 8–10). It is this understanding that informs Gibson's film, as the opening quote from Isaiah 53:5 makes clear: "He was wounded for our transgressions, He was bruised for our iniquities . . . By His stripes we are healed" (NKJV).

The "imitation of Christ" interpretation of Jesus's death has also enjoyed a large following. This view perceives Jesus's death as providing an example for humans to model, not so much a sacrifice for them to accept. Peter Abelard, a contemporary of Anselm, first popularized this view. According to Abelard, God's love in letting Jesus die along with Jesus's love in being willing to die motivates humans to practice the same love toward others. This was love answering love's appeal, said Abelard. So for him, sin was not so much the issue as ignorance. If humans would contemplate the cross, their selfishness would be replaced by love, which would lead to their salvation before God. Such an approach is called "exemplary atonement."

In Catholic circles, this interpretation of Jesus's death is wedded with the theory of substitutionary atonement. Together these two traditions form the "imitation of Christ" theme: Christ died for our sins and we must show our love for God and others by emulating his suffering in our lives. Often Matthew, Mark, and Luke are appealed to as supporting this reading. First Peter 2:21 is interesting in this regard: "For to this you have been called [to suffer], because Christ also suffered for you, leaving you an example, so that you should follow in his steps" (NRSV).

There is a sense in which all three of the preceding views of Jesus's death are legitimate theories of atonement, because they have scriptural support. But for us, two of the views require qualification before they can be accepted. The Christ the Victor theory is true, except for Origen's idea that Jesus's death was God's ransom paid to Satan. And the imitation of Christ theory is helpful, as long as one does not interpret it to mean that humans are saved by their own effort in emulating Jesus. The substitutionary theory of atonement, however, does not seem to need any qualifying statements.

A combination of all three of these views on Jesus's death might account, in part, for the enormous success of Mel Gibson's *The Passion of the Christ* for, as the *Time* magazine article concluded:

> Gibson's *The Passion of the Christ* has certainly done its bit to combat Christianity lite. The film's stance on atonement could best be described as substitutionary (that initial Isaiah quote sets the theme) with a strong dose of Catholic Passion piety (the very gory details), a pinch of exemplarism (the flashbacks to Jesus's teachings) and those sulfurous whiffs of the ancient good-vs.-evil model. In other words, an understanding almost as eclectic as the average American's. Will it convince anyone of any particular philosophy? Perhaps not, but it is a reminder that the question of why Jesus died requires some sort of response from anyone who reasons out his or her faith.[22]

CONCLUSION

So to recap our answers to the three questions raised in this chapter: Was *The Passion of the Christ* too violent? No; not if one is trying to capture the agony of ancient crucifixion, which is what Gibson attempted to accomplish, and thereby remind audiences of the enormity of God's love for humankind. Who killed Jesus? The answer is both the sins of some ancient Jews and Romans as well as the transgressions of all of humanity. In other words, you and me. Why did Jesus die? To pay the price for our sins, defeat Satan, and liberate us from our selfishness so that we might love others the way he loves us. But there is another question this topic raises, one the reader needs to address: Have you personalized *The Passion of the Christ* by inviting him to be your Savior? If not, what better time than now to do so?

DISCUSSION QUESTIONS

1. Do you think Gibson's *The Passion of the Christ* is too violent?
2. Do you think it is anti-Semitic?
3. Summarize the Romans' method of crucifixion.
4. Who was responsible for the death of Jesus?
5. Which of the three theories of atonement are you most drawn to?

THE SHROUD OF TURIN

Is It Jesus's Burial Cloth?

||||||||||||||||||||||||||||||||||||||||||||||||||||||||||||||||||||||||||||||||||||

INTRODUCTION

The Shroud of Turin is a linen cloth, fourteen feet long and three-and-a-half feet wide. The threads were handspun and the fabric hand-woven in three-to-one herringbone twill.

On the long fabric are two faint, straw-colored images, one of the front and the other of the back of a nude man who was apparently scourged and crucified, with the hands crossed over the pelvis. The images appear head to head, as though a body had been laid on its back at one end of the fabric, which was then drawn over to cover the front of the body.

The cloth has many burn holes and scorches; the holes have been patched. There are also large water stains. Although the cloth appeared in France 630 years ago, its history is obscure.[1]

The cloth in question is known by the Italians as the *Santa Sindone*, or Holy Shroud. It rests today in Turin's Cathedral of Saint John the Baptist, Italy. It has done so since 1578, except for 1939–1945 when it was taken to the Abbey of Monte

> *On the long fabric are two faint, straw-colored images, one of the front and the other of the back of a nude man who was apparently scourged and crucified, with the hands crossed over the pelvis.*

117

Vergine (Avellino) for safety at the outbreak of World War II. The Shroud's privacy has contributed to its mystique, punctuated by public expositions now and then. The reticence of Turin's cardinals to display it has rendered the cloth virtually inaccessible. In normal circumstances not even the most privileged visitor is allowed to see it. Ian Wilson writes:

> Since the time of Napoleon the Shroud has been seen publicly on no more than a handful of occasions, always attracting vast crowds of pilgrims, who have queued for hours just to file past it as it hung in the cathedral, or catch a glimpse of an exposition on the cathedral steps. An elaborate procedure must be followed for any exposition. Permission has to be obtained from the pope, from the cardinal of Turin and from the ex-king of Italy, Umberto II of Savoy. Although Umberto is technically still the cloth's owner, even he has not seen it since 1933 because of his fall from power.[2]

But the Shroud's visibility dramatically changed in November 1973 when Cardinal Pellegrino of Turin agreed to show the cloth on a thirty-minute RAI-TV program. That move opened the Shroud up to scientific investigation for the first time. Since then, the Shroud of Turin has generated dozens of books, hundreds of articles and reports, and endless debates over its alleged authenticity.

The issue of the Shroud seems straightforward: either it is real or a forgery; authentic or a hoax. If it is real, then the Shroud is none other than the burial cloth of Jesus, the only artifact bearing testimony to both his death by

> *If it is real, then the Shroud is none other than the burial cloth of Jesus, the only artifact bearing testimony to both his death by crucifixion (the blood stains caused by the scourging and crucifixion) and his resurrection (hence the burn marks).*

crucifixion (the blood stains caused by the scourging and crucifixion) and his resurrection (hence the burn marks). But if it is a forgery, as one leading particle expert puts it, "The Shroud is a beautiful painting created about 1355 for a new church in need of a pilgrim-attracting relic."[3]

Is it possible the truth lies in between authentic relic and brilliant hoax? Perhaps a personal testimony from the authors might be of interest at this point.

When we began researching the subject, we assumed that the cloth is not real. It is like what one scientist said of Catholic relics, "If one took all the pieces of the true cross and put them in one place, we would have a lumberyard!"[4] But now, in light of the evidence, it has become very interesting for us.

Is the Shroud of Turin the greatest "interface between science and religion?"[5] And does it confirm the Gospel's description of Jesus's death and resurrection? To aid in answering these questions, we will investigate the following: the Shroud and the Gospels; the known history of the Shroud; the debate over the interpretation of the data concerning the Shroud; its significance, genuine or not.

THE GOSPELS AND THE SHROUD OF TURIN

No matter what the opinion on its authenticity, all agree that the man whose image appears on the Shroud of Turin bears remarkable resemblance to the four Gospels' portraits of Jesus's death by crucifixion. Dr. Robert Bucklin, forensic pathologist (a specialist investigating the cause of violent deaths) of Los Angeles, filed this report on the violent death of the man in the Shroud of Turin:

> Irrespective of how the images were made, there is adequate information here to state that they are anatomically correct. There is no problem in diagnosing what happened to this individual. The pathology and physiology are unquestionable and represent medical knowledge unknown 150 years ago. . . .
>
> This is a 5–foot, 11–inch male Caucasian weighing about 178 pounds. The lesions are as follows: beginning at the head, there are blood flows from numerous puncture wounds on the top and back of the scalp and forehead. The man has been beaten about the face, there is a swelling over one cheek, and he undoubtedly has a black eye. His nose top is abraded, as would occur from a fall, and it appears that the nasal cartilage may have separated from the bone. There is a wound in the left wrist, the right one being covered by the left hand. This is the typical lesion of a crucifixion. The classical artistic and legendary portrayal of a crucifixion with nails through the palms of the hands is spurious: the structures in the hand are too fragile to hold the live weight of a man, particularly of this size. Had a man been crucified with nails in the palms, they would have torn through the bones, muscles, and ligaments, and the victim would have fallen off the cross.
>
> There is a stream of blood down both arms. Here and there, there are blood drips at an angle from the main blood flow in response to gravity. These angles represent the only ones that can occur from the only two positions which can be taken by a body during crucifixion.
>
> On the back and front there are lesions which appear to be scourge marks. Historians have indicated that Romans used a whip called a *flagrum* [*or flagellum*]. The whip had two or three thongs, and at their ends there were pieces of

metal or bone which look like small dumbbells. They were designed to gouge out flesh. The thongs and metal end-pieces from a Roman flagrum fit precisely into the anterior and posterior scourge lesions on the body. The victim was whipped from both sides by two men, one of whom was taller than the other, as demonstrated by the angle of the thongs.

There is a swelling of both shoulders, with abrasions indicating that something heavy and rough had been carried across the man's shoulders within hours of death. On the right flank, a long, narrow blade of some type entered in an upward direction, pierced the diaphragm, penetrated into the thoracic cavity through the lung into the heart. This was a post-mortem event, because separate components of red blood cells and clear serum drained from the lesion. Later, after the corpse was laid out horizontally and face up on the cloth, blood dribbled out of the side wound and puddled along the small of the back. There is no evidence of either leg being fractured. There is an abrasion of one knee, commensurate with a fall (as is the abraded nose tip); and finally, a spike had been driven through both feet, and blood had leaked from both wounds onto the cloth. The evidence of a scourged man who was crucified and died from the cardiopulmonary failure typical of crucifixion is clear-cut.[6]

Compare Dr. Bucklin's report, and others before him, with the four Gospels' descriptions of Jesus's death:[7]

Gospel Evidence	Source	Evidence on the Shroud
1. Jesus was scourged.	Matt. 27:26; Mark 15:15; John 19:1	The body is literally covered with the wounds of a severe scourging.
2. Jesus was struck a blow to the face.	Matt. 27:30, Mark 15:19; Luke 22:63; John 19:3	There appear to be a severe swelling below the right eye and other superficial face wounds.
3. Jesus was crowned with thorns.	Matt. 27:29; Mark 15:17; John 19:2	Bleeding from the scalp indicates that some form of barbed "cap" has been thrust upon the head.
4. Jesus had to carry a heavy cross.	John 19:17	Scourge wounds in the area of the shoulders appear to be blurred, as if by the chafing of some heavy burden.
5. Jesus's cross had to be carried for him, suggesting he fell under the burden.	Matt. 27:32; Mark 15:21; Luke 23:26	The knees appear severely damaged, as if from repeated falls.
6. Jesus was crucified by nailing in hands and feet.	(by implication John 20:25)	There are clear blood flows as from nail wounds in the wrists and at the feet.
7. Jesus's legs were not broken, but a spear was thrust into his side as a check that he was dead.	John 19:31–37	The legs are clearly not broken, and there is an elliptical wound in the right side.[8]

Almost as remarkable as the parallels between the Gospels' accounts and the preceding medical report on the Shroud is the blatant contrast between it and medieval portraits of Christ. The former has nails in the man's wrists while the latter has nails in Jesus's hands. The point to be made from this observation is that, if the Shroud of Turin is a medieval forgery, then it stands alone in artistic representation of the nailing of Jesus's wrists.[9]

But we have gotten ahead of our story of the Shroud of Turin. Let us now take a step back and trace its historical origin.

> If the Shroud of Turin is a medieval forgery, then it stands alone in artistic representation of the nailing of Jesus's wrists.

THE KNOWN HISTORY OF THE SHROUD

The first mention historically of the Shroud of Turin was in a letter written from the bishop of Troyes, France, to Pope Clement VII in 1389. In the letter, the bishop complains of a piece of linen, approximately 14 feet long and 3 feet wide with the front and back images of a crucified man, being falsely displayed in the village of Lirey since the year 1355 as the true burial shroud of Christ. This was a time in history when pilgrimages made forgery of relics lucrative. Although the bishop stated that the image was "cunningly painted," it was determined a forgery because the artist had admitted as much. In response, Pope Clement VII allowed the Shroud to be exhibited only if an announcement was continually made which denounced the authenticity of it as Christ's burial cloth, referring to the Shroud as an artist's rendition of the crucifixion.

The Shroud arrived in Turin, Italy, in 1578 after narrowly escaping a fire in 1532. It was placed on exhibit several times, which resulted in support for its authenticity even though it was officially proclaimed a fraud. During the 1898 exhibit, the Shroud of Turin was introduced to the scientific community, where the first photographs of the Shroud were taken by Secondo Pia, revealing a much clearer negative of a man. Since then, numerous scientific investigations have taken place in order to verify, or disprove, the authenticity of the Shroud of Turin. Most notably, in 1978 the Shroud of Turin Research Project (STURP) was organized to determine the cause of the image, and thus its true status. With the exception of one or two researchers, however, all of the scientists involved believed in the authenticity of the Shroud before the project began. After conducting its research, the STURP group concluded that the Shroud was in fact the burial cloth of Jesus. Most recently, the Shroud of Turin was again rescued from a fire in 1997 before being placed on exhibit in the years 1998 and 2000, again leading to a surge in popularity and belief in its authenticity.[10]

THE DEBATE OVER THE SHROUD

From the first known reference to the Shroud of Turin, this purported burial cloth of Jesus has had its detractors (recall the Bishop of Troyes's accusation that it was a forgery). Although the debate over the authenticity of the Shroud has continued through the centuries, since the 1970s scientific analysis has generated three key issues: Are the red stains blood or paint? Does the linen cloth date to the first century AD or only to the fourteenth century? Is there a "pre-history" to the Shroud that takes one back from the fourteenth century to the first century? We now enter into the fray of debate.

Nothing but the Blood?

Are the stains on the Shroud of Turin real blood or an artist's pigment? In 1978, the Shroud of Turin Research Project (STURP) was formed to objectively determine the cause of the image on the Shroud. The team was composed of forty scientists whose expertise ranged from photography to forensic pathology to botany. They were allotted 120 hours to perform their investigations.[11] They paid particular attention to the apparent blood stains on the Shroud. Members of the STURP team conducted x-ray fluorescent analysis of the stains. They were especially concerned to see what light the presence of iron in the faint sepia image would shed. They concluded that the presence of both iron and protein in the substance comprising the stains indicated that it was blood.[12]

> *They concluded that the presence of both iron and protein in the substance comprising the stains indicated that it was blood.*

Dr. Walter McCrone, expert in microanalysis and painting authentication, and one-time member of STURP, begged to differ. His investigation of the Shroud led him to report that it was a painting by a medieval artist with the image made up of paint pigment particles (red ochre and vermillion) in a collagen tempera medium rather than blood. He based this on numerous tests, including microchemical tests for iron, mercury, and body fluids.[13] McCrone identified the painting as grisaille, which was common in the Middle Ages and, to prove his point, recreated an image similar to the Shroud of Turin upon a linen cloth.[14]

But the debate was not thereby ended. Members of the STURP team countered McCrone's findings. They argued that there was no relevance between the iron oxide particles and the red pigment. The latter was blood and the former was the result of water damage.[15] These conclusions were reinforced by a later analysis conducted by Drs. John Heller and Alam Adler.

Applying pleochroism (a property of some minerals to show different colors), birefringence (light shone on a material will split into two beams), and chemical analysis, they determined that, unlike artists' pigment, which contains iron oxide contaminated with manganese, nickel, and cobalt, the iron oxide on the Shroud was relatively pure. They discovered, through research into the procedures of flax preparation and linen manufacture, that pure iron oxide is normal to the process of fermenting (retting) the flax in large outdoor vats of water.

Their conclusion: The iron oxide, abundant on the linen of the shroud, is not the remnant of an artist's pigment.

So members of the STURP team had proven the Shroud to be splattered with blood, not some artist's paint. But could the blood be that of an animal, especially since a large quantity was needed to portray all the different wounds? Drs. Adler and Heller addressed that question in their investigation. If animal blood is mixed with human blood, a watery reaction is produced. Therefore, the two researchers introduced human blood samples onto the samples of blood extracted from the Shroud. If the latter was animal blood, it should have produced the above reaction when coming into contact with human blood. But such was not the case. Adler and Heller thus concluded the blood on the Shroud was human, not animal.

Dr. Adler then proceeded to apply microspectrophotometric analysis of a "blood particle" from one of the fibrils of the Shroud and unmistakably identified hemoglobin in the acid methomoglobin form due to great age and denaturation. Further tests by Heller and Adler established, within scientific certainty, the presence of porphyrin, bilirubin, albumin, and protein. In fact, when proteases were applied to the fibril containing the "stain," the blood dissolved from the fibril leaving an imageless fibril.[16]

Kilmon goes on to report, "Working independently with a larger sample of blood containing fibrils, pathologist Pier Baima Bollone, using immunochemistry, confirmed Heller and Adler's findings and identified the blood of the AB blood group."[17]

The opinion that the stains on the Shroud were genuine blood seemed to receive support from DNA analysis from tests conducted on the cloth in the late 1990s. The tabloids had a field day with this conclusion, pronouncing that the DNA of Jesus was now revealed![18]

Critics of the Shroud, however, were quick to counter the above data. One 2002 website debunking the Shroud maintained the conclusions of the researchers who believed the Shroud to be authentic were rendered invalid

> **The tabloids had a field day with this conclusion, pronouncing that the DNA of Jesus was now revealed!**

because the first fire which the Shroud had survived had melted the silver box in which it was kept, making the temperature well above that at which proteins denature. Also, they countered that DNA found on the Shroud by researchers was subject to question because it had previously been open to public viewing and had been touched by hundreds of individuals over the centuries, each leaving a sample of their own DNA behind.[19]

With the experts in such disagreement, it is most difficult to decide whether or not the image on the Shroud is comprised of blood stains. Considering the evidence presented thus far, especially regarding the possible presence of blood stains, are you perhaps leaning toward believing the Shroud of Turin to be genuine? We concur with that, given the evidence offered thus far in the chapter.

But there may very well still be a problem with the whole issue of blood stains: If it is blood on the Shroud of Turin, what if it isn't that of Jesus Christ? For reasons soon to be discussed, it seems possible that an artist (either a forger or a well-meaning individual who wanted to graphically demonstrate the sufferings of Jesus) could use his own blood, or that of someone else, to paint the spots of the crucifixion on the cloth.

Carbon 14 and the Date of the Shroud

The linen comprising the Shroud of Turin is a herringbone-weave twill with a 3:1 weave. The flax fibrils contain entwisted cotton fibrils from a previous work of the loom. The cotton seems to be *Gossypium herbaceum*, a Middle Eastern species not found in Europe.[20] The two main theories of the origin of the image on the Shroud are either that the image on the cloth is that of Jesus Christ or it is a hoax created by a fourteenth-century artist.[21] Others who suspect the Shroud to be a forgery argue that the image is the result of someone procuring a life-size statue in the likeness of the dead Christ or even an actual corpse. According to this popular theory the "body" would then have been coated with silver nitrate to produce the image on the cloth, with blood added in appropriate areas.[22]

A critical stage in the investigation of the Shroud occurred in 1988 when the Carbon 14 dating method was applied to pieces of the linen. Radiocarbon dating measures the amount of C14, a radioactive isotope of carbon. Measurement of the C14 present in the remains of a plant or animal is a method of determining when the plant or animal died. The procedure is seen as valuable for dating organic material that originated up to about fifty thousand years ago.

When Carbon 14 dating was first used, the procedure required substantial samples of the test material and, understandably, the custodians of the Shroud of Turin were unwilling to have large portions of the Shroud destroyed in order for the testing to be done. However, advances in the procedure have made it possible to test smaller portions, and permission was granted to test twelve small samples of the non-image portion of the Shroud. Because linen is made from flax, assessment was done on when the linen was manufactured. Three Carbon 14 testing laboratories were utilized: one in Zurich, another in Oxford, and the third in Arizona. The results of the tests were published in the prestigious scientific journal *Nature*, entitled "Radiocarbon Dating of the Shroud of Turin." The results are as follows:

Sample dates from Arizona:
591 +/- 30 years
690 +/- 35 years
606 +/- 41 years
701 +/- 33 years

Sample dates from Oxford:
795 +/- 65 years
730 +/- 45 years
745 +/- 55 years

Sample dates from Zurich:
733 +/- 61 years
722 +/- 56 years
635 +/- 57 years
639 +/- 45 years
679 +/- 51 years[23]

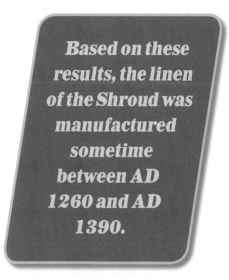

Based on these results, the linen of the Shroud was manufactured sometime between AD 1260 and AD 1390.

Based on these results, the linen of the Shroud was manufactured sometime between AD 1260 and AD 1390, with the mean value placing the manufacture of the linen in the fourteenth century!

The results were startling and fueled the opinion that the Shroud is a forgery. To ensure the accuracy of the testing, each of the three laboratories received control swatches from a known object (such as the wrappings of Cleopatra) to verify the precision of their methods and technology. Moreover, their dating of the Shroud between the thirteenth and fourteenth centuries AD corresponded with the Shroud's first appearance in historical documentation.[24]

Not surprisingly, this dating outraged many proponents of the authenticity of the Shroud of Turin.[25] They claimed that the dates were inaccurate because the samples had been taken from portions of the Shroud patched following the fires, and the linen was contaminated.

But skeptics of the Shroud were not swayed by the counter-response. Regarding the first claim, they noted that a textile expert was present upon removal of the samples; moreover, the entire procedure was videotaped, thus ensuring its validity. Regarding the second claim, through simple calculations, they argued that in order for the dating of the Shroud to be skewed by thirteen centuries, there would have to be an amount of contamination two times the weight of the Shroud itself.[26]

Now, we are not scientific experts, but if Carbon 14 dating is accurate, it seems, then, that the dating of the linen stands—that it is no earlier than the thirteenth century AD. The same method of Carbon 14 dating was applied to some of the Dead Sea Scrolls in the early 1990s, confirming a second century BC date for them. This was the same approximate time the Scrolls themselves purport to have been written (ca. 160 BC).[27] The same methodology was applied to the Shroud of Turin. However, there are still a number of unanswered questions.

Shrouded in Mystery

Another critical issue in the debate over the Shroud of Turin is the fact that there is no known mention of it before 1355 when the bishop of Troyes, France, complained of its presence there. Detractors from its authenticity naturally conclude from this that the Shroud did not exist before then. But Ian Wilson, a British reporter and theologian, using the findings of Dr. Max Frei, a noted criminologist from Zurich, Switzerland, has provided the most thorough attempt to prove the Shroud was the burial cloth of Jesus Christ.[28] In 1973 Frei was invited by Monsignor Caramello to study photographs of the Shroud. He concluded that there were forty-nine species of plants whose pollens are represented on the Shroud. They can be categorized into four main groups:

> *Wilson argued that the Shroud of Turin was originally known as Saint Veronica's Veil, famous as the sixth of the fourteen stations of the cross.*

1. Desert plants representative of the Palestine area
2. Plants from the area of Edessa, Turkey, which are from a dry zone (no natural pollen can grow there because of inadequate summer rainfall)
3. A small group of plants from the area of Istanbul, Turkey

4. Northern European plants. (This corresponds to the Shroud's known history in both France and Italy)[29]

Enter Ian Wilson. In his book *The Shroud of Turin*, Wilson argued that the Shroud was originally known as Saint Veronica's Veil, famous as the sixth of the fourteen stations of the cross. The most accepted description of that "event" in Catholic circles occurs in the AD 1696 work by Reverend Adrien Parvilliers:

> Veronica was in her house when she heard the shouting and wailing from a crowd surrounding the soldiers who were leading Jesus to Calvary. She rose hurriedly, put her head to the door, looked over the heads of the crowd, and saw our Redeemer. . . . Transported, beside herself, she seized her veil and threw herself into the street, oblivious to the insults and blows from the soldiers who pushed her back. Arriving in the presence of our Savior, whose face was pouring with sweat and blood, she wiped [his face] with her veil. . . . All honor to you, courageous woman. . . . The Savior granted you the most precious gift he could make to a creature of this world, his portrait imprinted . . . on your veil.[30]

Wilson attempts to correlate his theory that the Shroud was Veronica's Veil with the four geographical stages of Frei's pollen findings:

First Pollen Stage—Palestine, AD 30. Saint Veronica's Veil and the Shroud of Turin are one and the same, originating in Palestine at the death of Christ.

Second Pollen Stage—Edessa, Turkey, AD 30–944. Veronica's Veil / Shroud of Turin was taken by anonymous Christians to Edessa, Turkey, where a large Christian church formed. Wilson believes the Edessa (Abgar) Image—an image of a

---

Fourteen Stations of the Cross

According to Catholic tradition, Jesus's journey to the cross involved fourteen occasions of suffering:

The First Station: Jesus is condemned to die.

The Second Station: Jesus carries his cross.

The Third Station: Jesus falls the first time.

The Fourth Station: Jesus meets his mother.

The Fifth Station: Simon helps Jesus carry his cross.

The Sixth Station: Veronica wipes Jesus's face.

The Seventh Station: Jesus falls a second time.

The Eighth Station: Jesus meets the women of Jerusalem.

The Ninth Station: Jesus falls the third time.

The Tenth Station: Jesus is stripped.

The Eleventh Station: Jesus is nailed to the cross.

The Twelfth Station: Jesus dies on the cross.

The Thirteenth Station: Jesus is taken down from the cross.

The Fourteenth Station: Jesus is laid in the tomb.

face imprinted on a cloth, believed to be Christ's head, which dates to the fifth century AD—is the Shroud.

Third Pollen Stage. Istanbul, Turkey, AD 944–1204: The Arabs captured the Shroud / Veronica's Veil / Edessa Image and took it to Istanbul (Constantinople). Their name for it was the Mandylion.

Fourth Pollen Stage. Northern Europe (France, Italy): Veronica's Veil / Shroud of Turin / Edessa Image / Mandylion (all one and the same) was taken back by Christians in the Fourth Crusade. From 1204–1307, the Shroud of Turin was unaccounted for; during this period it became distinguished from its earlier name, Mandylion. After that, the Shroud was considered a separate artifact from the Mandylion. Wilson speculates that during this time the Knights of the Templar guarded it, keeping it in secret. In around 1307 the Shroud of Turin mysteriously turned up in the possession of Geoffrey de Charny, the Templar, of Lirey, France. The Shroud remained in France. A description of the Shroud appears in 1418 in connection with its relocation to Montband, France, for safe keeping. Humbert of Montband writes:

During this period of war, and mindful of ill-disposed persons, we have received from our kind chaplains, the dean and chapter of Our Lady of Lirey, the jewels and relics of the aforesaid church, namely the things which follow: first a cloth, on which is the figure or representation of the Shroud of our Lord Jesus Christ, which is in a casket emblazoned with the de Charny crest. . . . The aforesaid jewels and relics we have taken and received into our care from the said dean and chapter to be well and securely guarded in our castle of Monfort.[31]

In 1453 Margaret de Charny, after the death of her husband, gave the Shroud to the House of Savoy. There it rested until 1578, when it was brought to reside in Turin, Italy, where it has remained to this day.

As fascinating as Wilson's theory is, it suffers in the two main arguments upon which it is based: Frei's pollen analysis and Wilson's prehistory theory. First, after Frei's death in 1983, other scientists were able to view Frei's tapes, finding that they possessed the same sparse number of pollen grains as they had seen in their own research. These findings, compounded by Frei's already questionable reputation due to unrelated scandals, were deemed fraudulent by fellow scientists.[32] Second, Wilson's theory suffers at its outset by the fact that there is no record of a historical person Veronica. Even John H. Heller, who supports the claim that the Shroud contains blood, not paint stains, discounts Wilson's theory. Of the Veil/Shroud equation, he states, "I have spoken to no serious historian who gives credence to this essentially fictional story."[33] In truth, Veronica was not a person. Rather, she represents the personification of the combination of two words: one Latin—*vera* (true)—and one Greek—*icon* (image).

It is also interesting to note that the concept of Veronica's Veil containing the imprint of Jesus's face and the possibility of this later being called the Shroud of Turin does not make sense since the Shroud is the imprint of the entire body, front and back, of a man.

It seems likely, then, that the Shroud had no prehistory before the thirteenth century AD because it did not exist before then. This seems to be confirmed by the Carbon 14 test results.

We conclude this stage of our investigation by summarizing our findings concerning the three key issues regarding the Shroud of Turin. First, it may be that the tip of the scales of scientific judgment goes toward the stains on the Shroud being blood, rather than paint. But, second, the Carbon 14 dating and, third, the lack of firm prehistory combine to indicate that the Shroud most likely originated no earlier than the thirteenth century AD. A theory that could account for this mixed result—real blood, but medieval linen cloth—is that an artist studying the Gospels wished to portray the crucified Christ and used his or her own blood on a linen cloth. This is not at all a stretch in reason; one need only be reminded of those Christians in the Philippines, Mexico, and elsewhere who have themselves crucified on a yearly basis in honor of Christ.

The Significance of It All

If the Shroud of Turin should turn out to be genuine, it would scientifically

Crucifixion in the Philippines

Since 1946, the crucifixion of Jesus has been re-enacted in the Philippines every Easter, most notably at Gua Gua, Pampanga, north of Manila. Filipinos mimic Jesus's crucifixion on Good Friday at noon. Some ten to fifteen people per year submit to the brutal ritual. They do so to atone for sin. The victim's hands are pierced with spikes after being tied to a wood cross. The blood loss, however, is not as profuse as it could be since the tying of the arms in two places acts like a tourniquet and helps prevent bleeding. A field is cleared for the crucifixion and three crosses at a time are hoisted up for a few minutes. As the "Christ" is being prepared, there is an eerie humming chant that allows the "Christ" to reach a trance-like state to minimize the feeling of pain. About a dozen other Filipinos walk barefoot, some with masked faces, down the streets leading to the open field where the three crosses are erected. The tropical heat of the sun reflects the sweat and blood as they beat their backs to a bloody pulp with bamboo "cat-of-nine tails" whips. They make visible slices across each other's backs with homemade glass disks made from coke bottles imbedded in wooden mallets. No one has ever died from the bloody rites. The Catholic Church frowns upon the ritual, which combines "the imitation of Christ" theme with primitive beliefs.[34]

> If the Shroud of Turin should turn out to be genuine, it would scientifically prove two things: Jesus was crucified and Jesus was resurrected, like the Gospels say he was.

prove two things: Jesus was crucified and Jesus was resurrected, like the Gospels say he was. In other words, the Shroud of Turin, Jesus's burial cloth, would provide corroborating evidence for the Gospel accounts. But in light of the evidence presented in this chapter, we doubt the Shroud's authenticity.

Nevertheless, the above two statements about Jesus's crucifixion and resurrection remain true. For we do have scientific confirmation from the 1968 findings in Israel of a crucified man (see chapter 6) that the Gospels' portraits of Jesus's death match the type of death with which the ancient Jew called Jehohanan had met. His bones were discovered in an ossuary box in June 1968 as Israelis bulldozed a rocky hillside a mile north of the Old City's Damascus Gate for a new apartment block. The site *Giv'at ha-Mivtar* (the Hill of the Divide) was found to have been an extensive Jewish burial ground dating back to the New Testament period. Examination of the joined heel bones and the seven-inch nail holding them together confirmed beyond doubt that he had suffered death by crucifixion. Before the discovery of the bone box of Jehohanan, no known victim of crucifixion had ever been discovered. Now there is archaeological proof that Jesus was crucified, confirming what the Gospels and the Roman historians say about Jesus's crucifixion at the order of Pontius Pilate.

But what about the resurrection of Jesus? While no archaeological evidence has surfaced yet to "prove" that Jesus arose, there are plenty enough other facts to confirm what the Gospels declare about our Lord's resurrection. And that evidence leads us to the next chapter.

It is always helpful when facts surface that support our faith, such as the 1968 bones of the crucified Jehohanan and the soon-to-be noted evidence for the resurrection. But, in our judgment, the Shroud of Turin is *not* one of those corroborating artifacts.[35]

CONCLUSION

Authentic or a fake? The debate continues. While it seems likely to us that the Shroud of Turin is not authentic, there are curious unanswered questions.

If the image on the Shroud was a medieval artist's depiction of the scourging and crucifixion of Jesus, how was the individual aware that nails were driven through the wrists, not the hands, something not known during medieval times? On the other hand, if authentic, why would God permit such a relic to be found, for it would possibly invite worship of the object, rather than of the risen Christ?

We conclude that the Shroud is most likely an artist's representation of the suffering of Jesus dating from around the thirteenth century (based on Carbon 14 dating). It may be paint, but we would not rule out the possibility that an artist used his own blood or that of someone else in creating the Shroud. While it may have been created by someone who wished to create a brilliant forgery, it could also have been created by a well-meaning individual who wished to graphically portray the sufferings of Jesus—but not to mislead individuals that this was actually the burial cloth of Jesus.

> *While it seems likely to us that the Shroud of Turin is not authentic, there are curious unanswered questions.*

Certainly, there will be more twists and turns to come regarding the Shroud of Turin. It will be a fascinating headline to follow.

DISCUSSION QUESTIONS

1. What is the Shroud of Turin?
2. Describe the parallels between the four Gospels' accounts of Jesus's death and the medical report on the Shroud.
3. What were the findings of STURP?
4. What was the result of the Carbon 14 dating of the Shroud?
5. According to Wilson, are there other names for the Shroud of Turin? What are the problems with Wilson's theory?
6. If the Shroud of Turin should turn out to be genuine, what two things would it scientifically prove?
7. What is your opinion: Are the stains on the Shroud real blood or an artist's pigment?

THE RESURRECTION DEBATE

Did Jesus Really Rise from the Dead?

||||||||||||||||||||||||||||||||||||||||||||||||||||||||||||||||||||||||||||||||||||||||||||||||||||||||||||||||

INTRODUCTION

What do the Christian apologists Frank Morrison, Josh McDowell, and Lee Strobel have in common? All three men were once skeptics of Christianity, but were converted when they studied the Gospels' accounts of the resurrection of Jesus.[1] Both believers and skeptics alike understand that the bedrock of the Christian faith is the resurrection of Jesus. There is no middle ground on this debate: Christianity rises or falls on the resurrection. If it did not happen, then Christianity is no different from any other religion. In fact, it is nothing more than an antiquated relic from the past with no meaning for today. It's like the high school student said to his friend, "There ain't gonna be no Easter this year!" "Why not?" the friend asked incredulously. The first boy responded, "They found the body!" Actually, the boy was being facetious because he, in fact, believed in the resurrection of Jesus. But his quip profoundly captures the significance of the issue: no resurrection of Jesus, no Easter; no Easter, no Christianity.[2]

> There is no middle ground on this debate: Christianity rises or falls on the resurrection.

On the other hand, if Jesus really rose from the dead then, according to Saint Paul in 1 Corinthians 15:12–20, the Christian faith is uniquely true, our sins are forgiven, and we will be raised one day to join our departed believing loved ones. All of this brings eternal meaning into our present existence. In short, the resurrection of Jesus is like having a portion of heaven here on earth.

So the question is clear and the stakes high: Did Jesus really rise from the dead? In this chapter we seek to answer that question in the affirmative, offering three broad evidences for the bodily resurrection of Jesus Christ. And along the way we will provide information for refuting those theories that disagree. The three broad evidences are: the empty tomb, the post-resurrection appearances of Jesus, and other data which cumulatively confirm Jesus's resurrection.

> **What If There Were No Resurrection?**
>
> In 1 Corinthians 15:12–20 the apostle Paul underscores how disastrous it would be if Christ were not raised from the dead:
>
> **(1)** The preaching of the gospel would be in vain.
>
> **(2)** Our faith would be futile because we would still be in our sins.
>
> **(3)** Our loved ones would be lost because they too would still be in their sins.

THE EMPTY TOMB

The story of the empty tomb is found in Matthew 28:1–8; Mark 16:1–8; Luke 24:1–8; John 20:1–8; and 1 Corinthians 15:3–4. Four pieces of data combine to convince most biblical scholars, even non-conservative ones, that the tomb where Jesus was buried was found empty.[3] First, the testimony of the empty tomb is supported by the form criticism criterion of multiple attestation. The reader may recall from our chapter one that the Jesus Seminar, based upon form criticism, asserts that if an event or word of Jesus in the Gospels is attested to by two or more layers of tradition, then that event or word is likely to be authentic. Such is the case with the empty tomb event, for three separate strands of testimony confirm its actuality: the Synoptics' account (Matt. 28:1–8; Mark 16:1–8; Luke 24:1–8), the Johannine account (John 20:1–8), and the Pauline account (1 Cor. 15:3–4).

Second, it is ironic that women were the first to whom the risen Jesus appeared, because in the first century AD women were not allowed to give legal testimony.[4] Simply put, it would have been viewed as an embarrassment to the early church that the first witnesses of the empty tomb were women—Mary Magdalene, Mary the mother of James and of Jesus, Salome, who was probably the wife of Zebedee and the mother of James and John.

But this very fact serves to prove the historicity of the empty tomb, because if the church had conjured up the story, they surely would have had men, the disciples in particular, as the first witnesses of the empty tomb.

Third, if the tomb was not empty the Jewish leadership and the Roman authorities could have easily silenced the preaching of Peter and John in the days of the early church (Acts 1–7), by taking all concerned to the place where Jesus lay. Such a move would have silenced Christianity on the spot. Later Jewish medieval legend fancies just such a scenario.[5] But, in fact, the Jewish leadership and Roman authorities could do nothing of the kind because the tomb was indeed empty.

Fourth, the vast majority of biblical scholars agree that the report of the Gospels and Paul concerning the empty tomb reads like a straightforward narrative, without legendary features. One dissenter is John Dominic Crossan who argues in *The Cross That Spoke* that the empty tomb tradition is a midrashic (allegorical) interpretation of Deuteronomy 21:22–23 and Joshua 10:26–27.[6] Deuteronomy 21:22–23 reads:

> When someone is convicted of a crime punishable by death and is executed, and you hang him on a tree, his corpse must not remain all night upon the tree; you shall bury him that same day, for anyone hung on a tree is under God's curse. You must not defile the land that the LORD your God is giving you for possession (NRSV).

Joshua 10:26–27 reads:

> Afterward Joshua struck them down [the five enemy leaders] and put them to death, and he hung them on five trees. And they hung on the trees until evening.
>   At sunset Joshua commanded, and they took them down from the trees and threw them into the cave where they had hidden themselves; they set large stones against the mouth of the cave, which remain to this very day (NRSV).

But William Lane Craig easily refutes the second claim:

> The dissimilarities between the burial story and Josh. 10:26–27 suggest that Mark's account is not based on the latter. Joshua speaks of a cave, whereas Mark makes a point of the man-made, rock-hewn sepulcher in which Jesus was laid. . . . Joshua has a guard at the cave, whereas Mark has no guard; Mark's reference to Joseph of Arimathea, the scene with Pilate, and the linen shroud have no parallel in Joshua.[7]

Neither does a midrashic connection stand between the empty tomb tradition and Deuteronomy 21:22–23. Galatians 3:13–14 tells us that "Christ

> **The tradition of the empty tomb in the Gospels and in Paul is solid fact.**

redeemed us from the curse of the law by becoming a curse for us—for it is written, 'Cursed is everyone who hangs on a tree'" (NRSV). Jesus's death on a tree was for sin and therefore attracted the judgment of God. So Deuteronomy 21:22–23 is connected to the *meaning* of Jesus's death; it is not the literary origin of Jesus's death. All of this to say that the tradition of the empty tomb in the Gospels and in Paul is solid fact. But what might explain the empty tomb? Four theories have been proposed at one time or another, with only one of them proving to be true: the stolen body theory, the swoon theory, the wrong tomb theory, and the resurrection theory.

The Stolen Body Theory

Other than the resurrection theory, the most ancient theory explaining the empty tomb was that the disciples stole the body of Jesus and then perpetrated the fraud that Jesus had risen from the dead. This view circulated in New Testament times. Matthew records that the Jewish elders gave money to the soldiers who guarded the tomb and told the soldiers to say, "His disciples came by night and stole him away while we were asleep" (Matt. 28:13 NRSV). This explanation was also reflected in Origen's debate with Celsus in the early third century AD.[8] Origen disposes of this fanciful explanation by arguing that men do not risk losing their lives in defense of a lie.

This explanation has been defended in modern times by a German scholar named H. M. Reimarus. In 1778 he published a work entitled *The Goal of Jesus and His Disciples*.[9] He argued that, after Jesus's death, the disciples were unwilling to abandon the kind of life they had

The Church of the Holy Sepulchre

Jesus was crucified outside the city walls of Jerusalem at the place called Golgotha ("skull"). Ancient tradition places Jesus's death, burial, and resurrection on the site now covered by the Church of the Holy Sepulchre. Queen Helena, mother of Emperor Constantine, ordered the church built over the site Christians showed her when she visited Jerusalem about AD 335. Archaeology has demonstrated that the area under the church was outside the city walls at the time of Jesus's death and was used as a quarry with numerous tombs cut into the rock. The circumstances seem to fit the biblical description.

led with Jesus. So they stole the body of Jesus, hid it, and proclaimed to all the world that he would soon return as the Messiah. However, they waited fifty days before making this announcement in order that the body, if it should be found, would be unrecognizable.

But Origen's answer against this preposterous reasoning still stands: men (and women) do not risk their lives and suffer martyrdom for a lie (see Acts 7:60; 12:2).

The Swoon Theory

The "swoon theory" was promoted by a German scholar named Paulus who maintained that Jesus did not really die on the cross, but rather swooned and later resuscitated in the tomb. Paulus cited the fact that crucifixion was a slow, agonizing death that often took days. There are records that show there were cases where individuals were crucified, taken down from the cross, and survived. He believed that the loud cry Jesus uttered on the cross was proof that Jesus was not exhausted and near death, and states that the spear thrust in the side of Jesus was only a flesh wound. Paulus goes on to say that in response to the coolness of the tomb and the aromatic spices contained within, Jesus, who only appeared to be dead, resuscitated. An earthquake further contributed to his waking and caused the stone to roll away from the entrance of the tomb. Jesus took off his grave clothes and managed to secure a gardener's outfit (the reason Mary mistook him for a gardener recorded in John 20:15).

> **Men do not risk their lives and suffer martyrdom for a lie.**

If the swoon theory is accurate, Jesus must have lived out the rest of his life in hiding—at the very time when his disciples adamantly proclaimed his resurrection and his coming kingdom. It would appear, according to this theory, that Jesus was in solitary retreat, but that his disciples were unaware of this fact.

The "swoon theory," although not plausible, has actually been "resurrected" in popularity rather recently. Hugh Schonfield's *The Passover Plot* was aggressively promoted and has sold thousands of copies. Schonfield, a biblical scholar, maintained that Jesus was a self-proclaimed prophet whose mission was to preach repentance in Israel. But having failed, he decided that he should suffer atonement for his people and thus plotted his own demise through crucifixion, but not death. He goaded Judas into betraying him, and blasphemed Caesar (not God), causing the charge of political sedition. Jesus further planned to be crucified on Friday because his body wouldn't

David Friedrich Strauss on the Swoon Theory

Even the German skeptic David Friedrich Strauss rejected the swoon theory. He wrote of it, "It is impossible that One who had just come forth from the grave, half dead, who crept about weak and ill, who stood in the need of medical treatment, of bandaging, strengthening, and tender care, and who at last succumbed to suffering, could ever have given the disciples the impression that He was a conqueror over death and the grave; that He was the Prince of Life. This lay at the bottom of their future ministry. Such a resuscitation could only have weakened the impression which He had made upon them in life and in death—or at the most, could have given in an elegiac voice—but could by no possibility have changed their sorrow into enthusiasm or elevated their reverence into worship."[11]

be left on the cross beyond sunset of the Sabbath. His plan necessitated involving Joseph of Arimathea who on a signal from Jesus ("I thirst") administered a powerful drug to Jesus on a sponge which caused a death-like trance. Joseph asked Pilate for Jesus's body and laid the body in the tomb, where, according to Schonfield, Jesus had expected beforehand to resuscitate and rejoin his disciples. But there was an unforeseen problem—Jesus's side was pierced by a spear of a soldier. This further weakened Jesus, and only a few hours after he had been placed in the tomb, he was moved, the conscious Jesus asking that a message be given to his disciples saying that he soon would meet them in Galilee. But instead, he died and was placed in an unknown tomb, the neatly folded grave clothes left in the original tomb. Peter and John came to the original tomb and Jesus was not there, just the grave clothes, giving them the impression that Jesus had risen. Mary, who was "unbalanced," mistakenly identified a person near the tomb as Jesus. The two disciples who met a stranger on the Emmaus road also were mistaken that it was Jesus. Schonfield ignores the witness of Paul, a crucial witness, and doesn't explain how Jesus managed to appear to five hundred people at once. His story, done in the name of scholarship, makes Jesus into a deluded fraud.

People flocked to the book, and Schonfield made many public appearances promoting it, resulting in its immense popularity. It is disappointing that so many would be hoodwinked by this approach.[10]

The Wrong Tomb Theory

The "wrong tomb" theory was popularized by the Harvard scholar Kirsopp Lake, who wrote the book *The Historical Evidence for the Resurrection of Jesus Christ*. In it, he maintained that "the facts behind the tradition" of the resurrection of Jesus are as follows: Due to there being a number of tombs in the vicinity in which Jesus was buried, the women, who visited the tomb on Sunday morning, were confused as to which tomb was that of Jesus. [12] At an empty tomb, a young man who stood at the entrance tried to tell them they had the wrong location by stating, "He is not here." Pointing to another tomb, he said, "See the place where they laid him." The women, who were frightened that someone had discovered their errand, fled. They were confused as to the meaning of the young man, believing not only that the young man was more than they had seen, but also that he was announcing the resurrection of Jesus.

Professor Lake concluded, "The empty tomb . . . is doctrinally indefensible and is historically insufficiently accredited."[13]

But there is a stubborn detail that single-handedly refutes the wrong tomb theory: Joseph of Arimathea owned the tomb in which Jesus was placed. And certainly, he would know which tomb was his and where he placed the body, making it easy to refute the words of the women that Jesus had risen from the dead. All he had to do was to take people to the correct tomb with the body still inside. Yet Scripture does not indicate that he did that.

Is it possible that Joseph of Arimathea was a figment of Christian imagination designed to create the illusion of a resurrected Jesus? No. Even the most skeptical biblical scholars agree that Joseph of Arimathea was a historical person, actually a member of the Jewish Sanhedrin. As such, with the hostility which the early Christians felt toward these Jewish leaders who had put Jesus to death, it is highly unlikely that they would invent such an individual who would do the right thing regarding the burial of Jesus. Certainly Mark, who wrote that the whole Sanhedrin voted for Jesus's condemnation (Mark 14:55, 64; 15:1), would not have invented this man.

Details given in the Gospels confirm aspects of Joseph of Arimathea—he was rich (corroborated by the type and location of the tomb) and came from Arimathea (an unimportant town with no scriptural symbolism). That he was sympathetic to Jesus is attested to by Matthew and John, and also by Mark in the way he treated Jesus's body rather than those of the thieves.[14]

> *But there is a stubborn detail that single-handedly refutes the wrong tomb theory: Joseph of Arimathea owned the tomb in which Jesus was placed.*

William Lane Craig writes of Joseph's tomb:

> Joseph's laying the body in his own tomb is probably historical. The consistent descriptions of the tomb as an acrosolia, or bench tomb, and archaeological discoveries that such tombs were used by notables during Jesus's day makes it credible that Jesus was placed in such a tomb. The incidental details that it was new and belonged to Joseph are also probable, since Joseph could not have placed the body of a criminal in just any tomb, especially since this would defile the bodies of any family members also reposing there.[15]

The Resurrection Theory

The stolen body, swoon, and wrong tomb theories simply do not work. There really is only one explanation for the fact of the empty tomb—in accordance with the New Testament, Jesus Christ arose from the dead and, after spending time teaching his followers, ascended into heaven.

But were those purported post-resurrection appearances of Jesus real?

THE POST-RESURRECTION APPEARANCES OF JESUS CHRIST

The second piece of evidence is that the New Testament claims that Jesus rose from the dead three days after he was crucified and buried, after which he made his presence known to others.[16] The following chart lists eleven such appearances:

Event	Date	Matthew	Mark	Luke	John	Acts	1 Cor.
At the empty tomb outside Jerusalem	Early Sunday morning	28:1–10	16:1–8	24:1–12	20:1–9		
To Mary Magdalene at the tomb	Early Sunday morning		16:9–11?		20:11–18		
To two travelers on the road to Emmaus	Sunday at midday			24:13–32			
To Peter in Jerusalem	During the day on Sunday			24:34			15:5
To the disciples in the upper room	Sunday evening		16:14?	24:36–43	20:19–25		
To the eleven disciples in the upper room	One week later				20:26–31		15:5

Event	Date	Matthew	Mark	Luke	John	Acts	1 Cor.
To seven disciples fishing on the Sea of Galilee	One day at daybreak				21:1–23		
To the eleven disciples on the mountain in Galilee	Some time later	28:16–20	16:15–18?				
To more than 500	Some time later						15:6
To James	Some time later						15:7
At the Ascension on the Mt. of Olives	Forty days after the resurrection[17]			24:44–49		1:3–8	

Christians in general and many biblical scholars in particular accept the face value of these accounts—that Jesus Christ appeared to his followers in bodily form after his death. Thus Mary Magdalene touched him (John 20:11–18), as did Thomas (John 20:26–31). Jesus ate with his disciples (Luke 24:30, 42–43; John 21:1–15). The angels promised that Jesus's second coming would match his ascension, which was personal, visible, and corporal (Acts 1:3–8). According to Luke 24:38–42, Jesus invited his disciples to touch him precisely to dispel the notion that he was a ghost or apparition.

Skeptics often say, however, that these reports were apologetic defenses created by the later church to combat doceticism. Doceticism was a late first-century to second-century AD heresy that said that Jesus was fully God but only appeared to be human. First John especially refutes that heresy (see, for example, 1 John 1:1–4; 4:2). However, William Lane Craig correctly asserts that the Gospels were written before the rise of doceticism.[18] Moreover, in actuality, doceticism denied Jesus's physical incarnation but not his bodily resurrection.

Jesus Christ appeared to his followers in bodily form after his death.

Beyond the anti-docetic theory, two theories are often put forth to explain away the bodily resurrection of Jesus: it was a hallucination or it was a subjective vision (a spiritual "resurrection"). The hallucination theory asserts that the disciples were so grieved over the death of Jesus that their longing to see him made them hallucinate and think they saw him alive, when in fact he wasn't. The British New Testament professor William Milligan, however, destroyed the hallucination theory in the early part of the twentieth century. He pointed out some five problems with the hypothesis. First, the resurrection appearances of Jesus are varied; they do not fall into one pattern. Second, in contrast to the hallucination theory, the disciples did not expect Jesus to rise; they were as surprised as anyone when the news of his resurrection reached them. Third, hallucinations don't appear to five hundred people, unless they are all strung out on drugs; there is no evidence that such was the case. Fourth, hallucinations do not extend over a period of forty days. Fifth, such visions do not occur only to cease with suddenness.[19]

The second alternative theory proposed by skeptics of the resurrection of Jesus says that he appeared in spirit, but not in body, to his followers, or some such similar notion. The difference between this view and the hallucination hypothesis appears to be that the former apparently allows for some type of life for Jesus beyond the grave, but not a bodily one. For this perspective, it is the resurrection faith of the disciples that matters, not the resurrection fact. This allows the Jesus Seminar to say, on the one hand, that supernatural things like dead men rising from the grave don't happen, while on the other hand, they can affirm the faith of the disciples in the resurrected Christ. The former is the Jesus of history (he lived and died); the latter is the Christ of faith (he arose in Spirit or in the mind of the disciples). The introduction to *The Five Gospels* thus can assert:

> The contemporary religious controversy . . . turns on whether the worldview reflected in the Bible can be carried forward into this scientific age and retained as an article of faith. . . . The Christ of creed and dogma . . . can no longer command the assent of those who have seen the heavens through Galileo's telescope.[20]

In taking this stance, the Seminar aligns itself with one of the first skeptics of the Gospels, David Friedrich Strauss:

> Strauss distinguished what he called the "mythical" (defined by him as anything legendary or supernatural) in the gospels from the historical. . . . The choice Strauss posed in his assessment of the gospels was between the super-natural Jesus—the Christ of faith—and the historical Jesus.[21]

This explains how John Dominic Crossan, one of the co-chairs of the Jesus Seminar, could say in *Time* magazine that after the crucifixion Jesus's corpse was probably laid in a shallow grave, barely covered with dirt, and subsequently eaten by wild dogs; the story of Jesus's entombment and resurrection was the result of "wishful thinking."[22]

But here one can turn the tables on the Jesus Seminar by using their own criteria of authenticity to refute their denial of the bodily resurrection of Jesus: multiple attestation and the principle of dissimilarity. Multiple attestation works as well for the bodily resurrection of Jesus as we saw it work for the historicity of the empty tomb. Thus, three layers of New Testament tradition claim that Jesus arose from the dead in body, as the previous chart shows: the Synoptics, the Gospel of John, and Paul.

The power of the criteria of multiple attestation came home to Marvin during his doctoral studies. Early on in his training, one of Marvin's theology professors was a self-proclaimed skeptic. He was known for saying things like "Jesus predicted his return before the end of the first generation of Christians, but Jesus was wrong! So he blew it!" And "the eschatology of the New Testament is bunk!" His radical view of the Gospels discouraged most students from wanting to take his classes. But at the end of his coursework, Marvin enrolled in the same professor's course, only to hear that professor say, "I believe in the bodily resurrection of Jesus!" When Marvin and the three other students in the professor's class asked what caused his turnabout, he answered with two words: "Multiple attestation." In other words, the bodily resurrection of Jesus is attested at too many layers of tradition not to be true.

> *The bodily resurrection of Jesus is attested at too many layers of tradition not to be true.*

The reader may recall from chapter 1 our discussion of the criterion of dissimilarity, which states that if a purported word or deed of Jesus in the Gospels is neither Jewish nor from the Hellenistic church, it is authentic.[23] Although we still do not support the principle left unqualified, we will use it against the Jesus Seminar to support the bodily resurrection of Jesus. In the first place, Judaism at the time of the New Testament expected the Messiah to bring about the general resurrection of the dead at the *end* of history (see Daniel 12:1–3; Mark 9:9–13; John 11:24). There were, to be sure, instances in the Old Testament of the dead being brought back to life, but these dealt with a return to the earthly life and those so resuscitated eventually died again (e.g., Elijah's raising of the son of the widow at Zarephath [1 Kings 17:17–23]; Elisha's raising of the Shunammite's son [2 Kings 4:18–37]). But the Gospels' and Paul's proclamations that Jesus, an individual who was resurrected *in* history, is not paralleled in ancient Judaism.[24]

On the other hand, Hellenism did not believe in the resurrection of the body; rather, from Plato on (ca. 350 BC) it believed in the immortality of the soul only. It was this very idea, for example, that Paul wished to dismiss in his most Hellenistically inclined congregation, the church at Corinth (see 1 Corinthians 15). We also see from Acts 17 that the Greek philosophers laughed Paul out of town when he started preaching the resurrection of Jesus, because they only subscribed to the belief in the immortality of the soul. So the bodily resurrection of Jesus in history proves to be distinct from both Judaism and Hellenism. Its historicity is, therefore, confirmed by the criterion of dissimilarity.

But how is it that the Jesus Seminar does not practice what it preaches about the criteria of multiple attestation and dissimilarity regarding the Gospel's accounts of Jesus's bodily resurrection? They answer, "By definition, words [and events] ascribed to Jesus after his death are not subject to historical verification."[25] The Jesus Seminar wants to have their cake and eat it too—on the one hand, they want to hold onto their criteria of authenticity, but on the other hand, they refuse to use those principles in a "nonhistorical" situation!

OTHER EVIDENCE FOR THE RESURRECTION

The Mystery Religions have nothing to do with the New Testament record of Jesus's resurrection. The tomb was empty because, unlike Osiris, Adonis, and other Greek heroes, Jesus rose from the dead.

In the final section of this chapter, we critique a once popular explanation of the resurrection of Jesus of Nazareth, that the Mystery Religions were ready-to-hand for the early church's claim that Christ died and arose. A personal illustration may help to clarify what we mean. When Marvin was a senior in the undergraduate program at the University of Illinois, he was taking a philosophy course when he began to dialogue with a classmate on spiritual matters. She said she didn't believe in Christianity, so Marvin began to use his old Bible college course notes on the resurrection—surely this would wow her with the facts and convert her. But to his shock, the classmate responded, "Haven't you heard that the resurrection stories in the New Testament were borrowed myths from the Mystery Religions?" Marvin, now wide-eyed, asked, "What are the Mystery Religions?" By now the young woman had complete control of the conversation as she proceeded to tell him about the Egyptian Isis and Osiris, and other ancient Near Eastern and Greek heroes that allegedly died and rose from the dead. She continued, "The early church simply fit Jesus into one of these myths, even though he never really arose."

That interchange sent Marvin on a ten-year pursuit of the truth about Mystery Religions and Jesus's resurrection and Paul's declaration of it. This led him to read the writings of early twentieth-century theologians like Richard Reitzenstein and Wilhelm Bousset, who attempted to root Paul's thinking and the early church's portrayal of Jesus in the Mystery Religions. These authors claimed that such wide-ranging religions as the Eleusian mysteries and the cults of Isis and Osiris, Adonis, Attis, and Mithras, shared at least two commonalities: First, they focused on the dying/rising again of their respective hero/heroine or gods/goddesses; and second, worshipers entered into mystical union with these gods by participating in the cults' sacraments (baptism, cultic meal, etc.). Bousset tended to emphasize the former's supposed connection to the Pauline proclamation of the resurrection of Jesus, especially as the church gathered to worship Christ as risen Lord. Reitzenstein tended to emphasize the latter as the foundation for Paul's teaching on baptism and the Lord's Supper.[26]

In time, however, Marvin learned, quite the contrary to what the philosophy student had told him, that various weaknesses pinpointed in the Mystery Religions approach have rendered it largely unsuccessful. H. A. A. Kennedy and J. G. Machen subjected the proposed parallels between Paul and the Mysteries to a thorough critique and concluded that the Old Testament was the real source of the apostle's thought. Wesley Carr provided further damaging evidence showing that the Mystery Religions were not all that influential until the third and fourth centuries AD, long after the time of Paul and the Gospels. David Seeley and A. J. M. Wedderburn have recently effectively refuted the assumption that the Mystery Religions ever taught an actual resurrection of the deity. Finally, substantial differences between Paul's understanding of Christ and the Mystery Religions have also been identified: the Mystery deities' deaths were not in place of someone else; they died unwillingly rather than obediently; they were not historical personages; and they did not possess an apocalyptic (end-time) framework.[27]

Marvin's classmate did him a favor; she caused him to doubt the resurrection of Jesus, which sent him on a quest for the truth. And the truth is that the Mystery Religions have nothing to do with the New Testament record of Jesus's resurrection. The tomb was empty because, unlike Osiris, Adonis, and other Greek heroes, Jesus rose from the dead.

We may now list other considerations that cumulatively indicate that Jesus arose bodily after his death:

The message of Christianity rapidly spread.
The disciples were transformed from frightened, discouraged people (Mark 14:50, 66–72; John 20:19) into bold witnesses.
Paul's conversion from persecutor to preacher assumes a resurrection.

The disciples began observing the first day of the week (Sunday) as the day of worship rather than the Sabbath (Saturday).

Neither the Jews nor the Romans ever produced evidence to the contrary.

The church has existed for almost 2,000 years.

The earliest Christians, who were far closer to the scene than we are, believed in the physical, bodily resurrection of Jesus. They believed that the resurrection of Jesus was the divine reversal of the human verdict.[28]

CONCLUSION

Jesus did indeed rise from the dead. But approximately two thousand years later, his resurrection is still a hotly debated issue. However, when one considers the three main alternative theories to his resurrection—the wrong tomb, the swoon, and the stolen body theory—their explanations fail to convince. The wrong tomb theory stretches the imagination to see how it was possible that so very many individuals all went to the wrong tomb. If they had all done so, Joseph of Arimathea, who owned the tomb and buried Jesus there, could very easily have dispelled the idea that Jesus had risen by pointing out the correct tomb (with the body still inside). Yet, that didn't happen because it was, in fact, the correct tomb and it was, in fact, empty.

The swoon theory is a fanciful account of Jesus only appearing to be dead and reviving in the tomb, taking off his burial clothes, borrowing a gardener's clothes, and appearing to Mary. Such a theory is easily seen as flawed when one considers the graphic portrayal of Jesus's crucifixion in Mel Gibson's *The Passion of the Christ*. When we consider this accurate rendering of first-century torture and death by crucifixion (along with the piercing of Jesus's side with a lance), it is impossible that this could have resulted in Jesus merely having swooned on the cross, only to revive in the tomb three days later and victoriously appear to Mary. As to the stolen body theory, there is simply no way this could have occurred. If the Jewish leaders could have produced a body,

> *Contrary to other religions whose founders still occupy their graves, Christianity is the only faith whose founder met with a totally different destiny.*

they certainly would have. And Jesus's disciples would not have been transformed from terror-filled individuals to courageous martyrs if the body of

Jesus had been stolen. Only encountering the risen Savior could have effected that change.

Christianity rises or falls on the resurrection of Jesus. And the evidence is that, contrary to other religions whose founders still occupy their graves, Christianity is the only faith whose founder met with a totally different destiny. Like the angel said, "He is not here; he is risen." This is an awesome thought, one which Christians cherish and which provides certain hope for the future.

DISCUSSION QUESTIONS

1. What are the four pieces of data that show the tomb was empty?
2. What is the stolen body theory? What is Origen's answer to this theory?
3. Describe the swoon theory. Why is it implausible?
4. How would you refute the wrong tomb theory?
5. Regarding the post-resurrection appearances of Jesus, what are the problems with the hallucination theory?
6. What are the ways we know Jesus arose bodily, not just in spirit?
7. How would you answer someone who said that the resurrection of Jesus was just a myth borrowed from the Mystery Religions?

THE LORD OF THE RINGS

The Signs of the Times and the Return of the King

||||||||||||||||||||||||||||||||||||||||||||||||||||||||||||||||||||||||||||||||

INTRODUCTION

Wizards, hobbits, elves, dwarves, orcs, and humans—these are the characters J. R. R. Tolkien conjures up in his breathtaking trilogy set in the world of Middle-earth—*The Lord of the Rings*. Tolkien's fantasy world is the stage for the drama of ultimate good versus quintessential evil, of an apocalyptic showdown between Ilúvatar, the good creator, and Melkor, the evil ruler of Mordor. The plot of *The Lord of the Rings* was already known by fifty million people from 1949, the date of its first publication, to 2001, the time of its first movie. Those millions of readers made Tolkien's work the most popular book in the twentieth century. And, since 2001, Peter Jackson has brought to life Tolkien's work in three spectacular mega-buster films: *The Fellowship of the Ring*, *The Two Towers*, and *The Return of the King*. Little wonder the third film received the Oscar award for best picture of 2003.

The Fellowship of the Ring presupposes much history, which is provided in Tolkien's later work, *The Silmarillion*. There the author describes the good world Ilúvatar created, life before the Fall. It was a time of beauty,

> *Tolkien's fantasy world is the stage for the drama of ultimate good versus quintessential evil.*

J. R. R. Tolkien and C. S. Lewis: A Legendary Friendship

Perhaps the two greatest Christian fiction writers of our time were C. S. Lewis and J. R. R. Tolkien. As best of friends they shared three interrelated commitments—romanticism, reason, and Christianity. They were "interested in the literature of the romantic period because many of the poems and stories attempted to convey the supernatural, the 'otherworldly'—and thus provided a window into spiritual things. Lewis explored romantic themes like joy and longing, and Tolkien emphasized the nature of people as storytelling beings who by telling stories reflect the creative powers of God. But they both rejected an 'instinctive' approach to the imagination. Many romantic writers were interested in a kind of nature mysticism. They looked within themselves and at the world around them and sought flashes of insight into 'the nature of things'—illuminations of truth that could not be explained, reasoned, or systematized. But Lewis and Tolkien insisted that the reason and the imagination must be integrated. In any understanding of truth, the whole person must be involved.

This is where their third shared commitment came into play—this sense of wholeness was a Christian approach, distant from the neo-pagan mysticism of some romantics, the 'Pan worship' of the early twentieth century. Indeed, Tolkien worried increasingly towards the end of his life that people were missing the Christian balance of his work, and were taking it almost as the basis of a new paganism. You could argue in fact that one reason Tolkien didn't finish *The Silmarillion* was his concern to make his imaginative creations consonant with Christianity. Obviously not wanting to make them into allegory or preachment, he was concerned his literary insights be clearly consistent with Christianity."[1]

purity, and harmony for elves, dwarves, hobbits, and men alike. But Melkor, a god-like being (an Ainur), rebelled against Ilúvatar the supreme God and plunged Middle-earth into near ruin. Ugliness, selfishness, and dissonance now vied for control over the destinies of the inhabitants of Middle-earth. One learns relatively quickly from *The Fellowship of the Ring* that the focal point of the contest is the twentieth Ring, the one Ring of evil (made by Sauron, Melkor's agent). Through a series of providential circumstances, that Ring falls into the possession of Bilbo Baggins and then to his nephew Frodo Baggins. In the course of time, Frodo assumes the near impossible task of taking the Ring to evil Mordor and throwing it into Mount Doom to end the existence of evil. Those who join him for that adventure—Sam, Gandalf, Aragorn, and others—form the Fellowship of the Ring.

In *The Two Towers*, the second of Tolkien's trilogy, the plot thickens. What were skirmishes in the first film, though deadly and even wounding Frodo, become all out war in *The Two Towers*, as good and evil clash for control of Middle-earth. And a new character enters the story—grotesque Gollum. Gollum once possessed the Ring; as another of Tolkien's earlier works, *The Hobbit*, describes it, he murdered his friend to gain possession of the Ring. (The former owner had discovered the Ring while fishing in a river.) The Ring inspired Gollum to commit evil, as it did to whomever came to own it. By the time Gollum appears in our story, his withered appearance is matched only by his despicable character. Yet even Gollum would become an unwitting instrument of good before all was ended. By the end of *The Two Towers*, the combined forces of Aragorn, Gandalf, Treebeard, and others deal a blow to the enemy.

In *The Return of the King*, the third book/film of Tolkien's trilogy, wars give way to the ultimate of all battles—an apocalyptic showdown between the forces of good and Sauron and his henchmen. Here we learn that Aragorn is no longer a king incognito, but he now commands both living and dead in the eschatological fight against evil. And just when Aragorn seems defeated, Frodo, after much struggle, watches Gollum and the Ring career into the Cracks of Doom on Mount Orodruin in the land of Mordor, thus ending evil's sway over Middle-earth.

J. R. R. Tolkien (1892–1973) was Catholic. His mother died shortly after he made his First Communion at Christmas in 1903. Tolkien and his brother came under the guardianship of Father Francis Morgan at the Birmingham Oratory. There Tolkien imbibed the sacramental view of the world that Catholicism had to offer—the grace and goodness of God is present even in a sinful, evil world, which will eventually be overcome by God's grace and goodness. It was also at the Birmingham Oratory that Tolkien's literary and linguistical interests began to develop. The two disciplines, mingled together with faith, came to fruition in Tolkien's adult years at Oxford University, where he specialized in Anglo-Saxon languages. There he created the symbolic and mythical world of Middle-earth in order to tell the story of God's grace as reflected in the Gospels. Tolkien writes of this:

> *Tolkien created the symbolic and mythical world of Middle-earth in order to tell the story of God's grace as reflected in the Gospels.*

The Gospels contain a fairy-story, or a story of a larger kind which embraces all the es-

> **Tolkien thought, imagined, and wrote as a Catholic, and The Lord of the Rings bears the clear signs of his faith, as he fully intended it should.**

sence of fairy-stories. They contain many marvels, particularly artistic, beautiful, and moving: "mythical" in their perfect, self-contained significance. . . . But this story has entered History and the primary world. . . . This story is supreme; and it is true. Art has been verified. God is the Lord, of angels, and of men—and of elves.[2]

It is this understanding of reality that makes *The Lord of the Rings* one of the greatest fantasies of all time.

In this chapter we will explore the possible connections between *The Lord of the Rings* and eschatology, or the end of time. Although Tolkien insisted that his trilogy is not an allegorical work, the fact is that Tolkien thought, imagined, and wrote as a Catholic, and *The Lord of the Rings* bears the clear signs of his faith, as he fully intended it should.[3] Consequently, it is difficult to view the three-fold movie and not perceive wonderful parallels between the signs of the times in Jewish-Christian literature and *The Return of the King*. Taking the three films together, we see six correspondences between them and the end of history as portrayed in ancient Judaism, the Gospels, and Revelation. We turn now to those parallels.

HISTORY IS HIS STORY

Two key apocalyptic, or end-time, books in the Bible proclaim the truth that God's plan for the world is unfolding in history and will culminate in the ultimate triumph of good over evil—Daniel and Revelation. Daniel 2:28–29 tells the story of how God revealed to Daniel his plan for the ages and that this plan must take place. It would unfold through four human kingdoms, beginning with the Babylonian kingdom, continuing with Media, Persia, and Greece, and culminating with the messianic reign, the fifth and final kingdom. The last-mentioned kingdom will be initiated by a time of great tribulation for God's people (Dan. 12:1–3), but in the end they will prevail over the enemies of God (Dan. 12:4–13; cf. 7:13–14). Revelation fills in the details of that vision, focusing on the return of Christ as the climax of history. Using similar language to Daniel, Revelation asserts that this plan must take place (Rev. 1:3; 22:6). The key verse of Revelation spells out that plan; the risen Christ commands the apostle John:

Write, therefore, what you have seen, what is now and what will take place later.

1:19 NIV

These three tenses unfold the outline of Revelation: "what you have seen"—the risen Jesus (ch. 1); "what is"—the people of God in the midst of the great tribulation (chs. 2–18);[4] and "what will take place later"—the triumph of Christ's return and the full establishment of his kingdom (chs. 19–22).

Remarkably, we hear almost the same words of Revelation 1:19 from Galadriel, the elven queen of Lothlórien, as she tells Frodo that her mirror can reveal to him "things that were, and things that are, and things that yet may be."[5] The mirror's reflection reveals to Frodo his intertwined destiny with the Ring's past, present, and future, a destiny that involves the ultimate destruction of evil.

This sense of hope for Middle-earth in the third age is communicated early on in *The Fellowship of the Ring* when Gandalf, the good wizard, explains to Frodo the significance of the evil Ring being discovered by his Uncle Bilbo, a humble hobbit:

> There was something else at work, beyond any design of the Ring-maker. I can put it no plainer than by saying that Bilbo was *meant* to find the Ring, and *not* by its maker. In which case you also were *meant* to have it. And that may be an encouraging thought.[6]

As the story unfolds, Frodo's role will be to destroy the Ring by throwing it into the Cracks of Doom before Sauron, the Ring's maker, can get it back and thereby finally rule Middle-earth. But evil rears its ugly head in Frodo's destiny. This is seen nowhere more clearly than in the climactic scene at Mount Doom, where the two central characters—Frodo and Gollum—fight over the Ring, neither wanting to relinquish it to the Cracks of Doom. Gollum wins the struggle for the evil prize but in doing so accidentally falls into the fire, destroying the Ring. Gandalf's prophetic words spoken earlier to Frodo had come true: "Even Gollum may have something yet to do."[7] And in the overruling providence of good, he did.

The victorious plan of good reveals Tolkien's opposition to dualism—two equal powers at war for the world. Rather, the Judeo-Christian concept of creation, the fall, and the pre-eminence of good in the end is the driving engine of *The Lord of the Rings*. Evil is the distortion of good and will one day be defeated, at which time all good will be restored. This underlying principle is at work in a key exchange between Samwise Gamgee (Sam), Frodo Baggins's faithful friend, and Frodo, as they travel through the dark land of Mordor. When Sam wonders if the evil ones eat and drink food and water like ordinary creatures, or if perhaps they live on poison and foul air, Frodo replies:

No, they eat and drink, Sam. The Shadow that bred them can only mock, it cannot make: not real new things of its own. I don't think it gave life to the orcs, it only ruined them and twisted them; and if they are to live at all, they have to live like other living creatures. Foul water and foul meats they'll take, if they can get no better, but not poison.[8]

In Tolkien's vision, evil's perversion of good will not have the last word. This sense of eschatological hope is clear in one memorable passage during the journey through Mordor where Sam and Frodo stand at the crossroads. Behind them is the West, ahead Mordor. Standing there, the two hobbits gaze upon a stone figure of a king from Argonath. Time, vandals, and the enemy had all but destroyed the image. Its head was gone. In its place, in a mocking fashion, the followers of Sauron had put an unshaped stone. Suddenly Frodo saw the statue's head lying off the roadside.

> *The Judeo-Christian concept of creation, the fall, and the pre-eminence of good in the end is the driving engine of The Lord of the Rings.*

"Look, Sam!" he cried, startled into speech. "Look! The king has got a crown again!"

The eyes were hollow and the carven beard was broken, but about the high stern forehead there was a coronal of silver and gold. A trailing plant with flowers like small white stars had bound itself across the brows as if in reverence for the fallen king, and in the crevices of his stony hair yellow stonecrop gleamed.

"They cannot conquer for ever!" said Frodo.[9]

What temporarily allays Frodo's fears is the eschatological hope that fills his heart.

SIGNS OF THE TIMES

Jewish[10] and Christian sources speak about the signs of the times of the great tribulation heralding the end of history and the appearance of the king-dom of God: the intensification of evil (Dan. 12:1–10; Matt. 24:12; Revelation 6–18); wars (Mark 13:8 and parallel passages; Rev. 6:4); famines (Mark 13:8 and parallel passages; Rev. 6:8; 18:8); internecine strife (Mark 13:12 and parallel passages); apostasy (Dan. 9:24–27; Mark 13:6 and parallel passages; Rev.

6–18); and cosmic disturbances (Mark 13:24–25 and parallel passages; Rev. 6:12–14).

It is hard not to detect a similar progression of the signs of the end times in *The Lord of the Rings* trilogy associated with the return of King Aragorn. The intensification of evil: As the trilogy progresses so does the evil intention of Sauron, who unleashes his wicked armies on Middle-earth in an effort to recapture the Ring. Wars: In *The Fellowship of the Ring* we witness significant skirmishes between the forces of good and evil that erupt into outright wars in *The Two Towers*, which culminate in the battle of the end in *The Return of the King*. Famine: Famine ensues in those towns overrun by Sauron's orcs—the Shire, Rohan, and others. In fact, the destruction inflicted on Isengard is the catalyst for Treebeard and the Ents' decision to join forces with Gandalf and Aragorn in the fight against evil; they want to prevent such violence and famine from spreading. Internecine strife: Only Frodo's self-sacrificing decision at the Council of Elrond to take the Ring to Mordor breaks its spell, and consequently nine friends band together as brothers for the same cause of destroying the Ring. But even after that, the Ring, symbol of all evil, pits friend against friend in *The Fellowship of the Ring*. Apostasy: The Ring's seductive, evil sway causes more than one character to leave the side of the good, to stray from the faith: Gollum, Boromir, and even Frodo at the very end. It tempts others to do the same: Gandalf, Galadriel, queen of Lothlórien, Sam, and others. But the latter resist the temptation. Cosmic disturbance: A sort of cosmic disturbance occurs in Tolkien's trilogy as the growing threat of Sauron's shadow of evil falls over Middle-earth, with its impending message of doom.

> *It is hard not to detect a similar progression of the signs of the end times in The Lord of the Rings trilogy associated with the return of King Aragorn.*

THE PAROUSIA

The hope for the appearance of the Messiah to establish the kingdom of God originated in the Old Testament (Zechariah 9–14; Dan. 9:24–27), flourished in Judaism,[11] and is the basis of the New Testament's message. The difference is that the New Testament claims that Jesus the Messiah came once to die. During his first stay on earth Jesus was the divine king incognito. But when he appears (in Greek, *parousia*) the second time, Jesus will become the visible King of Kings and Lord of Lords (Mark 13:26–27 and parallel passages; Acts 1:9–11; 2 Thess. 1:7–8; Rev. 1:7; 19:11–16).

In *The Lord of the Rings* three individuals serve as Christlike characters: Frodo, Gandalf the Grey, and Aragorn.

Each in a remote way embody one of the three aspects of Christ's ministry as priest, prophet, and king. Each also undergoes a kind of sacrificial "death" and rebirth.

The priestly role belongs to Frodo, who bears a burden of terrible evil on behalf of the whole world, like Christ carrying his cross. Frodo's *via dolorosa* or way of sorrows is at the very heart of the gospels accounts. As Christ descended into the grave, Frodo journeys into Mordor, the Land of Death, and there suffers a deathlike state in the lair of the giant spider Shelob before awakening to complete his task. And, as Christ ascended into heaven, Frodo's life in Middle-earth comes to an end when he departs from his beloved Shire to go travel over the sea into the mythical West with the Elves, which is as much to say, into paradise.

Gandalf is the prophet, revealing hidden knowledge, working wonders, teaching others the way. Evoking the saving death and resurrection of Christ, Gandalf does battle with the powers of hell to save his friends, sacrificing himself and descending into the nether regions before being triumphantly reborn in greater power and glory as Gandalf the White. As with Frodo, Gandalf's sojourn in Middle-earth ends with his final voyage over the sea into the West.

Finally, there is Aragorn, the crownless destined to be king. Besides being a Messianic king of prophecy, Aragorn also reflects the saving work of Christ by walking the paths of the Dead and offering peace to the spirits there imprisoned, anticipating in a way the Harrowing of Hell. (The oath-breaking spirits Aragorn encounters on the Paths of the Dead, who cannot rest in peace until they expiate their treason, suggest a kind of purgatorial state.) [12]

> *In The Lord of the Rings three individuals serve as Christlike characters: Frodo, Gandalf the Gray, and Aragorn.*

Of these three, Aragorn best embodies the *parousia* or second coming of Christ motif. In reality, the third volume, *The Return of the King*, follows Aragorn's journey from Strider as a mere ranger who is the incognito king to his rule over the Paths of the Dead to his victorious return to help defeat Sauron.

The narrative hints at this at the battle of Minas Tirith. Standing upon its walls, looking eastward from where Aragorn would come, Faramir the steward and Éowyn, Lady of Rohan, saw a great eagle come winging its way over the city, crying aloud as it flew:

Sing and be glad, all ye children of the West,
for your King shall come again,
and he shall dwell among you
all the days of your life.[13]

One could be reminded here of Revelation 8:13, which also describes the coming of an eagle which proclaims the imminent arrival of Jesus the King to inflict judgment on evil and to establish God's domain.

But now returns King Aragorn, victorious over Sauron, the evil one. The Ring had been destroyed. Righteousness had long-last won. Now, on the field before the gate of Minas Tirith, the striped pavilions of the Lord of the West stood bright in the morning sun. Inside the city, every street, every doorway, every window flowed with garlands of fresh flowers. The gate itself was thronged with men in flashing armor, with women and children in garments of every hue. The music of harps, flutes, and silver horns filled the air.

"Behold!" cried Faramir as Aragorn approached the gate at the head of his kinsmen, the Dúnedain. "One has come to claim the kingship again at last. Shall he be king and enter into the City and dwell there?"

The reply was one of loud and unanimous acclaim. "Yes!"

The crown was then produced from a black and silver casket. It was made of silver itself, with the wings of a seabird, fashioned of silver and pearl, attached at each side. At Aragorn's request, Frodo bore it to the king and Gandalf placed it upon his head. Another great shout went up. This was the moment they had all been awaiting.[14]

The contrast between Aragorn's "first coming" as king incognito and his "second coming" as unrivaled lord is profoundly expressed by the crowd: "But when Aragorn arose all that beheld him gazed in silence, for it seemed to them that he was revealed to them now for the first time."[15] He was like a new man, ancient of days (cf. Dan. 7:13–14; Rev. 1:7–19); one they had known well and yet had never known before.

"Out of the Great Sea to Middle-earth I am come," he said. . . . "In this place will I abide . . . unto the ending of the world."[16]

ARMAGEDDON

Jewish literature (Ezekiel 38–39; Zechariah 14; The Dead Sea Scrolls [*The War Scroll*]) and chapters 19–20 of Revelation forecast an end-time battle between God's Messiah and his adversaries. Revelation calls it "Armageddon," the mountain (Hebrew, *har*) of Megiddo. Megiddo is the fortress that overlooks the beautiful plain dividing Galilee from Samaria. Whoever controlled that military site in ancient Israel controlled the roads traversing the nation.

The War Scroll

One of the most famous documents found among the Dead Sea Scrolls (ca. 160 BC) is *The War Scroll,* which is a description of the end-time battle between the Essenes (probably the authors of the Scrolls) and the enemies of God. It reads like the book of Revelation. *The War Scroll* predicts that the apocalyptic battle will last forty years, with neither side prevailing against the other. But, in God's timing, the two Messiahs—the Prince of Light and the Priest—will come and win the day for the righteous, and Israel will finally be restored to its original splendor.

The ancients said that to control Megiddo was to control a thousand cities.

It is undoubtedly against that eschatological backdrop that we are to read of the final war between the forces of Gandalf, Frodo, and Aragorn and Sauron and his thousands of orcs. The latter marched out of Mordor to engage the armies of good at Minas Tirith, chief city of Gondor, which lay just opposite of the border between the two opposing lands. There on the Field of Cormallen, outside Mordor, the ultimate of all battles was about to be waged.

But the hosts of Mordor vastly outnumbered the armies of the good from the West, and hope grew dim:

All about the hills the hosts of Mordor raged. The Captains of the West were foundering in a gathering sea. The sun gleamed red, and under the wings of the Nazgûl the shadows of death fell dark upon the earth. Aragorn stood beneath his banner, silent and stern, as one lost in thought of things long past or far away; but his eyes gleamed like stars that shine the brighter as the night deepens. Upon the hill-top stood Gandalf, and he was white and cold and no shadow fell on him. The onslaught of Mordor broke like a wave on the beleaguered hills, voices roaring like a tide amid the wreck and crash of arms.[17]

Then Gandalf the white wizard looked to the north and cried to his troops of the arrival of the Eagles from the encircling mountains, which swept down upon the evil Nazgûl to destroy them. The Eagles were joined by the good Captains of the West, and then by King Aragorn; all shared the intent to defeat evil Sauron. Then Gollum and the Ring fell into the Cracks of Doom in the Mountain of Fire in Mordor. The apocalyptic end unfolds:

But Gandalf lifted up his arms and called once more in a clear voice:
"Stand, Men of the West! Stand and wait! This is the hour of doom."
And even as he spoke the earth rocked beneath their feet. Then rising swiftly up, far above the Towers of the Black Gate, high above the mountains, a vast soaring darkness sprang into the sky, flickering with fire. The earth groaned and quaked. The Towers of the Teeth swayed, tottered, and fell down; the mighty rampart crumbled; the Black Gate was hurled in ruin; and from far away, now dim, now growing, now mounting to the clouds, there came a drumming rumble, a roar, a long echoing roll of ruinous noise.

"The realm of Sauron is ended!" said Gandalf. "The Ring-bearer has fulfilled his Quest." And as the Captains gazed south to the Land of Mordor, it seemed to them that, black against the pall of cloud, there rose a huge shape of shadow, impenetrable, lightning-crowned, filling all the sky. Enormous it reared above the world, and stretched out toward them a vast threatening hand, terrible but impotent: for even as it leaned over them, a great wind took it, and it was all blown away, and passed; and then a hush fell.[18]

And the end of evil had come. No one viewing this scene in the movie or reading the account in the book could miss the apocalyptic tone of this battle. Like Revelation 19–20, King Aragorn returns and, together with the forces of good, destroys Mordor—Mordor's end is matched in description only by the battle of Armageddon portrayed in Revelation 19:19–21; 20:7–10:

> Then I saw the beast and the kings of the earth and their armies gathered together to make war against the rider on the horse and his army. But the beast was captured, and with him the false prophet who had performed the miraculous signs on his behalf. With these signs he had deluded those who had received the mark of the beast and worshiped his image. The two of them were thrown alive into the fiery lake of burning sulfur. The rest of them were killed with the sword that came out of the mouth of the rider on the horse, and all the birds gorged themselves on their flesh.
>
> Rev. 19:19-21 NIV

> When the thousand years are over, Satan will be released from his prison and will go out to deceive the nations in the four corners of the earth—Gog and Magog—to gather them for battle. In number they are like the sand on the seashore. They marched across the breadth of the earth and surrounded the camp of God's people, the city he loves. But fire came down from heaven and devoured them. And the devil, who deceived them, was thrown into the lake of burning sulfur, where the beast and the false prophet had been thrown. They will be tormented day and night for ever and ever.
>
> Rev. 20:7-10 NIV

> *No one viewing this scene in the movie or reading the account in the book could miss the apocalyptic tone of this battle.*

URZEIT-ENDZEIT

German theologians have a wonderful way of capturing in words the regaining of paradise by the return of King Jesus: *urzeit* (beginning of time)—*endzeit* (end of time). This is most clear in Revelation 21–22, which tells of the restoration of Eden at the return of Christ. Note some of the many parallels:

Genesis 1–3	Revelation 21–22
Beginning of time	End of time (second coming of Christ)
Old creation (1:1)	New creation (21:1)
Loss of the presence of God (3:23–24)	God's presence among God's people, the new temple (21:2–3, 9–27)
Entrance of death (2:17)	Defeat of death (21:4)
Rivers of paradise (2:10–14)	Water of life (22:1)
Tree of life (3:24)	Heavenly food of eternal life (22:2–4, 14; cf. 2:17)
Son of God (1:26–28)	Sons of God (21:7)

Back in the Shire, home of the hobbits Frodo, Sam, Merry, and Pippin, things had become un-Shire like. Sharkey, the evil bully, had ruled the Shire, bringing about its ruin. But with the announcement that Mordor had fallen, Sharkey, too, was removed from "office." And now, with the return of the hobbits, the Shire was restored to its pristine beauty. Kurt Bruner and Jim Ware well relate the reaction of the hobbits:

> "*All's well as ends better!*"

> "All's well as ends better!" Old Gaffer never spoke so true. . . .
> The Shire had become a better place than before, its dreadful loss enriching the soil in which a new era could grow. The folk of Hobbiton were enjoying the deepest happiness they had known, as though the experience of grief had somehow increased their capacity for joy. Were the trees really growing taller or were the hobbits simply more aware of grandeur? Were the colors more vivid or the hobbits' eyes more attuned to beauty? Were the children born stronger and more fair or their parents more grateful for the gift of life? Perhaps it was both. Like recovering a misplaced treasure thought forever gone, the folk of the Shire were drinking deeply from the cup of gladness.[19]

Whether "*urzeit-endzeit*" as the Germans put it, or "All's well as ends better!" according to old Gaffer, the message is the same: humanity longs for the recovery of paradise lost. Ilúvatar, the good creator, was the first in Tolkien's works to express such a hope. Speaking of the assured defeat of evil Melkor, he declares:

> And thou, Melkor, shalt see that no theme may be played that hath not its uttermost source in me, nor can any alter the music in my despite. For he that

attempteth this shall prove but mine instrument in the devising of things more wonderful, which he himself hath not imagined.[20]

Revelation 21:3–4 expresses the restoration of paradise even better:

And I heard a loud voice from the throne saying, "See, the home of God is among mortals. He will dwell with them; they will be his peoples, and God himself will be with them; he will wipe every tear from their eyes. Death will be no more; mourning and crying and pain will be no more, for the first things have passed away." (NRSV)

THE ULTIMATE WEAPON OF REDEMPTION

"It must often be so, Sam, when things are in danger: someone has to give them up, love them, so that others may keep them."[21] So said Frodo as he departed forever from Sam and the Shire to cross to the West with Gandalf, Bilbo, Elrond, and Galadriel. The essence of every heroic act is self-sacrifice. It was so for Frodo. Frodo was a hobbit, which some called with derision a "halfling." Hobbits were known for their small stature, as well as their love

---

Aslan the Lion-Lamb

At last she [the White Witch] drew near. She stood by Aslan's head. Her face was working and twitching with passion, but his looked up at the sky, still quiet, neither angry nor afraid, but a little sad. Then, just before she gave the blow, she stooped down and said in a quivering voice, "And now, who has won? Fool, did you think that by all this you would save the human traitor? Now I will kill you instead of him [Edmund] as our pact was and so the Deep Magic will be appeased. But when you are dead what will prevent me from killing him as well? And who will take him out of my hand then? Understand that you have given me Narnia forever, you have lost your own life and you have not saved his. In that knowledge, despair and die" . . . "Oh Aslan!" cried both the children. . . . "Aren't you dead then, dear Aslan?" said Lucy. "Not now," said Aslan . . ."though the Witch knew the Deep Magic, there is a magic deeper still which she did not know. Her knowledge goes back only to the dawn of Time. But if she could have looked a little further back, into the stillness and the darkness before Time dawned, she would have read there a different incantation. She would have known that when a willing victim who had committed no treachery was killed in a traitor's stead, the Table [of Stone] would crack and Death itself would start working backwards."[22]

for eating and making merry. They were innocent and trusting like children. In other words, Frodo was chosen by good because of—not just despite—his perceived weakness. Bruner and Ware put it well:

> It is one of the great ironies of Christian faith. For some reason, God chooses those we least expect to accomplish his most important tasks. Some, like our hobbit friends, emerge from total obscurity to great fame. Others remain anonymous. All are used in ways they never imagined possible. And here is the mystery: They are chosen not in spite of weakness, but because of it.[23]

And Frodo showed his true strength by being willing to sacrifice his life for others. He chose to carry the burden of the evil Ring to Mount Orodruin in the land of Mordor and cast it into the Cracks of Doom. And so it happened.

And so it is with Jesus Christ, of which Revelation 5:9–12 (NIV) proclaims:

> "You are worthy to take the scroll and to open its seals,
>   because you were slain, and with your blood you purchased
>   men for God
>   from every tribe and language and people and nation.
> You have made them to be a kingdom and priests to serve
>   our God,
>   and they will reign on the earth."

Then I looked and heard the voice of many angels, numbering thousands upon thousands, and ten thousand times ten thousand. They encircled the throne and the living creatures and the elders. In a loud voice they sang:

> "Worthy is the Lamb, who was slain,
>   to receive power and wealth and
>   wisdom and strength
>   and honor and glory and praise!"

Jesus's self-sacrifice was the divine means for bringing redemption, the ultimate weapon against evil. It is also the case for his followers:

> Then I heard a loud voice in heaven say:
> "Now have come the salvation and the
>   power and the kingdom of our
>   God,
> and the authority of his Christ.
> For the accuser of our brothers,
>   who accuses them before our God
>   day and night,
>   has been hurled down.

> **Jesus's self-sacrifice was the divine means for bringing redemption, the ultimate weapon against evil.**

> They overcame him
> > by the blood of the Lamb
> > and by the word of their testimony;
> > they did not love their lives so much
> > as to shrink from death."

Revelation 12:10–11 NIV

CONCLUSION

J. R. R. Tolkien's trilogy is indeed beloved, as is evident from the immense popularity of the books, as well as the three movies based upon these works. Its quintessential theme of good against evil has people cheering for the *Fellowship of the Ring* to defeat the evil forces. Tolkien's Christian faith is manifest throughout his books, revealing itself through striking parallels between his writings and the Bible. Both tell the story of the world from its creation to the Fall, to the signs of the times, the ultimate battle, and the ultimate triumph of good. Although there is seemingly unending struggle, and one wonders if evil will perhaps overcome good through wars and hardship, nevertheless good and thus, God, prevails. In *The Lord of the Rings* there are three Christlike characters: Frodo, Gandalf the Grey, and Aragorn. Through their self-sacrifice and perseverance, the Ring is finally destroyed, and thus, too, evil. Heaven on earth is restored.

> *Tolkien's Christian faith is manifest throughout his books, revealing itself through striking parallels between his writings and the Bible.*

It is not difficult to see the faith of Tolkien: His works parallel the story of humanity and the sacrifice of Jesus Christ, who provides redemption, as well as the hope and faith that through Jesus's atonement evil has ultimately been defeated, and one day humans will again experience heaven on earth.

Tolkien's works also encourage us to know that, just as his characters were flawed and appeared to be unlikely heroes, so God chooses human beings with weaknesses, those who also seem to be unlikely candidates to fulfill his purpose in the world. His strength is made perfect in our weakness. We are emboldened by the realization that God has a plan for every human being in this imperfect world, giving them the power to overcome evil with good, and thus alter the course of history itself.

DISCUSSION QUESTIONS

1. For what purpose did J. R. R. Tolkien write?
2. God's plan for the world is unfolding in history, and will culminate in good triumphing over evil. How is this portrayed in Tolkien's trilogy?
3. Jewish and Christian sources speak about the signs of the times which will herald the end of history and the appearance of the kingdom of God. How is this also seen in Tolkien's trilogy?
4. What three individuals serve as Christlike characters in Tolkien's trilogy? Which of these individuals best embodies the second coming of Christ motif?
5. Armageddon, the ultimate battle between good and evil, will take place between God's Messiah and his adversaries. How do we also see this in Tolkien's writings?
6. The regaining of paradise by the return of King Jesus is eagerly anticipated. Is there a corresponding event in which paradise is restored in Tolkien's trilogy?
7. Jesus's self-sacrifice was the divine means for bringing redemption. Which of Tolkien's characters do you think best epitomizes self-sacrifice?

THE BIBLE CODE

Does It Tell Us When Jesus Will Come to End the World?

||||||||||||||||||||||||||||||||||||||||||||||||||||||||

INTRODUCTION

This chapter takes our previous discussion of the signs of the times a step further by connecting the end-times with the enormously popular book, *The Bible Code*, by Michael Drosnin. (It reached number three on the *New York Times* best-seller list.) Does *The Bible Code* correctly tell us when the end of the world will occur?

According to Drosnin the answer is emphatically yes! In his internationally best-selling books—*The Bible Code* and *The Bible Code II: The Countdown*[1]—he claims there is a predictive code in the Bible. He believes it accurately forecasted the following past events: the assassination of Israel's Prime Minister Yitzhak Rabin on November 4, 1995; the election of underdog Bill Clinton as president of the United States in 1992; the Great Depression of 1929 in the United States; the rise of the leaders in World War II—Roosevelt, Churchill, Stalin, Hitler; the election of unlikely candidate Benjamin Netanyahu to be Prime Minister of Israel on May 29, 1976; the attack on Pearl Harbor on December 7, 1941; the assassination of President John F. Kennedy on November 23, 1963; the terrorist attacks on the Murrah Federal Building in Oklahoma City on April 19, 1995, and on the Twin Towers in New York on September 11, 2001; the election of George W. Bush to the presidency of the United States in 2000; the impeachment of Bill Clinton; the rise of Osama Bin Laden. And these are only some of the more well-known predictions.

But, naturally, like all doomsday forecasters, Drosnin says the Bible also predicts the end of history—Armageddon— within our lifetime. As if the topic needed any more drama, Drosnin made three predictions to that effect in 1998. He had his attorney seal them in an envelope not to be opened until 2002. They were:

1. The world will face global "economic collapse" starting in the Hebrew year 5762 (2002 in the modern calendar).
2. This will lead to a period of unprecedented danger, as nations with nuclear weapons become unstable, and terrorists can buy or steal the power to destroy whole cities.
3. The danger will peak in the Hebrew year 5766 (2006 in the modern calendar), the year that is most clearly encoded with both "world war" and "atomic holocaust."[2] According to Drosnin, the fulfillments

> *In his internationally best-selling books—The Bible Code and The Bible Code II: The Countdown—Drosnin claims there is a predictive code in the Bible.*

> *Drosnin says the Bible also predicts the end of history—Armageddon—within our lifetime.*

of these three predictions were set in motion on September 11, 2001. They will culminate with a nuclear attack on Jerusalem engineered by Al Qaeda terrorists. This will be the beginning of the end.

Got your attention? Who in their right mind would not be riveted on such predictions? The fate of our world seems to be proceeding according to *The Bible Code*. Or is it? We intend to answer that question in this chapter. But first, we will examine the actual methodology employed by those espousing *The Bible Code*.

Are We Living in the Last Generation?

Mark 13:30 ("This generation will certainly not pass away until all these things have happened" [NIV]) has fueled interest in the theory that 1948 began the last generation before the end of history as we know it. According to this hypothesis, the Jews returning to the land of Israel in 1948 set the prophetic clock ticking and whenever this generation is completed—anywhere from thirty to forty years—then Christ will return. Of course, this time frame has already proved outdated and therefore erroneous. Actually, this reading of Mark 13:30 is but one of five views of this passage: (1) the reconstitution of Israel in 1948 began the last generation; (2) the generation Jesus referred to was the end-time generation, whenever that may be; (3) the words "this generation" could mean the nation of Israel, indicating that Israel will never pass away in the plan of God; (4) Jesus referred to his own generation that would witness his return; (5) Jesus referred to his contemporaries as the generation that would experience the fall of Jerusalem, which indeed occurred in AD 70, to the Romans. We suspect the last view is the best interpretation of Mark 13:30.

THE METHODOLOGY BEHIND *THE BIBLE CODE*

The basic assumption of *The Bible Code* is that there is more to the Bible than the literal reading of it. The literal reading is a good start, but underneath the text, or between the lines of the text, there is a hidden message to be decoded. This is especially the case with numbers in the book of Revelation, like seven—the number for God, six—the number for humankind, three—the number for the Trinity. Because Revelation is a book filled with symbols, it is fair game for the study of numerology (numbers convey a spiritual message). For example, take the number 666 in Revelation 13:18, which represents the beast, the enemy of Christ. While all sorts of interpretations have competed for the real meaning of 666 (Hitler, Social Security numbers, computer chips, etc.), many biblical scholars perceive the number to be an example of *gematria*, the idea that biblical numbers convey a symbolic message. Biblical Hebrew also uses its alphabet to represent numbers.

> More than one scholar has seen a possible reference of this number in *Neron Kaiser*. The Hebrew numerical valuation for *Nrwn Qsr* is as follows: N = 50, R = 200, W = 6, N = 50, Q = 100, S = 60 and R = 200, which add up to 666. Both ancient Christians and non-Christians alike thought Nero to be a good candidate for the anti-Christ.[3]

In our opinion, a symbolic reading of Revelation is legitimate because the book itself invites us to decode its message (which, it seems to us, had to do with the first-century battle confronting Christians: Could they worship both Caesar and Christ?).

But an allegorical or numerological interpretation of books in the Bible that are not symbolic in nature—for example the Pentateuch, the five books of Moses—is inappropriate. The method informing *The Bible Code* is called "equidistant letter sequencing" (ELS), which is applied to any and every part of the Hebrew Bible. First, depending on the researcher, either the Pentateuch (for example) or the entire Hebrew Bible is loaded into the computer. Spaces between words are eliminated, thus generating a continuous stream of consecutive letters. Then the operators tell the computer to find specific words or patterns of words by selecting equidistant letters; they start by looking at every other letter, and if no match is found, then every third letter, etc. Eventually, the computer can be looking at letters spaced thousands of real words apart to search for a specific word or pattern of words. In order for there to be a match, each letter has to be equidistant—separated by the exact same number of letters.

> *The method informing The Bible Code is called "equidistant letter sequencing," which is applied to any and every part of the Hebrew Bible.*

One of Drosnin's examples is the Israeli prime minister Yitzhak Rabin. The computer was directed to look for his name—Yitzhak Rabin— and found it: The first letter occurs in Deuteronomy 2:33, the next letter in Deuteronomy 4:42 (a skip of 4,722 letters), and so forth, skipping 4,722 letters each time until reaching the last letter in Deuteronomy 24:16.

In addition to finding a specific word or pattern of words, the proponents of the ELS code look for additional connecting or predicting aspects in the near vicinity of the specific texts involved. For example, in the case of Yitzhak Rabin's name, Deuteronomy 4:42 (the location of the second letter in his name), according to Drosnin contains the phrase "The assassin will assassinate," thereby predicting his assassination thousands of years before it happened. Unfortunately, however, the fact is that Drosnin translated Deuteronomy 4:41–42 rather poorly. The New International Version text reads: "Then Moses set aside three cities east of the Jordan, to which anyone who had killed a person could flee if he had unintentionally killed his neighbor without malice aforethought." This text deals with cities of refuge for those who kill someone unintentionally; it has nothing to do with assassination.[4]

This approach to the Bible was crafted by three individuals in the 1980s: Eliyahu Rips, a professor of mathematics at Hebrew University in Jerusalem, Yoav Rosenburg, a computer scientist from the Jerusalem College of Technology, and Doron Witztum, an Israeli graduate student who left physics to "study Torah." These three wrote an article explaining the equidistant letter sequencing approach to the Bible which, after careful scrutiny, was published in August 1994 in an American journal, *Statistical Science*.[5]

Michael Drosnin became a friend of Rips and, under his influence, published *The Bible Code* and *The Bible Code II: The Countdown*. One interesting difference between Rips and Drosnin is that the former believes in God while the latter does not. In fact, Drosnin frequently mentions in his books his lack of faith in God but, ironically, his belief that there is a code in the Bible. This contrasting claim is supposed to give an air of objectivity to Drosnin's research: since he doesn't believe in God he has nothing to prove on behalf of God—in other words, the Bible code is "fact" not faith.

But Christians, too, have gotten in on the ELS bandwagon. Grant Jeffrey, an evangelical author, applies the Bible code to the Greek New Testament. His Bible code discoveries include the death of Princess Diana and the AIDS epidemic, and it confirms other discoveries regarding the Rabin assassination, Gulf War I, the Oklahoma City bombing, and more.[6]

A CRITIQUE OF THE BIBLE CODE METHOD (ELS)

While popular audiences have enthusiastically received Drosnin's books, the majority of the scholarly community has rejected it.[7] Why is that so? The three categories of scholarly critique involve statistical problems, textual variants, and a psychological phenomenon.

Statistical Problems with the Bible Code (ELS)

The central claim of Drosnin (and others) is that the patterns they have found are beyond normal probability and are therefore divine in nature. They cite fantastic odds against finding names and connections by random, yet those who critique the code believe they have shattered the claims of this method.[8] Who is right here?

At first glance Michael Weitzman, for example, seems to help the case of the proponents of the Bible code, when he states that the probability of finding a six-letter word (based on equal letter distribution) is 1 in 110,000,000. However, he goes on to state that the Pentateuch by itself contains over

> Using an ELS computer search, any random six-letter name or other letter combination will show up in the Pentateuch around 160 times.

300,000 letters. Based on ELS methodology, names can be read forward or backward, and the skip sequence can range from 2 to around 30,000 letters. Using these criteria, the 300,000-letter Pentateuch yields 18 billion six-letter combinations. As a result, using an ELS computer search, any random six-letter name or other letter combination will show up in the Pentateuch around 160 times (18 billion divided by 110,000,000).[9] Thus, with 160 options, it really shouldn't be difficult to find one that intersects a verse that can be loosely connected to the name.

Interestingly, the ELS method has been used on nonbiblical literature as well. Any literary work of significant length yields hundreds of modern names with hundreds of different associations in adjacent phrases. Take, for example, the work of Brendan McKay, who loaded the English text of *Moby Dick* into his computer and ran ELS searches to find "predictions" about assassinations of other twentieth-century leaders. Not surprisingly, he found numerous names with significant connections to the topic of death in the nearby text. Among them, the name Samoza (president of Nicaragua, assassinated in 1956) showed up near the words "he was shot," "dies," and "gun."[10] This is certainly similar to Drosnin's search for Yitzhak Rabin's name and his conclusion that the text predicts his assassination. Thus, unless we are willing to view *Moby Dick* as divinely inspired, this evidence pretty well demolishes the heart of *The Bible Code*.

Textual Variants

Another flaw in the ELS approach is that its proponents ignore variations in the Hebrew text of the Old Testament. The Bible was transmitted for many years through handwritten manuscripts; because of the size of the Old Testament and the challenges involved in hand-copying, no two handwritten, ancient Hebrew manuscripts are identical down to the very letters. Spelling was not standardized during the production and early transmission of the Old Testament. In fact, many words had a number of spellings; after the return of the Jews in 536 BC to Israel following the Babylonian captivity, the scribes not only changed letter style from paleo-Hebrew to Aramaic letters, but they also inserted consonantal vowels[11] to aid in reading and pronunciation. It is clear that the specific letter length of the Old Testament was never uniform or fixed.

This causes a great problem for proponents of the ELS method because if one letter is missing or an extra letter added, their entire system collapses. Drosnin used an edition of the Hebrew Bible called *The Second Rabbinic Bible*. This was the standard, but not universal, printed text from the sixteenth century until the early twentieth century. While this edition was based on earlier printed Hebrew Bibles and late medieval manuscripts, none of the earlier printed editions were exactly the same in letter length as *The Second Rabbinic Bible*.

In addition, handwritten manuscripts predating *The Second Rabbinic Bible* by hundreds of years differ in numerous ways that do not affect meaning, but are critical in terms of letter spacing. Likewise, most twentieth-century editions of the Hebrew Bible are based on older manuscripts like the Leningrad Codex.[12]

Contemporary editions of the Hebrew Bible also differ from *The Second Rabbinic Bible* in the number of letters that appear. The modern edition, *Biblia Hebraica* (also available in electronic form), differs from *The Second Rabbinic Bible* by forty-one letters in Deuteronomy alone. Yet Drosnin himself has indicated his belief that every edition of the Hebrew Bible is identical letter for letter.[13] However, such is not the case. As J. Scott Duvall and J. Daniel Hays remark:

> Drosnin's Yitzhak Rabin "prediction" does not appear in any modern Hebrew Bible editions nor does it appear in any of the ancient handwritten manuscripts. In each edition of the Hebrew Bible and in each ancient manuscript the computer will find a different set of encoded names and "predictions." To argue for the validity of one particular set of supposedly encoded names from one specific edition of the Hebrew Bible seems highly questionable.[14]

No two handwritten, ancient Hebrew manuscripts are identical down to the very letters.

This is the same problem Grant Jeffrey faces with his usage of the Greek New Testament, particularly the *Textus Receptus* (*The King James Bible*). The majority of New Testament scholars, however, favor the Nestle's edition because it is based on much earlier Greek manuscripts. The King James Bible relies upon Greek manuscripts that date from the ninth to fifteenth centuries AD while the Nestle text is based on second to fifth century AD Greek manuscripts. Moreover, in those latter documents there are many variant readings. Even though text critics can with great confidence sort through those differences to arrive at the original Greek text, still, as Randall Ingermanson has shown, there is no Bible code to be found in either the *Textus Receptus* or the Nestle text.[15]

Cognitive Dissonance: A Psychological Phenomenon at Work in The Bible Code

Marvin has investigated other doomsday approaches to the Bible, especially millenarian groups (millennium—the 1000-year reign of the kingdom of God on earth) who have incorrectly predicted the end of the world.[16] At work in these failed predictions is the psychological theory or phenomenon labeled by social scientists as cognitive dissonance.

At work in these failed predictions is the psychological theory or phenomenon labeled by social scientists as cognitive dissonance.

Leon Festinger[17] is considered the leading expert and pioneer in applying cognitive dissonance to millenarian movements. In his *A Theory of Cognitive Dissonance*, Festinger explains that human beings usually strive for consistency (or consonance) in their beliefs (cognition). If we then acknowledge or do something that is inconsistent with our personal beliefs, we usually try to rationalize the inconsistency (or dissonance) so it becomes consistent with those beliefs instead of trying to accept the inconsistency at face value. If the rationalization process does not work and the inconsistency persists, discomfort sets in. To alleviate this feeling, we will work hard to reduce the dissonance, avoiding anything that would increase the tension.[18]

For example, members of a millenarian movement may set a date for the end of the world and the return of Christ. When the date passes and the prediction has not come true, they experience dissonance: reality is inconsistent with their belief. They also feel victimized by those who mock them for holding to such a seemingly odd belief. These circumstances create personal distress. They may accept that the prediction has failed and become disillusioned. On the other hand, if they cannot accept that conclusion, they may attempt to relieve the uncomfortable feeling by rationalizing away the failure of the prediction. They may set a new date, explain why the first one was incorrect, or claim that the prediction was fulfilled and provide an alternative interpretation for what happened. They also tend to ignore or condemn anything that forces them to deal with the reality of the situation.

Festinger further claims that people who are so committed to a certain conviction that they take irreversible action will, ironically, become even more convinced of the correctness of that conviction when presented with evidence that it is absolutely wrong.[19] He discusses five conditions under which this phenomenon occurs:

> *People who are so committed to a certain conviction that they take irreversible action will, ironically, become even more convinced of the correctness of that conviction when presented with evidence that it is absolutely wrong.*

1. A belief must be held with deep conviction, and it must have some relevance to action, that is, to what the believer does or how he or she behaves.
2. The person holding the belief must have committed to it; that is, for the sake of one's belief, one must have taken some important action that is difficult to undo. In general, the more important such actions are and the more difficult they are to undo, the greater is the individual's commitment to the belief.

Daniel's 70th Week

Daniel 9:24–27 predicts that Israel's fate will unfold during a period of 490 years (that is, 70 weeks of years: 70 weeks times 7 days per week = 490 years). Prophecy buffs believe that Daniel's 70th week is to be equated with a future seven-year great tribulation that will be poured out on Israel to bring her to faith in Jesus as Messiah. Many biblical scholars, however, think Daniel's 70th week already happened in history—from 171 to 164 BC, when the Syrian ruler Antiochus Epiphanes tried to force Palestinian Jews to give up their faith in God for pagan religion. First Maccabees tells the story of Israel's heroic and successful efforts to resist Antiochus's advances.

3. The belief must be sufficiently specific and concerned with the real world so that events may unequivocally refute the belief.
4. Such undeniable disconfirmatory evidence must occur and must be recognized by the individual holding the belief.[20]

Given these four conditions, we might expect that individuals would surrender their conviction. This will occur in many instances, but one further condition must be in place before people will hold onto a belief proved false.

5. The individual believer must have social support. If the believer is a member of a group of convinced persons who can support one another, we would expect the belief to be maintained and the believers to attempt to proselytize or to persuade nonmembers that the belief is correct.[21]

In the case of millenarian movements, the group must have set a date or a period of time within which Christ would return, giving details as to just what would take place. The commitment to the date must be held as important and is usually stated publicly.

Probably the most spectacular failed prediction uttered regarding the date of Christ's return was that by William Miller. Miller's theory was quite elaborate, but central to it was his interpretation of two verses in the book of Daniel, which he tied together to calculate the Lord's return: Daniel 8:14, "And he said to him, 'For two thousand and three hundred evenings and mornings; then the sanctuary shall be restored'" (RSV) and Daniel 9:24, "Seventy weeks of years are decreed concerning your people and your holy city, to finish the transgression, to put an end to sin, and to atone for iniquity, to bring in ever-

"Time rolls on His resistless course. We are one more year down its rapid stream towards the ocean of eternity. We have passed what the world calls the last round of 1843; and already they begin to shout victory over us. Does your heart begin to quail? Are you ready to give up your blessed hope in the glorious appearing of Jesus Christ? Or are you waiting for it, although it seems to us that it tarries? Let me say to you in the language of the blessed Book of God, 'Although it tarry, wait for it; it will surely come, it will not tarry.' Never has my faith been stronger than at this very moment."[22]

These words from a letter written by William Miller were published in late January 1844, less than two months before the deadline he had set for the second advent of Christ—March 21, 1844. When that prophecy failed, Miller reset the date of Christ's return for October 22, 1844. But that date, too, came and went with no second coming of Christ.

lasting righteousness, to seal both vision and prophet, and to anoint a most holy place" (RSV). Miller's basic reasoning can be outlined as follows:

1. The sanctuary cleansing mentioned in Daniel 8:14 referred to the return of Christ, which would eradicate all evil on the earth.

2. A prophetic day equaled one year, so one could correctly calculate the numbers in the passages as 2,300 years and 490 years (seventy times seven).

3. Using Bishop Ussher's popular Old Testament chronology, the 2,300–year period began with the return of the Jews to Jerusalem to rebuild the city in 457 BC (Christ's crucifixion, AD 33, marked the end of Daniel's seventy weeks. Moving back 490 years from AD 33, one comes to the year 457 BC).

4. Two thousand and three hundred years forward from 457 BC was AD 1843.[23] 1843, then, was to be the date of the return of Christ.

> *Drosnin's major prediction in* The Bible Code *about the future of the world is a clear-cut example of cognitive dissonance.*

There are two noteworthy examples of cognitive dissonance displayed by the Millerites when Miller's prediction failed. The first was that his followers recalculated the date of Christ's return to October 22, 1844 (Miller himself agreed).[24] When that prophecy failed, Millerite Hiram Edson rationalized that the "cleansing of the sanctuary" referred to in Daniel 8:14 actually did take place on October 22, 1844, *but in heaven.* When Christ entered the heavenly sanctuary he was "blotting out" sins, not just forgiving them. With this last task accomplished in heaven, the stage was set for Christ's return to earth.[25]

We also contend that Drosnin's major prediction in *The Bible Code* about the future of the world is a clear-cut example of cognitive dissonance.

Drosnin's Prophecy

Drosnin says that the Bible code predicted that Libya would engineer a nuclear attack on Israel in 1996, which, in turn, would be the catalyst for World War III—Armageddon and the end of the world.[26]

The Five Components of Cognitive Dissonance

(1) *A belief must be held with deep conviction and must be relevant to that person's actions.* Drosnin believed so strongly in the above prediction that he secured a meeting with Shimon Peres, then Prime Minister of Israel, to tell him of the Bible Code's prediction about the impending nuclear attack against Israel sometime before the end of 1996. That meeting took place on January 26, 1996.[27]

(2) *The person holding this belief must have committed to it*; that is, for the sake of one's belief, one must have taken some important action that is difficult to undo. When Drosnin put his prediction in print in his first book, *The Bible Code*, his bold prophecy became a matter of public record.

(3) *The belief must be sufficiently specific that events may clearly refute it.* Drosnin clearly states in *The Bible Code* that 1996 would be the date of the terrorist nuclear attack on Israel, sparking the end of history.

(4) *Undeniable disconfirmatory evidence must occur and must be recognized by the individual holding the belief.* Obviously, 1996 came and went without terrorists from Libya engineering a nuclear attack against Israel. Drosnin himself agrees:

> Right up to September 13, 1996, the last day of 5756, the year of the predicted "atomic holocaust," I stayed in close contact with Israeli leaders.
>
> Three days before the date encoded with "holocaust of Israel," I met in New York with the Prime Minister's national security advisor, Dore Gold. The next day, I sent a final message to Mossad chief Danny Yatom, and General Yatom sent back word that Israeli intelligence was on alert.
>
> But nothing happened on September 13, 1996. There was no atomic attack. The Hebrew year 5756 came and went and Israel and the world was still at peace.
>
> I was relieved, but puzzled. Was the Bible code simply wrong?[28]

> It is clear that Drosnin has changed his tune on the dates of World War III and the end of the world—from 1996 to 2006.

(5) *The individual believer must have social support*; that is, the conviction must be maintained by the individual and those who support him. The mathematics professor, Eli Rips, continued to support Drosnin's belief.[29] Faced with the decision to admit he misread the Bible regarding the prediction about Israel, sincere though it was, Drosnin rationalized his mistake. Like the Millerites and other

millenarian groups, Drosnin redefined the prediction by re-dating its fulfillment: the fulfillment was delayed.

> Or, was the danger real, and only delayed? I thought about it all weekend, and on Monday sent Yatom a fax: [Danny Yatom was Peres' top military advisor] "One last word, and I'm out of the fortune-telling business. The atomic attack predicted for the last days of 5756 was obviously a probability that did not happen—but my guess is that the danger is not over. On several occasions we have seen things happen as predicted, but not when predicted. I urge you to remain alert to what is almost certainly a real danger."[30]

Drosnin offers various reasons the prediction was delayed:

> Did the Israelis, warned by the Bible code of an atomic attack, prevent it by being on alert at the time of the predicted danger?

> Did Prime Minister Peres, by publicly stating the danger three days after I met with him, put a stop to a planned terrorist attack?

> Or was it all changed only by chance, when Netanyahu at the last minute delayed a diplomatic trip to Jordan?[31]

The revised date of the nuclear attack on Israel and the outbreak of Armageddon, says Drosnin in *The Bible Code II: The Countdown*, is 2006.[32] But it is clear that Drosnin has changed his tune on the dates of World War III and the end of the world—from 1996 to 2006.

Now Drosnin is no doubt a brilliant reporter whose sincere belief in the Bible code drives his humanitarian concern to thwart nuclear holocaust. And to say that a person is experiencing cognitive dissonance in no way suggests a person is psychologically unsound. Rather, cognitive dissonance, or rationalization, is a dynamic that can influence the most well-intentioned and mentally balanced individual without their knowledge, as is the case with Drosnin. It can affect us all if we are not aware of our tendencies to commit to beliefs that are not well grounded. Beware of making statements like, "That's my story and I'm sticking to it!" Or, as the popular adage puts it, "My mind is made up. Don't confuse me with the facts!"

CONCLUSION

Drosnin's books, *The Bible Code* and *The Bible Code II: The Countdown*, are fascinating; they have caused great speculation, keeping the world abuzz with talk of the end of the world. A mixture of excitement and horror gets the adrenaline flowing not only among its proponents, but also for the many who wonder if Drosnin has, in fact, cracked the code of the centuries, predicting

> *It's best to stick with Jesus's prediction about his return, which is, as of yet, still unknown even to him (Mark 13:32) and certainly, therefore, unclear to us.*

assassinations, economic collapse, and Christ's return to end history. But is Drosnin correct? It is difficult not to get caught up in the zeal of the ELS evangelists, tipping the scales toward believing the Bible code to be the real deal. However, when one considers the methodology of the equidistant letter sequencing, doubts begin to form. It is clear that the text is not speaking for itself—the researcher is *looking for* a specific word or pattern of words. And the chances of doing so are quite possible—given the number of possibilities based on a word count of the Pentateuch (over 300,000 letters).

In addition, Drosnin used an edition of the Hebrew Bible called *The Second Rabbinic Bible*, but there are no two handwritten ancient Hebrew manuscripts that are exactly alike; nor are the earlier printed editions exactly the same in letter length as *The Second Rabbinic Bible*.

The upshot is that Drosnin's Yitzhak Rabin prediction doesn't appear in any modern Hebrew Bible edition nor does it appear in any of the ancient handwritten manuscripts. The issue of different editions of the Hebrew Bible with different numbers of letters casts more doubt on the methodology of equidistant letter sequencing. This is a big problem for equidistant letter sequencing methodology—there simply can't be variance in the number or sequencing of letters in order for this approach to stand.

The thought that perhaps the Bible contains a unique hidden code is intriguing, to say the least. To think that there are predictions buried within the text is indeed tantalizing. However, when one considers that equidistant letter sequencing has been applied to a number of nonbiblical texts, resulting in names and predictions as well, the appeal of the Bible code diminishes. If you can find a "hidden meaning" in any text if you look hard enough and use a powerful enough computer, the response to any prediction becomes, So what?

Finally, there is Drosnin's unfulfilled prediction about the nuclear terrorist attack on Israel by Libya that would trigger the end of the world. It did not happen. Yet the proponents of the Bible code did not miss a beat. A new date was issued—2006 is now the beginning of the end of the world. One wonders, if this prophecy is also unfulfilled, what new date will be set by Drosnin?

A number of equally well-intentioned, convinced individuals throughout history have made similar predictions and those dates have come and gone.

In our opinion, it's best to stick with Jesus's prediction about his return, which is, as of yet, still unknown even to him (Mark 13:32) and certainly, therefore, unclear to us.

DISCUSSION QUESTIONS

1. What is the basic assumption of *The Bible Code*?
2. Is Revelation the only book in the Bible in which Drosnin believes there is a hidden message?
3. What is equidistant letter sequencing?
4. One of Drosnin's examples is that of the prediction regarding Yitzhak Rabin. What was it?
5. What is the statistical problem related to *The Bible Code*?
6. Was there just one version of the Old Testament? Is this a problem for the proponents of *The Bible Code*?
7. What is cognitive dissonance? What are the five conditions of cognitive dissonance as it relates to Drosnin?
8. Has Drosnin changed his mind regarding the dates of WWIII and the end of the world?

PLURALISM AND THE GOSPELS

Is Jesus the Only Way?

||||||||||||||||||||||||||||||||||||||||||||||||||||||||||||||||||||||||

INTRODUCTION

Marcus Borg is one of the more celebrated figures of the Jesus Seminar. In his book, *Meeting Jesus Again for the First Time*,[1] he writes of his rejection of the conservative Christian training he received as a young person. In its place, Borg advocates the view of Jesus by most in the Seminar:

> (1) Jesus did not think of himself in messianic terms. (2) It cannot be claimed that Jesus expected "the supernatural coming of the Kingdom of God as a world-ending event in his own generation." . . . Following these are four broad positive features ascribed to the historical persona of Jesus: he was (3) a spirit person, (4) a teacher of wisdom, (5) a social prophet, and (6) the founder of a movement.[2]

This paints a portrait of Jesus as a remarkable person, but not God. Borg says that Jesus's message to us was that we should seek personal, spiritual transformation by means of enlightenment experiences, much like Buddha and Muhammad taught. According to Borg, "in popular Christian usage, the 'uniqueness' of Jesus is most commonly tied to the notion that he is the uniquely and exclusively true revelation of God. It is this meaning of his uniqueness that I deny."[3]

Borg goes on to say:

> The notion that God's only son came to this planet to offer his life as a sacrifice for the sins of the world, and that God could not forgive us without that having happened, and that we are saved by believing this story, is simply incredible . . . taken literally, it is a profound obstacle to accepting the Christian message. To many people, it simply makes no sense.[4]

181

In its place, Borg shares a perspective prevalent in Western culture—pluralism: the idea that there are various paths to God, all legitimate and none mutually exclusive.

R. Douglas Geivett puts his finger on the pulse of our pluralistic society's view of dogmatic teaching:

> In a climate of suspicion about truth and reticence about claims to have the truth, exclusivist religious claims are bound to seem intolerant and unyielding. The claim that Jesus Christ is the way, the truth, and the life, the uniquely adequate remedy to the human spiritual condition, will almost certainly be met with suspicion and resistance by many who have not experienced the personal spiritual liberation that comes with acceptance of this claim. And in the present intellectual and religious climate, even those who *have* experienced such liberation often feel considerable pressure from the surrounding culture to eschew all forms of religious exclusivism.[5]

In light of our pluralistic society's distrust of dogmatic teaching, we must ask, "Is Jesus the only way to salvation, or are there other legitimate paths to God?" In this chapter we will attempt to answer that critical question by presenting three portraits of Jesus to be found in contemporary world religions. These Eastern religions are heavily shaping Western spirituality today. For each of them, we will offer comparisons with Jesus (the good news), but then we will point out differences between Christianity and them (the bad news). One of the important questions we will address in this chapter is, are these differences between Christianity and other religions irreconcilable?

We will focus on Buddhism, Judaism, and Islam. Then, in the last section of this chapter, we will examine four theories as to how we are to explain the relationship between Christianity and these other major religions.

> *Borg shares a perspective prevalent in Western culture—pluralism: the idea that there are various paths to God, all legitimate and none mutually exclusive.*

CHRISTIANITY AND WORLD RELIGIONS: GOOD NEWS/BAD NEWS

Jesus and Buddhism

The Buddha, or "enlightened one," was born about 560 BC in northeastern India. His family name was Gautama, his given name Siddhartha. Siddhartha was the son of a rajah, or ruler. His mother died when he was just a week old and Siddhartha was cared for by his mother's sister, who was also the rajah's second wife. There was supposedly a prophecy given at the time of his birth by a sage at his father's court.

The prophecy said that the child would be a great king if he stayed at home, but if he decided to leave home, he would become a savior for humankind. This bothered his father, for he wanted his son to succeed him as king. Therefore, to keep him at home his father surrounded him with wealth and pleasures and kept all painful and ugly things out of his sight.

> *This excursion would forever change his life, for it was during this journey that he saw "the four passing sights."*

Siddhartha eventually married and had a son but was still confined to the palace and its pleasures. One day he informed his father that he wished to see the world. This excursion would forever change his life, for it was during this journey that he saw "the four passing sights."

Although his father ordered the streets to be cleaned and decorated and all elderly or infirm people to stay inside, there were those who did not get the message. Consequently, Siddhartha did see some troubling sights, the first of which was that of a decrepit old man. When Siddhartha asked what happened to this man, he was told that the man was old, as everyone someday would become.

Later, he met a sick man and was told that all people were liable to be sick and suffer pain like that individual.

He then saw a funeral procession with a corpse on its way to cremation, the mourners weeping bitterly. When he asked what that meant, the prince was informed that it was the way of life, for sooner or later both prince and pauper would have to die.

The last sight was that of a monk begging for his food. The tranquil look on the beggar's face convinced Siddhartha that this type of life was for him. Immediately he left the palace and his family in search of enlightenment. The night that he left his home to seek enlightenment became known as the Great Renunciation.

The prince-turned-beggar spent his time wandering from place to place, seeking wisdom. Unsatisfied by the Hindu scriptures, he became discouraged, but continued on his quest. He tried asceticism but this gave him no peace. The fateful day in his life came while he was meditating beneath a fig tree.

Deep in meditation, he reached the highest degree of God-consciousness, known as nirvana. He supposedly stayed under the fig tree for seven days; after that, the fig tree was called the bodhi, or the bo tree—the tree of wisdom.

> *Such enlightenment is expressed in Buddha's Four Noble Truths and the Eightfold Path.*

The truths he learned during this time he would now impart to the world, no longer as Siddhartha Gautama, but as the Buddha, the enlightened one.[6]

Such enlightenment is expressed in Buddha's Four Noble Truths and the Eightfold Path:

The First Noble Truth concerns the existence of suffering: Birth is painful, and death is painful; disease and old age are painful. Not having what we desire is painful, and having what we do not desire is also painful.

The Second Noble Truth concerns the cause of suffering: It is the craving desire for the pleasures of the senses, which seeks satisfaction now here, now there; the craving for happiness and prosperity in this life and in future lives.

The Third Noble Truth concerns the ending of suffering: To be free of suffering one must give up, get rid of, extinguish this very craving, so that no passion and no desire remain.

The Fourth Noble Truth concerns the path to the ending of all pain: the Eightfold Path:

The first step on that path is Right Views: You must accept the Four Noble Truths and the Eightfold Path.

The second step is Right Resolve: You must renounce the pleasures of the senses; you must harbor no ill will toward anyone and harm no living creature.

The third step is Right Speech: Do not lie; do not slander or abuse anyone. Do not indulge in idle talk.

The fourth is Right Behavior: Do not destroy any living creature; take only what is given to you; do not commit any unlawful sexual act.

The fifth is Right Occupation: You must earn your livelihood in a way that will harm no one.

The sixth is Right Effort: You must resolve and strive heroically to prevent any evil qualities from arising in you and to abandon any evil qualities that you may possess. Strive to acquire good qualities and encourage those you do possess to grow, increase, and be perfected.

The seventh is Right Contemplation: Be observant, strenuous, alert, contemplative, and free of desire and of sorrow.

The eighth is Right Meditation: When you have abandoned all sensuous pleasures, all evil qualities, both joy and sorrow, you must then enter the four degrees of meditation, which are produced by concentration.[7]

It is not difficult to detect apparent parallels between the Jesus of the Gospels and Buddhism:

1. Both taught self-denial as the path to peace. Compare Mark 8:34–37 and its parallel passages with the Four Noble Truths.
2. Both Jesus and Buddha identified with the poor and needy. Compare Jesus's inaugural sermon in Luke 4:18–19 with Buddha's first sermon at Benares, which spelled out the Four Noble Truths and the Eightfold Path that resulted from his contact with the poor and needy.
3. Both target the need for rebirth. Compare John 3:5–6 with the message of reincarnation in Buddhism.
4. Both speak of the need for enlightenment. "Buddha" means "enlightened one"; compare that with the apostle John's presentation of Jesus as the light (John 8:12).[8]

Some have gone even further in their comparisons of Jesus and Buddha, arguing that Jesus was directly influenced by the teachings of Buddhism. Holger Kersten's best-selling trilogy, *Jesus Lived in India*, *The Jesus Conspiracy*, and *The Original Jesus*,[9] makes just such a claim.

In the first book, Kersten uses Notovich's story that Jesus traveled to India in his silent years (recall our chapter 3), where he encountered the teachings of Buddha. Kirsten further argues that Jesus taught reincarnation and that later church councils deleted this from the Gospels.

In Kersten's second book, he and his coauthor Elmar Gruber argue that Jesus didn't die from crucifixion; rather, he swooned, and upon his recovery went to India for a second time, where he died and was buried. The Shroud of Turin supposedly supports this. Kersten and Gruber maintain that the 1988 radiocarbon results, which indicate a medieval date for the Shroud, were deliberately faked, implicating Vatican officials in a conspiracy to invalidate the Shroud because the "evidence" showed that Jesus survived death and so discredited belief in the resurrection.

In *The Original Jesus*, Kersten and Gruber argue that there are many parallels between the life and teachings of the Buddha and Jesus because the Essenes at Qumran taught Jesus. The Essenes, they claim, were clearly influenced by Buddhist missionaries. They conclude that Jesus was not a Christian but a Buddhist teacher.[10]

There are problems with the above claims about Jesus and Buddhism. The first book of Kersten's trilogy, which traces the first trip of Jesus to India during his silent years, is based on the now refuted account of Notovich (see our chapter 3). Neither is Kersten's second proposed visit of Jesus to India (after his crucifixion but before his death) convincing. Further testing since 1988 has shown that the Shroud of Turin (see our chapter 7) does not date any earlier than the medieval period. Besides, when we understand the nature of ancient crucifixion or watch Mel Gibson's film *The Passion of the Christ*, we cannot conclude anything other than that Jesus died on the cross.

There is not a shred of evidence to support the alleged connections between Jesus and the Essenes, who were supposedly immersed in Buddhism. The Essenes were a Jewish group who were the probable authors of the Dead Sea Scrolls. The Dead Sea Scrolls have brought us fresh insights into the Jewish religious scene before and around the time of Christ, and for this we must be most grateful. The Scrolls were found near Qumran on the Dead Sea in 1947. They deal mainly with the life of a particular Jewish sect in the last two centuries BC. These Scrolls, though, make no mention of Jesus, John the Baptist, or any other New Testament figure.[11] Furthermore, we know of no reputable scholar linking the Dead Sea Scrolls to Buddhism.

Jesus had no direct contact with the teachings of Buddha. And even the indirect parallels between Jesus and Buddhism do not stand upon closer inspection.

The only conclusion to be drawn from the evidence is that Jesus had no direct contact with the teachings of Buddha. And even the indirect parallels between Jesus and Buddhism do not stand upon closer inspection. Thus:

1. The self-denial that Jesus calls for is not the negation of our humanity, like Buddhism calls for, because Jesus's Jewish background well knew of the dignity of humankind, according to Genesis 1:26–28. Rather, what Christ called for was placing our commitment to him above our commitment to ourselves.
2. Jesus, like Buddha, did indeed care for the poor and needy, but his ultimate concern was their spiritual well-being.
3. Jesus's light for the world does not consist of knowledge but spiritual transformation through his death and resurrection.
4. The Gospels offer resurrection through Christ, not reincarnation. Neither is the Christian message of rebirth to be confused with reincarnation. The former deals with spiritual transformation, the latter with the supposed physical rebirth of a person into another life form.[12]

Besides these contrasts, there are other irreconcilable differences between Christianity and Buddhism:

1. Buddhism is pantheistic, teaching that God is in nature, while Christianity teaches the transcendence of God relative to creation.

2. The Buddha saw no relevance for, nor gave any, revelation from God, whereas Jesus revealed a personal Creator.
3. The Buddha taught that the root problem for humanity is ignorance; Jesus taught that the root problem is sin.
4. The Buddha is not a savior figure, but rather points the way to attaining enlightenment; Jesus presents himself as the unique Savior of the world.[13]

Jesus and Judaism

Of all other religions, Judaism is closest to Christianity. Christians inherited from their Jewish kinsmen the Old Testament, a monotheistic faith, a great legal-ethical system, and the hope for a Messiah. Jesus, the Messiah, was a Jew. Christians often forget that.[14]

There is a growing number of Jewish biblical scholars and laity who are reclaiming Jesus the Jew. This is a welcome development for both Christians and Jews. Markus Bockmuehl writes of Jesus's Judaism:

> First and foremost, clearly Jesus was a believing and practicing Jew. He participated in synagogue and temple, and his teaching takes first-century Palestinian Judaism for granted. His brand of faith was at its core the covenant faith in the God of Israel. And despite all his controversy and disputes with the religious leadership, the Gospels . . . do not give the impression that his purpose was to start a new and fundamentally incompatible religion.[15]

Bockmuehl continues:

> In fact, Jesus said and did very little which would suggest that he wanted to distance himself from Judaism. He fully participated in Jewish piety including circumcision and temple sacrifice, without the slightest hint of criticism of those divinely ordained institutions as such. He approved of tithing (Matt. 23.23 par.), sacrifice, and voluntary gifts to the Temple (Mark 12.41–44 par.). Jesus said grace before meals (Mark 6.41 par.; 14.22 par), appealed to biblical purity laws, and apparently

Christianity's Jewish Heritage

According to Romans 9:4–5, Judaism enjoys numerous blessings from God which are also a part of the heritage of Christianity: "Theirs [Jews] is the adoption as sons; theirs the divine glory, the covenants, the receiving of the law, the temple worship and the promises. Theirs are the patriarchs, and from them is traced the human ancestry of Christ, who is God over all" (NIV).

Of all other religions, Judaism is closest to Christianity.

wore tassels on his garments (compare Matt. 9.20 par.; 14.36 with 23.5 and Num. 15.37–39). He explicitly stated that he was only interested in the "lost sheep of the house of Israel" (Matt. 10.6), and although the pro-Jewish centurion of Capernaum receives a favourable reply from him, this is such an exception that it is specially highlighted. His encounter with the Syro-Phoenician woman (Mark 7.25–30) further proves his reluctance to have contact with Gentiles, although the healing of a demon-possessed man in the Gentile region of the Decapolis (Mark 5 par.) may be particularly significant. In all this Jesus was very much a devout first-century Palestinian Jew.[16]

Yet Jesus, by any account, was not a typical Palestinian Jew. And he did not come to leave Judaism intact. John P. Meier admirably pinpoints why Jesus was on the margins of Jewish culture:

(1) Jesus in his own day "was at most a blip on the radar screen," in the estimation of the larger Greco-Roman world, as is shown by what Josephus, Tacitus and Suetonius say about him; (2) Jesus had obviously been pushed to the margins of his own society, as his death on the cross shows; (3) in a sense Jesus marginalized himself by giving up his trade (carpentry) and becoming jobless and itinerant to pursue his ministry; and he was further marginalized when this career decision led to his rejection by many, including his hometown folks and a number of his family members; (4) Jesus's teaching on such subjects as divorce, fasting, celibacy and the like was marginal in the sense that it was not mainstream, "it did not jibe with the views and practices of the major Jewish religious groups of his day"; (5) and Jesus's style of teaching and living pushed him to the margin so that he appeared "obnoxious, dangerous, or suspicious to everyone from pious Pharisees through political high priests to an ever vigilant Pilate."[17]

> *With all the marvelous heritage that Christianity and Judaism share, there were, however, and continue to be, three irreconcilable differences between the two regarding Jesus.*

We can press the matter further. With all the marvelous heritage that Christianity and Judaism share, there were, however, and continue to be, three irreconcilable differences between the two regarding Jesus. First, Jesus did in some sense bring an end to the Mosaic Law (see Mark 7; Matt. 5:17; John 1:17; cf. Galatians 3; Rom. 10:4; Hebrews in general). His seeming disregard of the kosher laws frustrated his Pharisaic opponents to no end, and they him (Matt. 25). Second, Jesus's death on the cross signaled to Jews in his day that he was accursed by God (Deut. 21:23). How could there be a cursed Messiah? Trypho's complaint to the church father Justin Martyr (AD 140) about Jesus's crucifixion still holds true for many Jews today:

> Be assured that all our nation awaits the Messiah; and we admit that all the Scriptures which you have quoted refer to him. Moreover, I also admit that the name of Jesus by which the son of Nun was called, has inclined me very strongly to adopt this view. But we are in doubt about whether the Messiah should be so shamefully crucified. For whoever is crucified is said in the Law to be accursed, so that I am very skeptical on this point. It is quite clear, to be sure, that the Scriptures announce that the Messiah had to suffer, but we wish to learn if you can prove it to us whether by suffering he was cursed.[18]

Third, Jesus's claim that he was God bespoke blasphemy to the ears of the Jewish leadership (Mark 14:62–64). The bottom line is that harmony between Jews and Christians over these three issues does not seem likely in the near future.

Jesus and Islam

Since September 11, 2001, the relationship between Christianity and Islam has been under intense scrutiny. Not since the Crusades have these two world religions collided as they do today. However confusing the issues between Christianity and Islam may be, most people believe (rightly we think) that the vast majority of Muslims are peaceful-minded, well-intentioned individuals, and that it is only the terrorist minority that has sought to communicate otherwise. Either way, Islam cannot be ignored. It is the fastest growing religion in the world, numbering some one billion adherents. How did Islam get started? What are its teachings? And how does this religion compare and contrast with Christianity? Muhammad was born about AD 570 in the city of Mecca in Arabia. Muhammad's father died before his birth; his mother died when he was six. He was raised first by his grandfather and later by his uncle. Muhammad's early background is not well known. Some scholars believe he came from a well-respected family, but this is not certain. What is clear is that he was of the Hashimite clan of the Al Qu'raysh tribe. At the age of 25, he married a wealthy 40-year-old widow named Khadijah. Of his life, Sir Norman Anderson relates:

> There is evidence in a tradition which can scarcely have been fabricated that Muhammad suffered in early life from fits. Be that as it may, the adult Muhammad soon showed signs of a markedly religious disposition. He would retire to caves for seclusion and meditation; he frequently practiced fasting; and he was prone

to dreams. Profoundly dissatisfied with the polytheism and crude superstitions of his native Mecca, he appears to have become passionately convinced of the existence and transcendence of one true God. How much of this conviction he owed to Christianity or Judaism it seems impossible to determine.... There can be no manner of doubt, moreover, that at some period of his life he absorbed much teaching from Talmudic sources and had contact with some form of Christianity; and it seems overwhelmingly probable that his early adoption of monotheism can be traced to one or both of these influences....

For the rest, his character seems, like that of many another, to have been a strange mixture. He was a poet rather than a theologian: a master improvisor rather than a systematic thinker. That he was in the main simple in his tastes and kindly in his disposition there can be no doubt; he was generous, resolute, genial and astute; a shrewd judge and a born leader of men. He could, however, be cruel and vindictive to his enemies; he could stoop to assassination; and he was undeniably sensual.[19]

By the age of forty, Muhammad had his first divine vision. These revelations are recorded in the Qur'an (Koran). This new faith encountered opposition in Muhammad's hometown of Mecca. Because of his rejection there and the ostracism generated by his views, Muhammad and his followers withdrew to the city now known as Medina, which means in full, "City of the Prophet."

The Dome of the Rock

The Dome of the Rock was built in AD 691 over the site of the Jews' First and Second Temple by Abdel Malik ibn Marwan. The rock on the top of Mount Moriah is in the center of the Dome of the Rock, which is one of the most beautiful and important mosques in the Muslim world. It is built, according to Jewish tradition, on the rock on which Abraham was about to sacrifice his son, Isaac. The Ark of the Covenant in the First Temple stood here. The rock is holy to Muslims as well; according to their tradition, Muhammad ascended to heaven on his winged steed from here.

The Hijira, which means "flight," marks the turning point in Islam. All Islamic calendars mark this date, July 16, 622, as their beginning. Thus, AD 630 would be 8 AH (8 years after the Hijira).

In his early years in Medina, Muhammad was sympathetic to both Jews and Christians. But they rejected him and his teaching. Upon that rejection, Muhammad turned from Jerusalem as the center of worship of Islam, to Mecca, where the famous black stone Ka'aba was enshrined. Muhammad denounced all the idols which surrounded the Ka'aba and declared it was a shrine for the one true god, Allah.

With this new emphasis on Mecca, Muhammad realized he must soon return to his home. The rejected prophet did indeed return in triumph, conquering the city. John B. Noss details some of Muhammad's actions upon his return to Mecca:

One of his first acts was to go reverently to the Ka'aba; yet he showed no signs of yielding to the ancient Meccan polytheism. After honoring the Black Stone and riding seven times around the shrine, he ordered the destruction of the idols within it and the scraping of the paintings of Abraham from the walls. He sanctioned the use of the well Zamzam and restored the boundary pillars defining the sacred territory around Mecca. Thenceforth no Muslim would have cause to hesitate about going on a pilgrimage to the ancient holy city.

> *The basis for Islamic doctrine is found in the Qur'an (Koran).*

Muhammad now made sure of his political and prophetic ascendancy in Arabia. Active opponents near at hand were conquered by the sword, and tribes far away were invited sternly to send delegations offering their allegience. Before his sudden death in 632 he knew he was well on the way to unifying the Arab tribes under a theocracy governed by the will of God. Between the return to Mecca and Muhammad's death, the prophet zealously and militantly propagated Islam, and the new faith quickly spread throughout the area.[20]

Throughout history, Islam has been divided into three basic groups: the Sunnis (the less strict group), the Shi'a (the strict conservatives) and the Sufis (the religious mystics).

The basis for Islamic doctrine is found in the Qur'an (Koran). Kenneth Boa describes the central place of the Qur'an in the Islamic faith, as well as the position of supplementary works:

> The Koran is the authoritative scripture of Islam. About four-fifths the length of the New Testament, it is divided into 114 surahs (chapters). Parts were written by Muhammad, and the rest, based on his oral teaching, was written from memory by his disciples after Muhammad's death.
>
> Over the years a number of additional sayings of Muhammad and his early disciples were compiled. These comprise the *Hadith* ("tradition"), the sayings of which are called *sunna* ("custom"). The Hadith supplements the Koran much as the Talmud supplements the Law in Judaism.[21]

The Qur'an is the word of God for Islam, their holy scriptures. As the authoritative text, it is the main guide for all matters of faith and practice. For Muslims, the Qur'an was revealed to Muhammad as the word of God for mankind.

Other revelations include the *Torat* (of Moses), the *Suhuf* (books of the prophets), *Zabur* (psalms of David), and *Injil* (gospel of Jesus). The Qur'an supposedly supercedes all these revelations and is the only one of which is the original text: all others have been corrupted, almost beyond recognition.

Islam, for example, would not consider our New Testament to be the Injil (gospel of Jesus) because it contains others' words about Jesus, not just the words of Jesus. Only the Qur'an is infallible. Muhammad and the Qur'an are that which Islam is to follow alone.[22]

Thus Stephen Neill comments:

> It is well known that at many points the Qur'an does not agree with the Jewish and Christian Scriptures. Therefore, from the Muslim point of view, it follows of necessity that these Scriptures must have been corrupted. Historical evidence makes no impression on the crushing force of the syllogism. So it is, and it can be no other way. The Muslim controversialist feels no need to study evidence in detail. The only valid picture of Jesus Christ is that which is to be found in the pages of the Qur'an.[23]

The 114 surahs, or chapters, in the Qur'an are arranged by length—the longer in front, the shorter in back:

> For the Muslims, the Koran is the Word of God, confirming and consummating earlier revealed books and thereby replacing them; its instrument or agent of revelation is the Prophet Muhammad, the last and most perfect of a series of messengers of God to mankind—from Adam through Abraham to Moses and Jesus, the Christian claims for whose divinity are strongly rejected. Indeed there is no people to whom a prophet has not come. Although Muhammad is only a human creature of God, he has nevertheless an unequaled importance in the Koran itself which sets him only next to God as deserving of moral and legal obedience. Hence his sayings and deeds (Sunna) served as a second basis, besides the Koran, of the belief and practice of Islam.
>
> The Koran (which, for the Muslim, is the miracle par excellence of Muhammad, unsurpassable in form as well as in content) is a forceful document basically expressing an *élan* of religious and social justice. The early chapters (surahs) of the Koran, reflecting Muhammad's grim struggle against the Meccans, are characterized by grave warnings of the imminent judgment, while the later surahs, of the Medina period, are chiefly directed to regulating the internal and external affairs of the young Muslim community-state, besides narrating the stories of the earlier prophets.
>
> The koranic theology is rigorously monotheistic: God is absolutely unique—"there is nothing like him"—omnipotent, omniscient, merciful. Men are exhorted to obey his will (*i.e.*, to be Muslim) as is necessarily done by all inorganic objects. Special responsibility is laid on man who willingly, although with his characteristically foolish pride, accepted "the trust," refused by all creation. Besides human beings and angels, the Koran speaks of the jinn, both good and evil, to whom sometimes the devil is represented as belonging.[24]

There are five articles of faith from which flow the main doctrines of Islam:

1. God: There is one true God, "Allah." Allah is all-knowing, all-powerful, and the sovereign judge. He is unknowable because of his vast superiority over human beings. Allah is the source of good and evil, and his will is supreme. The focus is on judgment and power.
2. Angels: The angel Gabriel appeared to Muhammad to deliver the revelations in the Qur'an. There was also an evil being, most likely a fallen angel or jinn, "Al Shaytan," the devil. Jinn refers to creatures who are between angels and men, and which can be either evil or good.
3. Scripture: The Qur'an is the most recent and final word from God to humans and replaces all the other works.
4. Prophets: God has spoken through numerous prophets over the years, the six greatest being: Adam, Noah, Abraham, Moses, Jesus, and Muhammad. Muhammad is the last and greatest of all the prophets.
5. Last days: The last days will be a time of resurrection and judgment. Those who follow Allah and Muhammad will enter Islamic heaven, "Paradise"—a place of pleasure. Those who have opposed them will experience torment in hell.[25]

> **There are five articles of faith from which flow the main doctrines of Islam.**

Besides the five major beliefs or doctrines in Islam, there are also "Five Pillars of Faith":

1. The creed: "There is no God but Allah, and Muhammad is the prophet of Allah."
2. Prayer: Prayer is central to a devout Muslim. Muslims pray five times a day: upon rising, at noon, in mid-afternoon, after sunset, and before retiring. The postures involved in these prayer times are standing, kneeling, and hands and face on the ground. The call to prayer is sounded by the Muslim crier from a tower called a minaret, which is part of the *Mosqut* (Mosque), the Muslim place of worship.
3. Almsgiving: Stemming from the fact that Muhammad was an orphan and had a deep desire to help the poor, Muslims are required to give one-fortieth of their income for the destitute.
4. Fasting: Muslims fast for the entire month of Ramadan (early spring). They do so from sunup to sundown for the month. No smoking or sexual pleasures may be enjoyed.
5. Pilgrimage: All Muslims are expected to make a pilgrimage to Mecca once during their lifetime. In the case of extreme sickness, Muslims can designate someone to take their place. The trip is an essential part in Muslims gaining salvation.

It is obvious that Islam and Christianity share a number of foundational beliefs: monotheism, Abraham as the father of their faith, holiness and obedience to God, and concern for the poor. The same, of course, could be said of Judaism. But there are irreconcilable differences between the ways of Jesus and Muhammad. First, Islam, like Judaism, rejects the concept of the Trinity—"there is no God but Allah." Second, Islam believes the Bible is filled with errors because of the transmission process, which they contrast to the Koran, which came directly to Muhammad free of translation error because it was revealed and written in Arabic. Because of this Muslims deplore translations of the Koran into other languages. Third, Islam rejects the New Testament portrayal of Jesus Christ, though Muslims have a high regard for Jesus. Max Kershaw notes:

> In this regard, the Muslim view of Jesus is significant. The Qur'an presents Jesus as one of the great prophets. He is called the Messiah. He is declared to have been born of the virgin Mary. He lived a sinless life (Surah 19:19). He accomplished many wonderful miracles, such as the giving of sight to the blind, healing of lepers and the raising of the dead (3:49). He is going to return to the earth again to establish Islam throughout the earth. He is called "the Word of God" (3:45) and "the Spirit from God" (4:171). Thus, Muslims have a high view of Jesus.[26]

But, in reality, Islam rejects the biblical portrait of Christ. For the Christian, the resurrection of Jesus Christ and his status as the incarnate Son of God are vital cornerstones of faith, yet the Muslim does not hold to either of these truths. In fact, Muslims do not even believe Jesus was crucified; rather, many believe Judas was crucified in his place. Some, however, believe it was Christ on the cross but that he did not die.

Islam does believe Jesus was a sinless prophet, although not as great a prophet as Muhammad. While Surah 3:45–47 in the Qur'an speaks of the virgin birth of Christ, Jesus is certainly *not* the only begotten Son of God, and an angel—rather than the Holy Spirit—was the agency of God's power in the conception. Indeed, the idea that Allah had a son is repugnant to Islam. Surah 4:171 states, "Jesus . . . was only a messenger of Allah. . . . Far is it removed from his transcendent majesty that He should have a son."[27]

Islam does believe Jesus was a sinless prophet, although not as great a prophet as Muhammad.

Of the crucifixion, the Qur'an states in Surah 4:157, "They killed him not nor crucified, but the resemblance of Jesus was put over another man." Most Muslims believe, as noted above, that Judas was put in the place of Christ, and Christ went to heaven.

Consequently, Muslims differ in their view of sin and salvation. Since Muhammad did not die for sin nor was he resurrected, in contrast to Jesus Christ, Islam operates under a legalistic system and Muslims must earn their salvation by adhering to the Five Articles of Faith and following the Pillars of Faith.

CHRISTIANITY AND WORLD RELIGIONS: FOUR THEORIES

Our original question was, is Jesus the only way to salvation or are there other legitimate paths to God? In this section, we survey four different answers to that query: pluralism, universalism, exclusivism, and inclusivism. Furthermore, we necessarily utilize the broader New Testament, not just the Gospels, in our discussion.

"Pluralism" means that everybody's "truth" is fine; that there are many equally acceptable religious paths to God by whatever name we call God. The only approach that is unacceptable is a dogmatic stance that claims to be the true religion. While this is a politically correct perspective, it is also at odds with the message of the New Testament, which is that Jesus is "the way and the truth and the life" in terms of knowing God (John 14:6 NIV). Moreover, "there is no other name under heaven given to men by which we must be saved" (Acts 4:12 NIV) because God has fully and finally revealed himself through Jesus Christ (Heb. 1:1–4). And the resurrection of Jesus, in contrast to the non-resurrection of Buddha, Muhammad, and any other religious leader, sets Christianity apart from all other faith perspectives.

"Universalism," like the next two categories, does operate from a Christian frame of reference. Based on 1 Corinthians 15:22 ("For as in Adam all die, so in Christ all will be made alive" [NIV]), universalism teaches that Jesus's death and resurrection automatically saved all humanity. The slogan of this perspective is, "Christ's death is *efficient* for all," meaning Christ's atonement was fully effective in covering all of humankind's sin. In other words, all people, regardless of religion, are saved. The church's job, therefore, is not to evangelize the lost but rather to announce to all that they are already Christians. This proclamation, then, will result in a transformed life.

As appealing as this theory is, it is neither supported by Paul in particular, nor by the New Testament as a whole. For it is clear from the New Testament that a person is only in Christ by faith; a person must volitionally decide to accept Jesus (John 3:16-18).[28]

"Exclusivism" takes a hard line when it comes to Christianity and other religions: Even if people respond positively to the truth that is in creation in general and religion in particular, they are nevertheless lost unless they hear and respond to the gospel of Jesus Christ. This approach is based on a passage like Romans 1:18–2:16, which asserts that both the "heathen" and "religious" will not have a leg to stand on when judgment day comes if they have not received Christ. While this is true, it is not, however, the whole of the story, as the fourth theory will point out.

"Inclusivism" certainly disagrees with pluralism and universalism in their offer of salvation apart from personal faith in Jesus, and agrees with exclusivism on this point. But there is a major difference between inclusivism and exclusivism: Inclusivism is associated with the belief that God will give more light to those who respond positively to the truth they have in creation, which culminates in the full disclosure of the gospel of Christ. This is made clear in Acts 10, where we read of the conversion of Cornelius the Roman centurion. Cornelius, apparently at first a pagan Gentile, responded positively to the truth that there is one God, the God of the Old Testament; Acts 10:2 calls him "God-fearing" (NIV). We are told that Cornelius regularly sought God (v. 2). Consequently, the Lord gave a vision to the centurion, telling him that he was about to receive more revelation (vv. 3–6, 22), which he did indeed through the apostle Peter (vv. 24–43). Cornelius and his family then accepted Christ (vv. 44–48).[29] This is biblical confirmation that God reveals his truth, apparently in stages, to those who receive the divine light they have exposure to, culminating in the offer of the gospel.

> *Inclusivism is associated with the belief that God will give more light to those who respond positively to the truth they have in creation, culminating in the full disclosure of the gospel of Christ.*

Marvin's personal experience confirms this pattern of revelation. On a short-term mission trip to the island of Pohnpei, Micronesia, some years ago, he worked with some seventy pastors for a part of a summer, teaching biblical courses. The pastors related to him how the gospel came to the island in the late 1800s. The "religion" of the island at that time was witchcraft. But the tribal chieftain had a dream that a boat would come to the island with "good news." At the same time, back in Boston, a number of Congregational churches were having a contest to see if Sunday school children could collect enough pennies to send a boatload of gospel tracts to the Western Pacific Islands. Sure enough, the children reached their goal and sent, not one, but five boatloads of gospel tracts to their intended destination. One day the islanders of Pohnpei reported to their chief that a big boat from afar had landed on the island, and the chief realized that his dream had more than come true: five boats filled with gospel tracts were distributed to the inhabitants of the island and beyond by canoe. And the whole island was converted to Christ. Every summer, Pohnpeians celebrate in

C. S. Lewis on Christianity and World Religions

C. S. Lewis's *The Last Battle* of the Narnia series records the encounter between a pagan named Emeth and Lord Aslan (Christ). Which of the four theories highlighted in this section regarding the relationship between Christianity and world religions best captures the following scene?

"Then I fell at his feet and thought, Surely this is the hour of death, for the Lion (who is worthy of all honour) will know that I have served Tash all my days and not him. Nevertheless, it is better to see the Lion and die than to be Tisroc of the world and live and not to have seen him. But the Glorious One bent down his golden head and touched my forehead with his tongue and said, Son, thou art welcome. But I said, Alas, Lord, I am no son of thine but the servant of Tash. He answered, Child, all the service thou hast done to Tash, I account as service done to me. Then by reason of my great desire for wisdom and understanding, I overcame my fear and questioned the Glorious One and said, Lord, is it then true, as the Ape said, that thou and Tash are one? The Lion growled so that the earth shook (but his wrath was not against me) and said, It is false. Not because he and I are one, but because we are opposites, I take to me the services which thou hast done to him. For I and he are of such different kinds that no service which is vile can be done to me, and none which is not vile can be done to him. Therefore, if any man swear by Tash and keep his oath for oath's sake, it is by me that he has truly sworn, though he know it not, and it is I who reward him. And if any man do a cruelty in my name, then, though he says the name Aslan, it is Tash whom he serves and by Tash his deed is accepted. Dost thou understand, child? I said, Lord, thou knowest how much I understand. But I said also (for the truth constrained me), Yet I have been seeking Tash all my days. Beloved, said the Glorious One, unless thy desire had been for me thou wouldst not have sought so long and so truly. For all find what they truly seek."[30]

their churches the arrival of the boats with the "good news" that converted the island.

So the inclusivists' approach to Christianity and the world's major religions is this: If people respond to the truth that is in their religion (assuming that all truth is God's truth), God will increasingly reveal more light to them, culminating in the revelation of the gospel of Jesus's death and resurrection for their salvation. But it is their decision at that point whether or not to respond to that truth. This way seems to us to account for both God's justice and grace which are rooted in the good news of Jesus Christ.

CONCLUSION

We live in a day of pluralism, in which it is politically correct to say that all religions are of equal value and whatever one believes, as long as one is sincere, is a valid path to God. This appears to be a tolerant, open-minded approach in which one avoids offending any particular religious group; thus, on the surface, it seems the "right" thing to do. However, in surveying Judaism, Buddhism, and Islam, it is clear that these religions are not as hospitable to Christianity as one might imagine—they certainly do not believe that Christianity is as valid a path to God as are their approaches. It can be surprising to learn that the religious flexibility of "political correctness" is not reciprocated. Indeed, Christianity is viewed as inferior to their religious perspectives. Thus, it is naïve to assume that these other faith systems are truly respectful toward the tenets of Christianity. Quite the opposite can be the case.

Although one certainly needs to respect others, including their religious faith, there are areas in which the differences between the beliefs of Christianity and other world religions are simply irreconcilable. Jesus does not claim to be just another prophet in a long line of those who would teach us who God is. He claims to be the only way to God, the final fulfillment for which the human heart has longed since the beginning of time. And, in the end, he is the one who rose from the dead and, as Christians believe, is now seated at the right hand of God the Father. Our hope is based on the belief that he will return again to earth one day, not just as another prophet, but rather as the visible Lord of all.

> *Although one certainly needs to respect others, including their religious faith, there are areas in which the differences between the beliefs of Christianity and other world religions are simply irreconcilable.*

DISCUSSION QUESTIONS

1. What is pluralism as it relates to religious belief?
2. What are the Four Noble Truths and the Eightfold Path to which Buddhists ascribe?

3. What are the "apparent" parallels between the beliefs of Buddhism and Christianity?

4. What are four irreconcilable differences between Christianity and Buddhism?

5. Was it Jesus's purpose to leave Judaism intact?

6. Are there beliefs which Judaism and Christianity share in common?

7. What are the irreconcilable differences between Christianity and Judaism?

8. For Muslims, what are the Five Articles of Faith and the Five Pillars of Faith that they are expected to believe and practice?

9. Are there any commonalities in the belief systems of Islam and Christianity?

10. What are four irreconcilable differences between Christianity and Islam?

11. There are four different answers offered in this chapter to the following question: "Is Jesus the only way to salvation, or are there other legitimate paths to God?" What are they? Which one do you support?

CONCLUSION

"Who Do Men Say That I Am?"

||||||||||||||||||||||||||||||||||||||||||||||||||||||||||||||||||||||||||||||||||||||||

Yes, Jesus is certainly in the news today. Questions are being asked about what he actually said and did, including whether he was married to Mary Magdalene; and controversy rages over a number of other issues regarding Jesus, such as who was actually responsible for his death by crucifixion, whether we have his actual burial cloth, if the earliest archeological reference to Jesus has been found, and if a possible biblical prediction as to Jesus's return has been identified, to name but a few. Let's briefly summarize each of the topics we have addressed in this book:

CHAPTER 1

Chapter 1 introduced the scholars of the Jesus Seminar. These individuals, who subscribe to the "seven pillars of scholarly wisdom," concluded that only eighteen percent of the sayings and acts traditionally attributed to Jesus are actually authentic; as a result, they have produced their own color-coded edition of the Gospels. Are they correct? Based on an examination of their agenda and methodology, our conclusion was "no!"

CHAPTER 2

In chapter 2 we addressed the issue of whether the *Gospel of Thomas* should replace the Gospel of John. It is really a question of who is right—historic Christianity or Gnosticism? Elaine Pagels has long championed the Gnostic cause in American religion, writing best-sellers on the subject, including her most recent work, *Beyond Belief.* Pagels asserts that the *Gospel of Thomas* is a more promising path to spirituality because of its teaching that truth is not revelation from God outside the individual but rather truth is within the individual, waiting to be discovered and experienced. This sounds appealing and interesting until one really understands what that means, for the content of that teaching is that Christians are actually none other than Christ, newly created in the image of God! Pagels claims that the Gospel of John was written precisely to squash the growing popularity of *Thomas* in the first-century church. She is undoubtedly a brilliant writer. However, she does not reveal that she is in the minority of scholars who date the *Gospel of Thomas* to the first century, a fact pivotal to her argumentation. Nor does she reveal the lifestyle of the Gnostics, the behavioral outcome of the belief system she advocates—asceticism and/or libertinism. We, however, cast our vote for historic Christianity as depicted in the Gospel of John.

CHAPTER 3

Chapter 3 introduced us to the New Testament apocryphal gospels. Do they provide clues to Jesus's silent years? We looked at *Proto-Evangelium of James*, which defends both Jesus's virginal conception and Mary's perpetual virginity, as well as the *Arabic Infancy Gospel* and *Pseudo-Matthew,* which claim that Jesus as a young child in Egypt was every bit the supernatural Son of God that he was in adulthood, performing miracles that sometimes were bizarre in nature. The *Infancy Gospel of Thomas* focuses on Jesus from the ages of five to twelve, revealing a rather badly behaved, miracle-working boy. Are these documents correct? Should they have been included in the New Testament canon? Our conclusion was no. While a reading of apocryphal gospels is fascinating and beneficial from the standpoint of understanding the culture, customs, and complexity of the early centuries of Christianity, they serve as a foil to the canonical Gospels, for the stories contained within them are clearly legends not based in fact. Although they purport to have been written as contemporaries of the canonical Gospels, they were actually written much later. As such, it is clear that the New Testament apocryphal gospels are an offshoot of orthodox Christianity, not merely a collection of additional supplementary and complementary materials to the four Gospels.

CHAPTER 4

In chapter 4 we considered the authenticity of an ossuary bearing the inscription: "James, son of Joseph, brother of Jesus." Is it bona fide? If so, it is not only the *real* deal, but also a *big* deal for it would be the first archeological proof of Jesus's existence. Proponents and opponents of the ossuary have their own agendas, while heated debate continues. It is our opinion that only time will tell whether or not it is actually the bone box of James, the brother of Jesus.

CHAPTER 5

Chapter 5 dealt with the novel *The Da Vinci Code.* Has the Catholic Church suppressed the truth about Jesus and Mary Magdalene? Were they actually lovers who married and bore children? There is no doubt that Dan Brown is a creative, engaging writer whose book is almost impossible to put down once one begins to read it. And, if it is simply a work of fiction, that is one thing—unsettling perhaps, but not to be taken seriously. But it is not fictitious from the perspective of the author. Dan Brown has repeatedly stated his belief that *The Da Vinci Code* is based in fact. Is he right? In our estimation, Brown's portrait of Jesus and his relationship with Mary Magdalene is flawed, and his premise that they were married and had children simply is not rooted in reliable evidence.

CHAPTER 6

In chapter 6, we examined the question, "Who killed Jesus?" Critics of Mel Gibson's film *The Passion of the Christ* claim, among other things, that the film is anti-Semitic in nature. We don't agree with this assessment. Bottom line—who is responsible for the crucifixion of Jesus? In our opinion, the answer is both the sins of some ancient Jews and Romans as well as the transgressions of all of humanity. In other words, you and me. Jesus died to pay the price for the sins of the whole world.

CHAPTER 7

Chapter 7 investigated the Shroud of Turin and the crucial question it raises: Is it the burial cloth of Jesus as some claim, or a brilliant forgery, or perhaps even the creation of a well-meaning individual who wished to graphically portray the sufferings of Jesus? The conclusion we reached was that the Shroud is most likely an artist's representation of the suffering of Jesus from around the thirteenth century. But it will be fascinating to follow the debate in the days to come; we could be wrong.

CHAPTER 8

Chapter 8 tackled the long-time controversy surrounding the resurrection of Jesus. Did Jesus rise from the dead, or is one of the alternative approaches (the stolen body theory, the swoon theory, or the wrong tomb theory) more plausible? Our conclusion—the alternative theories fail to convince. We, therefore, reaffirm that Jesus did indeed rise from the dead in bodily form. And such a determination is crucial to the Christian faith, for Christianity rises or falls on the issue of the resurrection of Jesus.

CHAPTER 9

In chapter 9, we entered J. R. R. Tolkien's world of Middle-earth, dwelling place of wizards, hobbits, elves, dwarves, orcs, and humans. Does Tolkien's religious faith permeate his works? In our opinion, it does. In Tolkien's trilogy, we learn that self-sacrifice defeats evil; that good will ultimately triumph; and that heaven will be restored to earth when Christ returns as Lord of all.

CHAPTER 10

Chapter 10 dealt with the very popular books *The Bible Code* and *The Bible Code II: The Countdown* by Michael Drosnin. In these books Drosnin claims there is a predictive code in the Bible which not only forecasted past world events, but which even answers the ultimate question: When will the end of the world occur? His decoding is accomplished through use of the method of equidistant letter sequencing (ELS). Is Drosnin right? While the ELS method may appear to be valid in finding predictions in the Bible, upon closer examination one realizes that, with so many possibilities of word combinations in a long text, it is statistically rather easy to identify "predictions" about the future, even in nonbiblical texts. And then there is the problem of variation in the Hebrew text of the Old Testament. Moreover, Drosnin's failed prediction that nuclear holocaust would engulf Israel and the world in 1996 is reason for skepticism. We concluded, therefore, that, although appealing, the ELS method is simply not convincing in its claims of predictions regarding either world events or the end of the world. In our opinion, such date setting is dangerous. Rather, we share the sentiment of Jesus, that even he does not know the day and time of his return to earth.

CHAPTER 11

In chapter 11, we discussed the issue of pluralism so prevalent in today's society. Are Buddhism, Islam, and Judaism just as valid paths to God as Christianity? Is sincerity of belief, no matter what the religion, the determining factor? Although we must be careful to respect others' religious beliefs, our answer to both questions, as Christians, was no. There are irreconcilable differences between Christianity and these religions. Jesus does not claim to be one way to God, but the *only* way to God. But we do believe that God provides increasing amounts of light to those who respond to him, culminating in the offer of the gospel.

CONCLUSION

With all the hotly debated issues regarding Jesus today, the underlying questions really amount to those asked and answered by C. S. Lewis years ago: Who is Jesus Christ? Were his claims false or true?

If his claims were false, two possibilities emerge. Either he knew his claims were false, which made him a **liar**, or he didn't know his claims were false, making him a **lunatic**.

On the other hand, if his claims are true, he is truly **Lord** of all, which demands a decision from each human being. Will we choose to embrace Jesus, committing our lives to him, or will we turn away, choosing not to follow him?

What is your decision?

Notes

Chapter 1

1. Robert W. Funk, Roy W. Hoover, and the Jesus Seminar, *The Five Gospels: What Did Jesus Really Say? The Search for the Authentic Words of Jesus* (San Francisco: HarperSanFrancisco, 1997). Some eighty scholars are listed on the roster on pages 533–37, though curiously in the introduction (p. 34) the authors say two hundred scholars joined the group.

2. The five Gospels, as they list them in order, are Mark, Matthew, Luke, John, and the *Gospel of Thomas* (more on this last work later).

3. Robert W. Funk, ed., *The Acts of Jesus: What Did Jesus Really Do? The Search for the Authentic Deeds of Jesus* (San Francisco: HarperSanFrancisco, 1998). The sources used are Q, or *Quelle*, 235 statements purportedly from Jesus that Matthew and Luke share in common. The *Gospel of Thomas* is excluded from this work because it records 114 sayings of Jesus but no deeds of Jesus, while the *Gospel of Peter* is added, a New Testament apocryphal gospel dating no earlier than the second century AD. While evangelicals are hospitable to the hypothetical Q document, they categorically reject the claim of canonical status for the *Gospel of Thomas* and the *Gospel of Peter*.

4. The American president Thomas Jefferson (1743–1826) was anti-supernatural so he excised any statement about miracles in the Gospels in his *The Life and Morals of Jesus of Nazareth, Extracted Textually from the Gospels in Greek, Latin, French and English*. It was not published until 1904.

5. David Friedrich Strauss's famous book was entitled *Life of Jesus Critically Examined* (1835). It is a 1,400-page book.

6. Here are two helpful books, conservative in content, that criticize the Jesus Seminar. Ben Witherington III, *The Jesus Quest: The Third Search for the Jew of Nazareth* (Downer's Grove, IL: InterVarsity, 1995), especially pp. 42–57; and Michael J. Wilkins and J. P. Moreland, eds., *Jesus under Fire: Modern Scholarship Reinvents the Historical Jesus* (Grand Rapids: Zondervan, 1995).

7. Funk, Hoover, and the Jesus Seminar, *The Five Gospels*, p. 36.

8. See Wilkins and Moreland, *Jesus under Fire* and Witherington, *The Jesus Quest* for a bibliography of those who argue against the methodology and results of the Jesus Seminar.

9. Witherington, *The Jesus Quest*, pp. 45–46.

10. Craig L. Blomberg, "Where Do We Start Studying Jesus?" in *Jesus under Fire*, p. 18.

11. The quip comes from Richard B. Hays, "The Correct Jesus," *First Things* 43 (1994): p. 44.

208

12. Albert Schweitzer, *The Quest of the Historical Jesus: A Critical Study of Its Progress from Reimarus to Wrede*, trans.W. Montgomery (1906; repr. New York: Macmillan, 1968).

13. Funk, Hoover, and the Jesus Seminar, *The Five Gospels*, pp. 2–4. Evangelicals do not reject all of these seven pillars, numbers 3 and 4 in particular.

14. See the Jewish historian Josephus, *Antiquities of the Jews* 18:16–19; 63–64; the Jewish Talmud, Babylonian Talmud *Sanhedrin*—43a, 107b; the Roman historian Tacitus, *Annals* 15:44, Pliny the Roman governor of Bithynia, *Letters*, 10.96.

15. For documentation of the historical reliability of the Gospel of John, see Craig L. Blomberg, *The Historical Reliability of John's Gospel: Issues and Commentary* (Downers Grove, IL: InterVarsity, 2001). On the some forty similarities between the passion narratives in Luke and John alone, see Raymond E. Brown, *The Gospel According to John, Vol. XIII–XX*, vol. 29a of the *Anchor Bible Series* (Garden City, NY: Doubleday, 1966), pp. 7, 90–91.

16. An older generation of scholars thought Matthew wrote Q (based on Papias's remark that Matthew recorded the oracles of the Lord), while an increasing number of scholars in our day, Martin Hengel included, suspect that Luke authored Q. Polykarp, John's disciple, reports that Mark was guided by Peter in writing his Gospel; see Eusebius, *Ecclesiastical History*, III. XXXIX 15. For a recent defense of Matthew's dependence on Luke, perhaps the author of Q, see Martin Hengel, *The Four Gospels and the One Gospel of Jesus Christ: An Investigation of the Collection and Origin of the Canonical Gospels* (Harrisburg, PA: Trinity Press International), pp. 186–207. But even if Q was not written by Luke, that need not detract from Q's reliability as a source of Jesus's sayings.

17. See again Schweitzer, *The Quest of the Historical Jesus*.

18. Funk, Hoover, and the Jesus Seminar, *The Five Gospels*, p. 40.

19. For further discussion see Robert H. Stein, *The Synoptic Problem: An Introduction* (Grand Rapids: Baker, 1988), pp. 197–203.

20. First Corinthians 15:3–4 has been long recognized by scholars as a credal statement Paul received from the Jerusalem church.

21. Ernst Käsemann shocked his former teacher, Rudolph Bultmann, by affirming a more conservative approach to the Gospels in his paper, "The Problem of the Historical Jesus," at a reunion of University of Marburg students—the place Bultmann taught for years! Martin Hengel's rather conservative view is expressed in *The Four Gospels*.

22. The Jesus Seminar dates the *Gospel of Thomas* as early as AD 50, over ten years before Mark, the first canonical Gospel to be written (ca. AD 64–68). See Funk, Hoover, and the Jesus Seminar, *The Five Gospels*, p. 474.

23. Unless otherwise specified, the translation of the *Gospel of Thomas* in this chapter comes from Wilhelm Schneemelcher, ed., *New Testament Apocrypha*, trans. R. McL. Wilson, vol. 1 of *Gospels and Related Writings* (Cambridge, England: James Clarke and Company; Louisville: John Knox Press, 1991).

24. Funk, Hoover, and the Jesus Seminar, *The Five Gospels*, p. 5.

25. Rudolph Bultmann was a twentieth-century liberal German theologian who popularized the notion that the later church created the sayings of Jesus and placed them on his lips as though authentic. His groundbreaking book was *The History of the Synoptic Tradition*, trans. John Marsh (Oxford: Basil Blackwell, 1963).

26. Darrell L. Bock, "The Words of Jesus in the Gospels: Live, Jive or Memorex?" in Wilkins and Moreland, *Jesus under Fire,* p. 91.

27. Funk, *Acts of Jesus*, p. 54.

28. Funk, Hoover, and the Jesus Seminar, *The Five Gospels*, pp. 285–87.

29. For further discussion, see Bock, "The Words of Jesus in the Gospels," in Wilkins and Moreland, *Jesus under Fire*, pp. 92–93.

Chapter 2

1. For the authoritative account of the story of the discovery, see James M. Robinson, "The Discovery of the Nag Hammadi Codices," *Biblical Archaeologist* 42 (1979): pp. 206–224.

2. There are two editions or rescensions of this document extant today. The first, already known in the early twentieth century, consists of three Greek papyri fragments found at Oxyrhyncus, an ancient Egyptian town, called, Oxyrhyncus Papyrus 1, which corresponds to sayings 26:30,77, and 31–33 from the Nag Hammadi Coptic complete copy of the *Gospel of Thomas*; Oxyrhyncus 654 equals *Gospel of Thomas* 1–7; Oxyrhyncus 655 equals *Gospel of Thomas* 36–40.

3. Elaine Pagels, *The Gnostic Gospels* (New York: Random House, 1979).

4. Elaine Pagels, *The Gnostic Paul: Gnostic Exegesis of the Pauline Letters* (Harrisburg, PA: Trinity Press International, 1992).

5. Elaine Pagels, *Adam, Eve, and the Serpent* (New York: Random House, 1989).

6. Elaine Pagels, *Beyond Belief: The Secret Gospel of Thomas* (New York: Random House, 2003).

7. For an excellent discussion of these issues and other related concerns regarding the canon, see F. F. Bruce, *The Canon of Scripture* (Downers Grove, IL: InterVarsity, 1988). Bruce's arguments support the traditional conclusions, namely, that the thirty-nine books of the Old Testament (following the English order) were recognized as canonical by 250 BC while the New Testament canon was in place by AD 200. See more discussion on the topic later in this chapter.

8. Pagels, *Beyond Belief*, pp. 23–25, 35–37.

9. Ibid., pp. 37–44.

10. Ibid., p. 34.

11. Ibid., pp. 44–45. She compares this to Paul's "high Christology" as reflected in Philippians 2:6–9.

12. We are following Pagels's comments, *Beyond Belief*, pp. 34–40.

13. Unless otherwise specified, the quoted translations of the *Gospel of Thomas* in this chapter come from Wilhelm Schneemelcher, ed., *New Testament Apocrypha*, trans. R. McL. Wilson, vol. 1 of *Gospels and Related Writings* (Cambridge, England: James Clarke and Company; Louisville: John Knox Press, 1991).

14. Pagels, *Beyond Belief*, p. 57.

15. *Gospel of Thomas*, 138, quoted in Pagels, *Beyond Belief*, p. 57.

16. Irenaeus *Against Heresies* 1.9.4; 1.10.1.

17. Pagels, *Beyond Belief*, pp. 72–73, 81, 112, 148–53.

18. Ibid., pp. 80–81, 86, 89–97, 111–13, 147, 166, 167. Also relevant is that here Pagels seems to contradict herself. On the one hand, in the previous point, she claims that Irenaeus imposed an orthodox straitjacket on the Gospel of John while, on the other hand, she argues that the Gospel of John was written precisely to refute the *Gospel of Thomas*. For the first position, see footnotes 13–16 above. For the second position, see chapter 2, "Gospels in Conflict: John and Thomas."

19. Ibid., pp. 6, 97, 168–80.

20. Athanasius *Festal Letter* 39.3 (AD 367), our emphasis in italics.

21. Pagels, *Beyond Belief*, pp. 176–77.

22. Also see *The Apocalypse of Baruch* 29.

23. See also The Dead Sea Scrolls *11 Q Mech.* 2.19–11; *1 Enoch* 48.2; 62.7; *4 Ezra* 13.3, 26; Mark 14:62; John 1:51; Rev. 1:12–18; 14:14.

24. Pagels, *Beyond Belief*, pp. 66–75.

25. Athanasius *Festal Letter* 39.5, 7.

26. By way of contrast, it is certain the Gospel of John was written in the late first century (ca. AD 95), because a fragment of John 17:31–33, 37–38 coming from Egypt (P52 = Papyrus 52

in the John Rylands collection) dates to AD 114. Allowing for a few years for the early church to copy the original manuscript in Ephesus, the origin of the Gospel of John, and then pass those copies along to the churches until they reached Egypt, surely dates John's Gospel in the late first century AD.

27. Pagels's Harvard mentor champions this cause; see Helmut Koester, *Ancient Christian Gospels: Their History and Development* (Harrisburg, PA: Trinity Press International, 1990). See also John Dominic Crossan, *The Cross That Spoke: The Origins of the Passion Narrative* (San Fransisco: Harper & Row, 1988), which is an exposition of the *Gospel of Peter.* Crossan argues that work dates to the first century AD. Crossan also argues that the *Gospel of Thomas* should be used as a source to investigate the historical Jesus in his best-selling book, *The Historical Jesus* (San Francisco: HarperSanFrancisco, 1991).

28. See Bruce, *The Canon of Scripture*, pp. 255–269. See also the helpful remarks by Paul D. Wegner, *The Journey from Texts to Translations: The Origin and Development of the Bible* (Grand Rapids: Baker, 1999), pp. 129–149.

29. Pagels, *Beyond Belief*, pp. 68–69.

30. Pagels quotes *Thomas* 70 with approval (*Beyond Belief*, p. 32) and, indeed, throughout her books she supports the *Gospel of Thomas*. See also the sayings in *Thomas* 11, 106, and 114.

31. See Pagels's references, ibid., pp. 130–33, 137–38, 160–63.

32. Ibid., p. 147.

33. Galatians 3:28 does not support androgyny as the goal of the Christian life. When Paul asserts, "There is neither Jew nor Greek, slave nor free, male nor female, for you are all one in Christ" (NIV), he does not obliterate racial, cultural, and gender distinctions; rather he relativizes them. They exist, unfortunately so in his day with regard to slavery, but they no longer count before God.

34. For a helpful discussion of this point, see Henry A. Virkler, *Hermeneutics: Principles and Processes of Biblical Interpretation* (Grand Rapids: Baker, 1988), pp. 48–53. Jewish interpreters also used nonliteral methods to interpret their Old Testament, for example Philo; see the discussion in text.

35. We follow Virkler, *Hermeneutics*, pp. 53–58.

36. See Virkler, *Hermeneutics*, pp. 60–73. This is not to say that Augustine always practiced what he preached about hermeneutics, as his allegorization of the Parable of the Good Samaritan (Luke 10:25–36) reveals.

37. Bernard Ramm, *Protestant Biblical Interpretation*, 3rd rev. ed. (Grand Rapids: Baker, 1970), p. 28.

38. We follow here Virkler, *Hermeneutics*, pp. 59–72.

39. Origen, a church father who was later branded a heretic, apparently spoke for many when he said of the fourth Gospel, "John does not always tell the truth *literally*, he always tells the truth *spiritually*"—that is, symbolically (*Commentary on John 10:4–6*).

40. See Pagels's discussion of this point, *Beyond Belief*, p. 119.

41. *Gospel of Truth*, 16:31–33. Unless otherwise specified, the quoted translations of the *Gospel of Truth* in this chapter come from Wilhelm Schneemelcher, *New Testament Apocrypha*.

42. *Gospel of Truth*, 24:5–9.

43. *Apocryphon of John* 2:9–14, in Wilhelm Schneemelcher, *New Testament Apocrypha*.

44. Reported in Pagels, *Beyond Belief*, pp. 126–127.

45. Recall our earlier comments on *Thomas*'s pantheistic interpretation of Scripture.

46. We already get an early semi-Gnostic espousal of asceticism in Colossians 2:21–23 where Paul refutes his opponents' teaching that harming the body enhances one's spirituality.

47. E. M. Yamauchi, "Gnosis, Gnosticism," in Gerald F. Hawthorne, Ralph P. Martin, Daniel G. Reid, *Dictionary of Paul and His Letters* (Downers Grove, IL: InterVarsity, 1993), p. 352.

Chapter 3

1. Origen, *Homily on Luke 1:11* quoted in Wilhelm Schneemelcher, ed., *New Testament Apocrypha*, trans. R. McL. Wilson, vol. 1 of *Gospels and Related Writings* (Cambridge, England: James Clarke and Company; Louisville: John Knox Press, 1991), p. 46.

2. Philip Jenkins, *Hidden Gospels: How the Search for Jesus Lost Its Way* (New York: Oxford University Press, 2001). Jenkins's work provides a devastating critique of the attempts of modern radical biblical scholars to lead the church into the way of Gnosticism via the New Testament apocryphal gospels.

3. Paul D. Wegner, *The Journey from Texts to Translations: The Origin and Development of the Bible* (Grand Rapids: Baker, 2000), p. 159.

4. *Apocryphon of James*, NHC I.2 in Schneemelcher, *New Testament Apocrypha*. Unless otherwise specified, the quoted translations of the New Testament Apocrypha in this chapter come from Schneemelcher, *New Testament Apocrypha*.

5. *Dialogue of the Savior*, in *The Nag Hammadi Library in English* (San Francisco: Harper & Row and E. J. Brill, 1988).

6. Wegner, *The Journey from Texts to Translations*, pp. 160–61.

7. Everett F. Harrison, *Introduction to the New Testament*, rev. ed. (Grand Rapids: Eerdmans, 1971), pp. 121–22.

8. *Gospel of Hebrews*, in Jerome *Ephesians* 5.4.

9. Otfried Hofius, "Unknown Sayings of Jesus," in *The Gospel and the Gospels,* ed. Peter Stuhlmacher (Grand Rapids: Eerdmans, 1991), p. 357.

10. Harrison, *Introduction to the New Testament*, pp. 122–23.

11. The text of *Proto-Evangelium of James* occurs in Schneemelcher, *New Testament Apocrypha*, pp. 426–37. For *Proto-Evangelium*'s usage of the infancy narratives in Luke and Matthew, see pp. 437–38.

12. See Oscar Cullmann's discussion in Schneemelcher, *New Testament Apocrypha*, p. 423.

13. A. K. Tebecis, *Mahikari: Thank God for the Answers at Last* (Tokyo: Yoko Shuppansha, 1982), p. 358.

14. Ibid., p. 417.

15. Ibid., p. 425. We will discuss the three views of Jesus's brothers and sisters in our next chapter, when we highlight the discovery of the ossuary of James, son of Joseph, brother of Jesus.

16. Ibid., p. 456.

17. According to Matthew 2:13–14, Joseph fled to Egypt with Mary and Jesus to escape Herod the Great's wrath at the birth of a rival king. If Jesus was born in 6 BC (as most scholars say) and since Herod died in 4 BC, then the holy family stayed in Egypt approximately two years.

18. This place is identified as Matarea in the text.

19. See Cullmann in Schneemelcher, *New Testament Apocrypha*, p. 458.

20. Is this perhaps the legend behind the beloved Christmas carol, "The Drummer Boy"?

21. See Cullmann in Schneemelcher, *New Testament Apocrypha*, pp. 439–40.

22. Ibid., p. 442.

23. This perspective is clear in the longer version of *The Infancy Gospel of Thomas,* 6.2, in Schneemelcher, *New Testament Apocrypha*, pp. 449–50. There, the boy Jesus utters a long discourse on his superior wisdom to his teachers.

24. See Jenkins, *Hidden Gospels*, p. 47. Nicholas Notovich, *The Unknown Life of Jesus Christ: From Buddhistic Records* (New York: G.W. Dillingham, 1894), pp. 155–218.

25. For discussion and refutation, see Schneemelcher, *New Testament Apocrypha*, p. 84, and Jenkins, *Hidden Gospels*, pp. 45, 47.

26. Pagels, *The Gnostic Gospels* (New York: Random House, 1979), pp. xx–xxi. Pagels makes this remark by way of introducing Thich Nhat Hanh's book *Living Buddha, Living Christ* (New York: Riverhead Books, 1995), pp. xxiii, xxvi; see also Pagels, *Beyond Belief* (New York: Random

House, 2003), pp. 75–76. Compare A. K. Tebecis, *Mahikari: Thank God for the Answers at Last* (Tokyo: Yoko Shuppansha, 1982).

27. Enakshi Bhavani, "A Journey to 'Little Tibet,'" *National Geographic* 99 (1951): p. 624.

28. See the criticism by Schneemelcher, *New Testament Apocrypha*, p. 83, and Jenkins, *Hidden Gospel*, p. 47; Ross Clifford and Philip Johnson, *Jesus and the Gods of the New Age: A Response to the Search for True Spirituality* (Colorado Springs: Victor, 2003), pp. 218–27; Enakshi Bhavani, "A Journey to 'Little Tibet,'" *National Geographic* 99 (1951): p. 624.

Chapter 4

1. See Shanks's story in Hershel Shanks and Ben Witherington III, *The Brother of Jesus: The Dramatic Story and Meaning of the First Archaeological Link to Jesus and His Family* (New York: HarperCollins, 2003), pp. xi–xiv, 3–22. The story of the James ossuary was first published in the magazine Hershel Shanks edits, "Burial Box of James the Brother of Jesus," *Biblical Archaeology Review*, November/December 2002, vol. 28, no. 6.

2. Shanks and Witherington, *The Brother of Jesus*, p. viii.

3. Ibid., pp. 11–22, 79–87.

4. Ibid., p. 80.

5. Ibid., pp. 11–12. For a thorough study on ossuaries at the time of Jesus in Jerusalem, see Craig A. Evans, *Jesus and the Ossuaries: What Jewish Burial Practices Reveal about the Beginning of Christianity* (Waco, TX: Baylor University Press, 2003).

6. Shanks and Witherington, *The Brother of Jesus*, p. 12.

7. Hence the title of chapter 3 in Shanks and Witherington: *The Brother of Jesus*: *"How Could the Son of God Have a Brother?"*

8. Ibid., p. xiii.

9. Ibid., pp. 14–16.

10. Ibid., pp. 17–20.

11. Ibid., pp. 15, 47.

12. Ibid., p. 48.

13. Ibid., p. 46.

14. Ibid., p. 34.

15. Ibid., chaps. 4–5, and the summary statement on p. 53.

16. Ibid., p. 40.

17. Ibid., p. 44.

18. Ibid., pp. 7–8.

19. For the story of the Dead Sea Scrolls find, see C. Marvin Pate, *Communities of the Last Days: The Dead Sea Scrolls, the New Testament and the Story of Israel* (Downers Grove, IL: InterVarsity, 2000), chap. 1.

20. See Evans on the history of the Rosetta Stone, *Jesus and the Ossuaries*, p. 2.

21. The Jehoash inscription describes repairs to the temple by the Judahite king Jehoash in the ninth century BC as described in 2 Kings 12 and 2 Chronicles 24.

22. The report was summarized in *Biblical Archaeology Review* 29, no. 5 (September/October 2003): pp. 26–31.

23. Lemaire, *Biblical Archaeology Review* 29, no. 6 (November/December 2003): pp. 50–59, 67, 70.

24. Shanks, *Biblical Archaeology Review* 29, no. 6, p. 52.

25. David Merling quoted in Gordon Govier, "Rush to Judgment?" *Christianity Today*, vol. 48, no. 5 (May 2004): pp. 20–21.

26. The following is indebted to Evans, *Jesus and the Ossuaries*, pp. 121–22.

27. Jesus, like most Palestinian Jews in his day, spoke Aramaic because this was the language their forebears brought back with them from Babylonian captivity (536 BC). Probably also nu-

merous Jews were familiar with Koine Greek, the language of the New Testament. From Luke 4, we learn that Jesus might have also known Hebrew, hence his reading from the Torah in the synagogue service.

28. Hegesippus, quoted in Josephus *Antiquities of the Jews* 20.199–203.

29. Hegesippus, quoted in Eusebius *Ecclesiastical History* 2.23.4–8.

30. Eusebius *Ecclesiastical History* 2.23.9–18.

31. Evans, *Jesus and the Ossuaries*, pp. 121–22. Jewish Christianity was dealt a severe blow by the Roman destruction of the Jerusalem temple in AD 70. The second Jewish revolt against Rome in AD 134–35 also failed miserably, nearly obliterating Jewish Christianity. In any event, by the mid-second century AD, Gentile Christianity dominated the theological landscape of the church.

32. Witherington, in Shanks and Witherington, *The Brother of Jesus*, p. 202.

33. Ibid., p. 202.

34. These statements are culled from Jerome's response to Helvidius in *Against Helvidius* and *DeCarne Christi* 7; see Shanks and Witherington, *The Brother of Jesus*, p. 203. Jerome argued that the James under discussion was James the Little, a Son of Mary Clopas, a sister-in-law to Joseph (Mark 15:40, John 19:25). This would make James Jesus's cousin. For a refutation of this identification, see Shanks and Witherington, *The Brother of Jesus*, pp. 200–204.

35. See *Proto-Evangelium of James*, 9.2; 17.1–2; 18.1.

36. Epiphanius's work is entitled *Panarion*; the quotations come from section 29.3.8–29.4.4; see Shanks and Witherington, *The Brother of Jesus*, pp. 205–6.

37. Quoted in Shanks and Witherington, *The Brother of Jesus*, p. 204.

Chapter 5

1. Dan Brown, *The Da Vinci Code* (New York: Doubleday, 2003), opening page.

2. In addition to our own reading of and interaction with *The Da Vinci Code*, the following critiques of that novel have been most helpful: Ben Witherington III, "Review of *The Da Vinci Code*," *Biblical Archaeological Review*, May/June 2004, vol. 30, no. 3, pp. 58–61, which is expanded in his *The Gospel Code: Novel Claims about Jesus, Mary Magdalene and Da Vinci* (Downers Grove, IL: InterVarsity, 2004); Darrell L. Bock, *Breaking the Da Vinci Code: Answers to the Questions Everyone's Asking* (Nashville: Nelson Books, a division of Thomas Nelson Publishers, 2004); and James L. Garlow and Peter Jones, *Cracking Da Vinci's Code* (Colorado Springs: Victor, 2004).

3. Brown, *The Da Vinci Code*, p. 231.

4. See Witherington, "Review of *The Da Vinci Code*," pp. 58–59; Bock, *Breaking the Da Vinci Code*, pp. 61–62.

5. All quotations of the *Gospel of Philip* and the *Gospel of Mary*, as well as all quotations from New Testament apocryphal gospels in this chapter, come from Wilhelm Schneemelcher, ed., *New Testament Apocrypha* trans. R. McL. Wilson, vol. 1 of *Gospels and Related Writings* (Cambridge, England: James Clarke and Company; Louisville: John Knox Press, 1991).

6. Witherington offers a helpful discussion of the word used here, *koinonos*:

Brown's 'scholarly' protagonist Teabing argues that the word "companion" in this passage means "spouse" because that's what the Aramaic word really means. Unfortunately, this document was not written in Aramaic. Like the other Gnostic gospels discovered at Nag Hammadi, Egypt, this document was written in Coptic! The word here for companion (*koinonos*) is actually a loan word from Greek and is neither a technical term nor a synonym for wife or spouse. It is true the term could be used to refer to a wife, since *koinonos*, like "companion," is an umbrella term, but it does not specify this fact. There was another Greek word, *gune*, which would have made this clear. It is much more likely that *koinonos* here means "sister" in the spiritual sense since that is how it is used elsewhere in this sort of literature. In any case, this text does not clearly say or even suggest that Jesus was married, much less married to Mary Magdalene. (Witherington, "Review of *The Da Vinci Code*," p. 60)

7. Bock, *Breaking the Da Vinci Code*, p. 75.

8. At one point, Teabing argues that the Nag Hammadi documents and the Dead Sea Scrolls were the truest forms of Christianity, preceding orthodox Christianity. But in chapters 1–3, we summarily dismissed the first notion. For refutation of the view that the Dead Sea Scrolls contain Christian works, see C. Marvin Pate, *Communities of the Last Days: The Dead Sea Scrolls, the New Testament and the Story of Israel* (Downers Grove, IL: InterVarsity, 2000), chaps. 1–2.

9. Brown, *The Da Vinci Code*, p. 234.

10. Ibid., p. 234.

11. We should mention here that this statement even surpasses Pagels's argument, for as we observed in chapter 2, she at least believes the Gospel of John presents Jesus as God even if, as she believes, the Synoptics do not.

12. This text of the Nicene Creed comes from *The Constitution of the Presbyterian Church (USA) Part I. The Book of Confessions* (New York: The Office of the General Assembly, 1983).

13. Witherington, "Review of *The Da Vinci Code*," p. 59.

14. Irenaeus *Against Heresies* 3.11.8

15. Justin Martyr *Dialogue with Trypho* 103.19.

16. See Bock, *Breaking the Da Vinci Code*, p. 120. Not just conservative scholars take this view; see Martin Hengel, *The Four Gospels and the One Gospel of Jesus Christ*, trans. John Bowden (Harrisburg, PA: Trinity Press International, 2000), and Larry Hurtado, *Lord Jesus Christ: Devotion to Jesus in Earliest Christianity* (Grand Rapids: Eerdmans, 2003). Both of these works oppose the "new school's" claim that Jesus was not considered divine early on. We should mention here that two threats to the church before AD 313 served as catalysts to the church's process of defining the New Testament canon: heresy, particularly Gnosticism, and persecution by the Roman empire.

17. Raymond Brown, book review of Elaine Pagels, *The Gnostic Gospels*, in *New York Times*, November 1979.

18. Brown, *The Da Vinci Code*, p. 250.

19. The book by Michael Baigent, Richard Leigh, and Henry Lincoln, *Holy Blood, Holy Grail* (New York: Dell Doubleday, 1982) helped to inspire Brown's *The Da Vinci Code*. See especially pages 313–15. In that book, the authors argue that Mary Magdalene is the Holy Grail and that her sarcophagus (burial casket) contains the *Sangreal* documents. Dan Brown's work builds on this thesis, arguing that the Holy Grail was not the cup Christ drank from at his Last Supper that was later used by Joseph of Arimathea to collect blood from the crucified Christ. Rather, the Holy Grail is the womb of Mary Magdalene. And, supposedly, Da Vinci's painting of the Last Supper has her at Jesus's left side, so that the viewer sees a V-shape created by Mary to the left and Jesus to the right. According to Teabing, "The [Catholic] Church needed to defame Mary Magdalene in order to cover up her dangerous secret—her role as the Holy Grail" (Brown, *The Da Vinci Code*, p. 244). But see the scriptural evidence below refuting any sexual or marital relationship between Jesus and Mary.

20. Brown, *The Da Vinci Code*, p. 244.

21. Ibid., p. 238 discusses this V.

22. Ibid., pp. 242-45.

23. Bock, *Breaking the Da Vinci Code*, pp. 34–35.

24. Mark 16:9–20 is not in the oldest Greek manuscripts of Mark (Sinaiticus and Vaticanus, both fourth-century manuscripts) so the reference to Mary in 16:9 may not be a legitimate reference, but 16:1, which mentions her, is.

25. One wonders if maybe the picture of Mary Magdalene as the supreme disciple of Jesus, highly revered (and perhaps even having the status of being Jesus's lover and/or wife) by *The Da Vinci Code* and the elevation of women as depicted by Pagels might be appealing to today's culture out of reaction to a patriarchal society, one in which the power base does not include women. Women are highly esteemed in these works, and are placed on equal par with men. (Although, conveniently, they do not mention that the Gnostic approach upon which they are based actually devalues women, telling them they must become males in order to have worth.)

26. Bock, *Breaking the Da Vinci Code*, pp. 19, 41–42.

27. See Garlow and Jones, *Cracking Da Vinci's Code*, p. 118.

28. Bock, *Breaking the Da Vinci Code*, p. 45.

29. Brown, *The Da Vinci Code*, p. 245.

30. Ibid, pp. 246–47.

31. Josephus *The Jewish Wars* 2.8.2.

32. See the descriptions by first-century Jewish writers like Josephus (*Antiquities* 18.1.5.20–21; *Jewish Wars* 2.8.2.) and Philo (*Hypothetica* 11.14–17).

33. See Pate's discussion, *Communities of the Last Days*, p. 81.

34. For example, Witherington, "Review of *The Da Vinci Code*," p. 60; and Bock, *Breaking the Da Vinci Code,* pp. 32–40.

35. Brown, *The Da Vinci Code*, p. 308.

36. Ibid., pp. 308–9.

37. Ibid., p. 308.

38. Ibid., p. 309.

39. We have been following the discussion by Garlow and Jones, *Cracking Da Vinci's Code*, pp. 35–36, 176, 178.

40. Ibid., pp. 182–84.

41. Brown, *The Da Vinci Code*, p. 238.

42. Ibid., p. 113.

43. Garlow and Jones, *Cracking Da Vinci's Code*, p. 203. See their documentation on p. 251.

44. Brown, *The Da Vinci Code*, p. 248.

45. *Gospel of Philip* 61a-b, 66-68, 127.

46. Irenaeus *Against Heresies* 1.21.3.

47. See Epiphanius in Irenaeus *Against Heresies* 24.3.2.

48. *Thunder, Perfect Mind* 15–34.

49. Brown, *The Da Vinci Code*, p. 309.

50. Ibid., p. 125.

Chapter 6

1. Richard Corliss, "The Goriest Story Ever Told," *Time*, vol. 163, no. 9 (March 1, 2004): p. 64.

2. Besides the four Gospels, the most notable influence on Gibson's film is the book by Anne Catherine Emmerich, *The Dolorous Passion of Our Lord Jesus Christ* (repr. Rockford, IL: TAN Books & Publishers, 1994). Emmerich was an Augustinian nun who was born on September 8, 1774, in Germany. She reportedly experienced the mystical phenomenon of the stigmata, the wounds of Christ. In addition, she claimed to have mystical visions. Her testimonies were written down by Clemens Brentano, her secretary, including the content of *The Dolorous Passion of Our Lord Jesus Christ*. Her own purported experience of the stigmata, as well as the influence of medieval passion plays, undoubtedly lies behind her graphic descriptions of Christ's passion. She died on February 9, 1824. The Catholic Church is presently considering venerating her.

3. Josephus *Jewish Wars* 5.11.1.

4. This description comes from the medical report by William D. Edwards, MD, Wesley J. Gabel, MDiv., and Floyd E. Hosman, MS, "On the Physical Death of Jesus Christ," *Journal of American Medical Association* 255, no. 11 (March 21, 1986): pp. 1455–57.

5. Ibid., pp. 1458–60. For a description of the 1968 archaeological discovery of the bones of a crucified man in Israel, see Peter Connolly, *Living in the Time of Jesus of Nazareth* (Israel: Steimatzky, 1993), p. 51. The findings confirm the Gospels' accounts of how Jesus was crucified.

6. See Acts 5:30; 13:29; 1 Peter 2:24; cf. the Dead Sea Scrolls: Q Pesher Nahum 3.4.1.7–8; 11 Q Temple Scroll 64.6–13. Also see Philo, *On the Special Laws* 3.152; *On the Posterity of Cain* 61; *Dreams* 2.213.

7. Bruce Corley, "Trial of Jesus," in Joel B. Green, Scot McKnight, and I. Howard Marshall, eds., *Dictionary of Jesus and the Gospels* (Downers Grove, IL: InterVarsity, 1992), p. 851.

8. Josephus *Antiquities of the Jews* 18.63–64; though it must be said that many scholars think these statements were added to Josephus's comments by later Christian writers.

9. Corliss, "The Goriest Story Ever Told," p. 64. In quoting Corliss, however, we do not intend to make any political statement about this or any American administration.

10. Corley, "Trial of Jesus," p. 854.

11. Ibid., p. 850.

12. For example, J. Joster, *Les Juifs dans l' empire Romain*, 2 volumes (Paris: Geuthner, 1914); and Paul Winter, *On the Trial of Jesus*, 2nd ed. (New York: DeGruyter, 1974).

13. The two were discovered in 1871. They read, "No foreigner is to enter within the balustrade and enclosure around the Temple area. Whoever is caught will have himself to blame for his death which will follow," in Connolly, *Living in the Time of Jesus of Nazareth*, p. 36. Josephus quotes this inscription (see *Jewish Wars* 5.52; *Antiquities of the Jews* 15.11.5). Today the inscriptions are in the Archaeological Museum, Istanbul.

14. See Josephus *Jewish Wars* 6.2.4; 126.

15. See *Mishnah Sanhedrin* 6:6; Josephus *Antiquities of the Jews* 4.8.6.

16. These comments are indebted to J. A. Weatherly, "Anti-Semitism," in *Dictionary of Jesus and the Gospels*, pp. 13–17.

17. See Josephus *Antiquities of the Jews* 18.55–62; 4.85–89.

18. This paragraph comes from C. Marvin Pate, *Luke* (Chicago: Moody, 1995), p. 450.

19. Jeff Chu et al, "Why Did Jesus Have to Die?" *Time*, April 12, 2004, pp. 55–61.

20. Ibid., p. 56.

21. Ibid., p. 58.

22. Ibid., p. 61.

Chapter 7

1. Prologue to John H. Heller, *Report on the Shroud of Turin* (Boston: Houghton Mifflin, 1983). Heller was involved with STURP (The Shroud of Turin Research Project), a group of scientists organized in 1978 to objectively analyze the Shroud of Turin. Heller makes the case in his book for the authenticity of the blood stains on the image on the Shroud, though he does not say it was the blood of Jesus Christ.

2. Ian Wilson, *The Shroud of Turin: The Burial Cloth of Jesus Christ?* rev. ed. (Garden City, NY: Image Books, 1979), p. 14. Wilson is an avid proponent of the authenticity of the Shroud.

3. As reported on *The Shroud of Turin Research at McCrone Research Institute*, http://www.mcri.org/Shroud.html, pp. 1–2. McCrone is a particles expert who removed himself from the STURP team due to his conviction that the Shroud was a hoax.

4. The quip is by Heller, who was originally a skeptic of the Shroud turned believer, *Report on the Shroud of Turin*, p. 5.

5. So, according to Dr. John Kilmon, in his article entitled, "The Shroud of Turin: Genuine Artifact or Manufactured Relic," published in three parts in *The Archaeological Institute of America*,

San Diego, vol. 1, no. 10 (Sept. 1997); no. 11 (Dec. 1998); no. 12 (March 1999). It can be accessed on the website, http://www.historian.net/shroud.htm. We quote from this website, p. 1.

6. Cited in Heller, *Report on the Shroud of Turin*, pp. 2–4, who approvingly quotes Dr. Robert Bucklin's autopsy report on the image of the Shroud of Turin. Bucklin was also associated with the STURP team.

7. See especially Dr. David Willis's 1969 medical report on the Shroud, in Wilson, *The Shroud of Turin*, p. 34.

8. The chart of Gospel parallels with the Shroud of Turin is Wilson's, which is based on Dr. Willis's medical report, *The Shroud of Turin*, pp. 51–52.

9. See Heller, *Report on the Shroud of Turin*, p. 4.

10. Taken from the website, *Debunking the Shroud of Turin: True Science vs. "Shroud Science,"* http://www.uiowa.edu/~anthro/webcourse/lost/shroudpage.htm, pp. 1–7, p. 1.

11. Heller's book *Report on the Shroud of Turin* is devoted to relating the incidents of those five days.

12. See *Debunking the Shroud of Turin*, website, p. 2.

13. Summarized on McCrone's website, p. 1.

14. Reported in *Debunking the Shroud of Turin*, website, p. 3; cf. McCrone's website, p. 1.

15. See *Debunking the Shroud of Turin*, website, p. 2. Heller's entire book is largely concerned with countering McCrone's denial that the stains were blood. Heller began his research in 1980.

16. See Heller's documentation in *Report on the Shroud of Turin*, pp. 187–89.

17. See the website by Kilmon, *The Shroud of Turin*, p. 3.

18. See *Debunking the Shroud of Turin* website, p. 2.

19. Ibid.

20. See Kilmon, *The Shroud of Turin*, website, p. 1.

21. There is some thought that the image on the Shroud of Turin was created by a burst of radiation emitted from the body of Christ upon his resurrection rather than originating from either blood stains or paint.

22. See Wilson, *The Shroud of Turin*, p. 31. He, of course, disagrees.

23. P. E. Damon, et al, "Radiocarbon Dating of the Shroud of Turin," *Nature* 16 February 1988, pp. 611–615. See Kilmon, *The Shroud of Turin,* website, p. 6; see also McCrone's website, pp. 1–2.

24. *Debunking the Shroud of Turin*, website, p. 2.

25. See, for example, Kilmon's response, *The Shroud of Turin*, website, pp. 5–6.

26. Reported in Ian Wilson, *The Blood and the Shroud* (NY: The Free Press, 1998), p. 225.

27. See C. Marvin Pate, *Communities of the Last Days: The Dead Sea Scrolls, The New Testament, and the Story of Israel* (Downers Grove, IL: InterVarsity, 2000), chap. 1.

28. Wilson, *The Shroud of Turin*, p. 80.

29. Cited in Wilson, *The Shroud of Turin*, p. 81.

30. Rev. Adrien Parvilliers, S.J., *La dévotion des présdestinés, ou les stations de Jérusalem et du Calvaire pour servir d'entretien sur le passion de Notre Seigneur, J.C.* This work appeared in 14 editions between 1696 and 1892, cited in Wilson, *The Shroud of Turin*, p. 106.

31. Humbert was Margaret's second husband. Wilson tells the story in *The Shroud of Turin*, pp. 211–12. The quote comes from p. 212.

32. See *Debunking the Shroud of Turin*, website, p. 2.

33. Heller, *Report on the Shroud of Turin*, p. 70.

34. See the following website for more information, as well as photos of the event: http://pages.zdnet.com/AsiaBill/id11.html.

35. The following bibliography may be sought with reference to the Shroud. In addition to McCrone's website and *Debunking the Shroud of Turin* website, those against the authenticity of the Shroud include Gary Vikan, "Debunking the Shroud," *Biblical Archaeology Review*, November,

1998; Joe Nickell, *Inquest on the Shroud of Turin* (Amhearst, NY: Prometheus Books, 1998). In addition to Wilson's and Heller's books cited in this chapter, those in favor of the Shroud's genuineness include John Travis, "Microbes Muddle Shroud of Turin's Age," *Science News*, June 3, 1995; Ian Wilson's newest book, *The Blood and the Shroud: New Evidence That the World's Most Sacred Relic Is Real* (New York: The Free Press, 1998).

Chapter 8

1. The English lawyer Frank Morrison began to write a book discrediting Jesus's resurrection, but became convinced of its historicity in the process. Ironically, his book has become a classic defense for the resurrection, *Who Moved the Stone?* (repr. Grand Rapids: Zondervan, 1987). Josh McDowell became a Christian during his skeptical college years after investigating the resurrection of Jesus; see his *Evidence That Demands a Verdict*: vol. 1 (San Bernadino, CA: Here's Life Publishers, 1979). Lee Strobel had a similar experience, *The Case for Christ: A Journalist's Personal Investigation of the Evidence for Jesus* (Grand Rapids: Zondervan, 2002). The most recent defense of the bodily resurrection of Jesus is the monumental work by N. T. Wright, *The Resurrection of the Son of God: Volume III of Christian Origins and the Question of God* (Minneapolis: Fortress Press, 2003). Richard N. Ostling of the Associated Press writes that Wright's achievement is "the most monumental defense of the Easter heritage in decades . . . *The Resurrection of the Son of God* marches through a clearly organized case that confronts every major doubt about Easter, ancient and modern" (endorsement in the front of the book).

2. Story told by William Lane Craig, "Did Jesus Rise from the Dead?" in *Jesus under Fire: Modern Scholarship Reinvents the Historical Jesus*, ed. Michael J. Wilkins and J. P. Moreland (Grand Rapids: Zondervan, 1995), p. 165.

3. There is debate today concerning where the empty tomb is located. Some think it is identified with the Garden Tomb, just about one mile northeast of the old City of Jerusalem. Most scholars, however, locate the tomb in the Holy Sepulcher inside the old city, not far from the Temple Mount. That site is attested archaeologically back to at least the second century AD.

4. See the comments by Ben F. Witherington III, *Women in the Ministry of Jesus: A Study of Jesus's Attitudes to Women and Their Roles As Reflected in His Earthly Life*. Society for New Testament Studies Monograph Series 51 (Cambridge: Cambridge University Press, 1984), pp. 9–10.

5. See further Craig, "Did Jesus Rise from the Dead?" p. 147.

6. John Dominic Crossan, *The Cross That Spoke: The Origins of the Passion Narrative* (San Francisco: Harper & Row, 1988).

7. Craig, "Did Jesus Rise from the Dead?" p. 169, footnote 16.

8. Origen *Against Celsus* II, LVI. This point is indebted to George Ladd, *I Believe in the Resurrection of Jesus* (Grand Rapids: Eerdmanns, 1975), pp. 133–34. Celsus was a vociferous critic against Christianity. Mocking Paul's words in 1 Corinthians 1:26–28, he sarcastically said of Christians: "Their injunctions are like this. 'Let no one educated, no one wise, no one sensible draw near. For these abilities are thought by us to be evils.' By the fact they themselves admit that these people are worthy of their God, they show that they want and are able to convince only the foolish, dishonorable, and stupid, and only slaves, women and little children" (Origen *Contra Censum* 3.44).

9. H. M. Reimarus, *The Goal of Jesus and His Disciples*, trans. G. W. Buchanan (Leiden: Brill, 1970).

10. This discussion follows Ladd, *I Believe in the Resurrection*, pp. 134–36.

11. David Friedrich Strauss, *The Life of Jesus for the People*, reprint, ed. Peter C. Hodgson, trans. George Eliot (Philadelphia: Fortress, 1972), p. 412.

12. Kirsopp Lake, *The Historical Evidence for the Resurrection of Jesus Christ* (London: Williams & Norgate / New York: Putnam's Sons, 1907), pp. 251–53.

13. Ibid., p. 263.

14. Raymond E. Brown, *The Death of the Messiah: A Commentary on the Passion Narratives in the Four Gospels*, Anchor Bible Reference Library (New York: Doubleday, 1994), 2:1240. This section is indebted to Craig, "Did Jesus Rise from the Dead?" p. 148.

15. Craig, "Did Jesus Rise from the Dead?" p. 148.

16. Jews reckoned any part of a day as one day; therefore Jesus lay in the tomb on Friday night (one day), Saturday (one day), and until early Sunday morning (one day).

17. The *NIV Study Bible* (Grand Rapids: Zondervan, 1985), p. 1588. We placed question marks by Mark 16:9–11, 14, 15–18 because they are not in the oldest Greek manuscripts of the New Testament.

18. Craig, "Did Jesus Rise from the Dead?" p. 174. He is responding to the claim of Peter Carnley that anti-docetism informs the resurrection accounts, *The Structure of Resurrection Belief* (Oxford: Clarendon, 1987), p. 68.

19. William Milligan, *The Resurrection of Our Lord* (New York: Macmillan, 1927), pp. 81–114.

20. Robert W. Funk, Roy W. Hoover, and the Jesus Seminar, *The Five Gospels: What Did Jesus Really Say? The Search for the Authentic Words of Jesus* (San Francisco: HarperSanFrancisco, 1997), p. 2.

21. Ibid, p. 3.

22. Reported by Richard N. Ostling, "Jesus Christ, Plain and Simple," *Time* 10 January 1994, pp. 32–33. That Ostling does not agree with Crossan can be seen from his endorsement of N. T. Wright's book, *The Resurrection of the Son of God*, quoted in our note 1 above.

23. In chapter 1 we identify this principle as distinguishing Jesus from Judaism and the church. Here we nuance the second half of the criterion: the followers of Jesus in the Greek or Hellenistic churches.

24. See Craig, "Did Jesus Rise from the Dead?" pp. 160–162, though we supplement his argument by adding the Hellenistic component to the criterion.

25. Robert W. Funk, Roy W. Hoover, and the Jesus Seminar, *The Five Gospels*, p. 398.

26. See the discussion and bibliography in C. Marvin Pate, *The End of the Age Has Come: The Theology of Paul* (Grand Rapids: Zondervan, 1995), p. 27.

27. Ibid., p. 28 for the bibliography.

28. Quoted from Terry Carter and Preben Vang, "The Story of the Bible" class notes handout, Ouachita Baptist University, 2003.

Chapter 9

1. Chris Armstrong, "Christian History Corner: J. R. R. Tolkien and C. S. Lewis, a Legendary Friendship," *Christianity Today* (August 2003), an interview with Colin Duriez, accessed at http://www.christianitytoday.com/ct/2003/134/52.0.html.

2. J.R.R. Tolkien, *The Tolkien Reader* (New York: Ballantine Books, 1966), p. 88.

3. Steven D. Greydanus explores the Catholic influence on Tolkien's works, especially *The Lord of the Rings*, "Faith and Fantasy: Tolkien the Catholic, *The Lord of the Rings*, and Peter Jackson's film trilogy, " www.decentfilms.com/commentary/faithandfantasy.html.

4. Some interpreters prefer, however, to place Revelation 2–3 at the present time of the apostle John while Revelation 4 and following refer to the future end-time events.

5. J. R. R. Tolkien, *The Lord of the Rings, Part II. The Two Towers*, 2nd ed. (Boston: Houghton Mifflin, 1965), Book Two, Chapter VII, p. 377.

6. J. R. R. Tolkien, *The Lord of the Rings, Part I. The Fellowship of the Ring*, 2nd ed. (Boston: Houghton Mifflin, 1965), Book One, Chapter II, p. 65.

7. J. R. R. Tolkien, *The Lord of the Rings, Part III. The Return of the King*, 2nd ed. (Boston: Houghton Mifflin, 1965), Book Six, Chapter III, p. 225.

8. *The Return of the King*, Book Six, Chapter I, p. 190.

9. *The Two Towers*, Book Four, Chapter VII, p. 311.

10. Following are some Jewish sources that speak about the signs of the times of the great tribulation heralding the end of history and the appearance of the kingdom of God: wars (*1 Enoch* 90; *4 Ezra* 9:3); famines (*4 Ezra* 6:22; *2 Baruch* 27:6); internecine strife (*1 Enoch* 100:1–2; 56:7; *4 Ezra* 6:24); and cosmic disturbances (*Sibylline Oracles* II.796–808; *1 Enoch* 80:4–6; *4 Ezra* 5:4).

11. See *Psalms of Solomon* 17; the Dead Sea Scrolls; *4 Ezra* 13.

12. These comments come from Greydanus, "Faith and Fantasy," website p. 5.

13. *The Return of the King*, Book Six, Chapter V, p. 241.

14. Ibid., pp. 245–47; as summarized by Kurt Bruner and Jim Ware, *Finding God in the Lord of the Rings* (Wheaton: Tyndale, 2001), p. 94.

15. *The Return of the King*, Book Six, Chapter V, p. 246.

16. Ibid., p. 246.

17. Ibid., Book Six, Chapter IV, p. 226.

18. Ibid., p. 227.

19. Ibid., Chapter IX, pp. 302–3, as summarized by Bruner and Ware, *Finding God in the Lord of the Rings*, p. 103.

20. J. R. R. Tolkien, *The Silmarillion* (Boston: Houghton Mifflin, 1977), pp. 17–18.

21. *The Return of the King*, Book Six, Chapter IX, p. 309.

22. C. S. Lewis, *The Lion, the Witch, and the Wardrobe*.

23. Bruner and Ware, *Finding God in the Lord of the Rings*, p. 53.

Chapter 10

1. Michael Drosnin, *The Bible Code* (New York: Simon & Schuster, 1997); Michael Drosnin, *The Bible Code II: The Countdown* (New York: Viking Press, 2002).

2. Drosnin, *Bible Code II*, p. 223; cf. p. 20.

3. C. Marvin Pate and Calvin B. Haines, Jr., *Doomsday Delusions: What's Wrong with Predictions about the End of the World?* (Downers Grove, IL: InterVarsity, 1995), pp. 42–44.

4. This section is indebted to J. Scott Duvall and J. Daniel Hays, *Grasping God's Word: A Hands-On Approach to Reading, Interpreting, and Applying the Bible* (Grand Rapids: Zondervan, 2001), pp. 189–90.

5. We follow here the discussion by Randall Ingermanson, *Who Wrote the Bible Code? A Physicist Probes the Current Controversy* (Colorado Springs: Waterbrook Press, 1999), p. 9. Doron Witztum, Eliyahu Rips, and Yoav Rosenberg, "Equidistant Letter Sequences in the Book of Genesis," *Statistical Science* 9, no. 3 (1994): p. 429.

6. Grant Jeffrey, *The Mysterious Bible Codes* (Nashville: Word, 1998).

7. See Ingermanson's bibliography in *Who Wrote the Bible Code?* pp. 10–11; also, see the book reviews by H. Van Dyke Parunak in the *Journal of Evangelical Theological Society* 41 (June 1998), and by Michael Weitzman in *The Jewish Chronicle*, July 25, 1997. See the scathing articles by Ronald S. Hendel, "The Secret Code Hoax," *Bible Review*, August 1997, p. 23; and Shlomo Sternberg, "Snake Oil for Sale," *Bible Review*, August 1997, p. 25. See also the rebuttal of the statistical data in the article by Brendan McKay, Dror Bar-Natan, Maya Bar-Hillel, and Gil Kalai, "Solving the Bible Code Puzzle," *Statistical Science* 14, no. 2 (May, 1999): pp. 150–73.

8. McKay et al, "Solving the Bible Code Puzzle." The following two criticisms are indebted to Duvall and Hays, *Grasping God's Word*, pp. 190–92.

9. Michael Weitzman, book review of *The Bible Code*, cited by Parunak's book review in *Journal of Evangelical Theological Society*, p. 324.

10. Cited by Sternberg, "Snake Oil for Sale," p. 25; see also Ingermanson, *Who Wrote the Bible Code?* for a thorough refutation of the mathematical method employed in ELS.

11. Bruce K. Waltke, "The Textual Criticism of the Old Testament," in *The Expositor's Bible Commentary*, vol. 1, ed. Frank E. Gaebelein (Grand Rapids: Zondervan, 1979), p. 214.

12. We don't know of any Christian scholars today who use *The Second Rabbinic Bible* as a Hebrew text.

13. Drosnin reveals his lack of awareness of the current status of text criticism of the Hebrew Bible when he says, "Every Hebrew Bible that now exists is the same letter for letter," *The Bible Code*, p. 35.

14. Duvall and Hays, *Grasping God's Word*, p. 192.

15. Ingermanson, *Who Wrote the Bible Code?* pp. 165–67.

16. Pate and Haines, *Doomsday Delusions*, chap. 5. In another book, Marvin conducted a similar investigation of the *Dead Sea Scrolls*, in *Communities of the Last Days: The Dead Sea Scrolls, The New Testament, and the Story of Israel* (Downers Grove, IL: InterVarsity, 2000), pp. 231–36. These insights on the Bible code and the theory of cognitive dissonance is our intended contribution to this subject.

17. Leon Festinger, *A Theory of Cognitive Dissonance* (Stanford: Stanford University Press, 1957); cf. Leon Festinger, Henry W. Riecken, and Stanley Schachter, *When Prophecy Fails* (Minneapolis: University of Minnesota Press, 1956).

18. Festinger, *A Theory of Cognitive Dissonance*, p. 103.

19. Festinger et al, *When Prophecy Fails*, p. 3.

20. Ibid., p. 4.

21. Ibid.

22. William Miller, *Signs of the Times*, January 31, 1844, p.195, quoted in Francis D. Nichol, *The Midnight Cry* (Washington, D.C.: Review and Herald Publishing Association, 1945), p. 158.

23. See Pate and Haines, *Doomsday Delusions*, pp. 93–94.

24. Pate and Haines, *Doomsday Delusions*, pp. 120–21.

25. Ibid., pp. 129–33.

26. Drosnin, *The Bible Code*, pp. 55-59. This prediction governs much of Drosnin's book; see his chaps. 3, 6, 7, and 8.

27. Ibid., pp. 54-57.

28. Ibid., p. 133.

29. Ibid., pp. 137-38.

30. Ibid., p. 133.

31. Ibid., p. 133. The reference to Prime Minister Peres concerns a speech he gave in Jerusalem on January 3, 1996, warning Israel of the possibility of a terrorist attack on that nation using nuclear weapons, which itself was a response to Libya's leader Muamman Kaddafi's call to Arab countries to buy nuclear weapons to protect themselves against Israel. That announcement was made in a rare public statement on January 27, 1996, by Kaddafi. The reference to Benjamin Netanyahu has to do with his planned trip as prime minister of Israel to Jordan on July 25, 1996. According to *The Bible Code*, Netanyahu would have been killed had he carried through with the trip. That trip was rescheduled, however, for August 5, 1996, due to the fact that Jordan's King Hussein fell ill.

32. See Drosnin, *The Bible Code II*, pp. 165, 169, 170, 199, 220, 223.

Chapter 11

1. Marcus J. Borg, *Meeting Jesus Again for the First Time: The Historical Jesus and the Heart of Contemporary Faith* (San Francisco: HarperSanFrancisco, 1994). The quotation is taken from R. Douglas Geivett, "Is Jesus the Only Way?" in *Jesus under Fire: Modern Scholarship Reinvents the Historical Jesus*, ed. Michael J. Wilkins and J. P. Moreland (Grand Rapids: Zondervan, 1995), p. 183.

2. Ibid., pp. 29–31.

3. Ibid., pp. 44–45, footnote 42.

4. Ibid., p. 131.

5. Geivett, "Is Jesus the Only Way?"

222

6. This description comes from Josh McDowell and Don Stewart, *Handbook of Today's Religions* (San Bernardino, CA: Here's Life Publishers, 1982), p. 305.

7. Ibid., p. 307.

8. For more parallels see Marcus J. Borg, *Jesus and Buddha: The Parallel Sayings* (Berkeley, CA: Ulysses Press, 1997).

9. Holger Kersten, *Jesus Lives in India: His Unknown Life Before and After the Crucifixion* (Dorset: Element, 1986); Holger Kersten and Elmar R. Gruber, *The Jesus Conspiracy: The Turin Shroud and the Truth about the Resurrection* (Dorset: Element, 1994); Elmar R. Gruber and Holger Kersten, *The Original Jesus: The Buddhist Sources of Christianity* (Dorset: Element, 1995).

10. For a more detailed analysis, see Ross Clifford and Philip Johnson, *Jesus and the Gods of the New Age: A Response to the Search for True Spirituality* (Colorado Springs: Victor, 2003), pp. 228–29.

11. For documentation of this point, the reader is referred to C. Marvin Pate, *Communities of the Last Days: The Dead Sea Scrolls, The New Testament and the Story of Israel* (Downers Grove, IL: InterVarsity, 2000), chap. 2.

12. On this point see further Clifford and Johnson, *Jesus and the Gods of the New Age,* pp. 180–81.

13. Donald S. Lopez and Steven C. Rockefeller, eds., *The Christ and the Bodhisattua* (Albany: State University of New York Press, 1987), p. 258.

14. On one of Marvin's trips to Israel, he signed up with a Jewish tour group. It was a wonderful experience, in part, because the tour guide, knowing that Marvin was about the only Gentile Christian on the bus, made it a point to say on a number of occasions that Jesus was Jewish and should, therefore, be respected by his fellow Jews.

15. Markus Bockmuehl, *This Jesus: Martyr, Lord, Messiah* (Downers Grove, IL: InterVarsity, 1994), p. 103.

16. Ibid., p. 119.

17. John P. Meier, *A Marginal Jew, vol. 1, Rethinking the Historical Jesus* (New York: Doubleday, 1991), pp. 7–9.

18. Justin Martyr *Dialogue with Trypho, a Jew* 89.1. For further discussion, see Pate, *Communities of the Last Days*, p. 223.

19. Sir Norman Anderson, *The World's Religions* (Grand Rapids: Eerdmans, 1976), pp. 54, 60.

20. John B. Noss, *Man's Religions* (New York: Macmillan, 1974), p. 517; see also McDowell and Peterson, *Handbook of Today's Religions*, p. 517.

21. Kenneth Boa, *Cults, World Religions and You* (Wheaton: Victor, 1977), p. 52.

22. See McDowell and Peterson, *Handbook of Today's Religions*, p. 387.

23. Stephen Neill, *Christian Faith and Other Faiths* (London: Oxford University Press, 1970), p. 64.

24. "Islam," from the *Encyclopaedia Britannica* (Chicago: William Benton Publishing Company, 1967), p. 663.

25. This description is based on the comments by McDowell and Stewart, *Handbook of Today's Religions*, pp. 389–90.

26. Max Kershaw, *How to Share the Good News with Your Muslim Friend* (Colorado Springs: International Students, Inc., 1978), quoted in McDowell and Stewart, *Handbook of Today's Religions*, p. 395.

27. Unless otherwise stated, the quotations from the Qur'an are taken from *The Interpretation of the Meanings of the Noble Qur'an in the English Language* (Saudi Arabia: Maktaba Dar-us-Salam).

28. For more on the emphasis on the need for personal faith in Christ see 1 Cor. 15:14–17; Mark 1:15 and its parallel passages; Rom. 3:22; Acts 2:38; 3:19; 1 John 5:1–5.

29. Compare this with Acts 17:24–31.

30. C.S. Lewis, *The Last Battle* (London: Penguin, 1956), p. 149.